RUDY TOMJANOVICH

with Robert Falkoff

A
ROCKET

MY LIFE AND MY TEAM

AT
HEART

SIMON & SCHUSTER

SIMON & SCHUSTER
Rockefeller Center
1230 Avenue of the Americas
New York, NY 10020

SIMON & SCHUSTER and colophon are registered trademarks
of Simon & Schuster Inc.

Designed by Kate Nichols

Manufactured in the United States of America

10   9   8   7   6   5   4   3   2   1

Library of Congress Cataloging-in-Publication Data
Tomjanovich, Rudy, date.
A Rocket at heart : my life and my team / Rudy Tomjanovich with
Robert Falkoff.
p.   cm.
Includes index.
1. Tomjanovich, Rudy, date.   2. Basketball coaches—United
States—Biography.   3. Basketball players—United States—Biography.
4. Houston Rockets (Basketball team)   I. Falkoff, Robert, date.
II. Title.
GV884.T65A3   1997
796.323'092—dc21
[B]   97-2063
            CIP

ISBN 0-684-83428-6

Photo Credits:
1, 3, 17 courtesy of the Tomjanovich family
2, 4, 5, 7, 8, 12 courtesy of the Houston Rockets
6, 9, 11, 13, 14, 15, 16 © AP/Wide World
10 © *Houston Chronicle*

Acknowledgments

THE AUTHOR AND COAUTHOR wish to gratefully acknowledge the contributions and encouragement of the many people who helped make this project a reality.

Special thanks to Jesse Brown, who provided behind-the-scenes assistance in every area. Thank you to Tim Frank, Angela Blakeney, Matt Alexander, and Robyn Wherritt of the Rockets' media services staff for their help. Thank you to Susan Coon and Frances Mack for their technical expertise. Thanks to Peter Knobler for introducing us to Simon & Schuster's Jeff Neuman, who introduced us to agent Faith Hamlin, who reintroduced us to Jeff Neuman. Thanks, Jeff, for pushing us to probe deep. Thanks also to Simon & Schuster's Frank Scatoni for his editorial guidance.

Thank you to Carroll Dawson, Bill Berry, Larry Smith, and Jim Boylen for rekindling the memories. Thanks to Chris Boylen for her positive feedback.

Thank you to Sophie Tomjanovich, Nichole Tomjanovich, Melissa Tomjanovich, and Trey Tomjanovich and to Jackie Falkoff, Joey Falkoff, Laurie Falkoff, and Ada Falkoff for their unwavering support.

Thank you to the entire organization of the Houston Rockets and to the many players who have helped this NBA franchise on a rags-to-riches journey over nearly three decades.

To Sophie, Nichole, Melissa, and Trey,
whose character and integrity continually
inspire me.

—R.T.

To the memory of Edward Falkoff, my father,
the kindest man I've ever known.

—R.F.

A ROCKET AT HEART

1

ON THE NIGHT of February 17, 1992, as I sat down in my seat on the Houston Rockets bench, I had no clue that in a few hours I was going to take on a burden that would change the course of my life.

I was the second assistant coach for the Rockets, and for three quarters I felt good about the way our game against the Minnesota Timberwolves was going. Their coach, Jimmy Rodgers, had been kicked out, and we had built a 24-point lead. We told our guys, "Get ready for the press," but when we looked at our scouting reports to see where the pressure would come from, we saw that Minnesota hadn't even used a press. Sidney Lowe, the Minnesota assistant coach, was in charge, and I think Sidney just drew up a halfcourt zone on the spot. We didn't execute, the lead slipped away, and we wound up losing the game.

It was probably the most depressing, humiliating game we had been involved in, and as we walked through the tunnel to our dressing room, some of the catcalls were brutal. We heard all the things that really strike the nerves of a coach.

When I got home that night I couldn't sleep. As was often the case, I talked to first assistant Carroll Dawson, another guy who takes losses hard. Carroll and I talked about the game; suffice it to say, it was a very depressing conversation.

Then our strength coach Robert Barr called me around 3 A.M. and he was just as depressed.

"Rudy, I just feel something in the air," Robert said.

"I hope you aren't saying what I think you're saying," I responded. "I don't want to talk about it. Let's sleep on this thing. It'll be better tomorrow."

I had been with the Rockets organization since 1970 as a player, scout, and assistant coach. During that span of more than two decades of making a living in professional sports, I had felt a lot of exhilaration and a lot of apprehension. This situation definitely belonged in the latter category.

I tossed and turned all night and was lying there with my eyes open as the sun came up. We had an 11-A.M. practice over at Texas Southern University, and our players were really down about the Minnesota game. Don Chaney, our head coach, came in and gave the prepractice talk; Don did a great job of staying positive and saying things to try to get us back on track. You really feel for a head coach in that situation; those are the toughest moments, when your team has been shaken and needs to get its confidence back.

I think everyone was relieved when we didn't have to talk about it anymore and could go through the physical exercise of practice. It was sort of therapeutic, as if we could run that terrible loss out of our systems.

As the practice ended, we got word that our general manager, Steve Patterson, wanted to see Carroll and me.

"What could this be?" Carroll wondered. It was a little strange that a meeting would be called for Carroll and me, but not Don. Right there, I started to get a bad feeling.

"Let's talk about this before we go in," Carroll said. "What do you think is going to happen?"

"Well, we're going to have to answer some very hard questions here," I said. Then I thought back to the previous night's conversation with Robert Barr and his eerie feeling that something was in the air. "I think we'll have to do more than that. I think we're going to have to do some fighting. We're going to have to fight for Don's job."

I know some people will wonder if that's the way assistant coaches really are. Well, that's the way Carroll and I have always been. Loyalty is very big with us. That was our job, to support the head coach.

So we went to the general manager's office. I looked at Steve and I didn't like the serious expression on his face. The three of us just sat there and stared at each other for over a minute. Carroll started trying to break the ice by talking about the Minnesota game, but Steve just shook his head and got right to the meat of it.

"Guys, I know how you are," he said. "You're going to come in here and support Don. But it's too late. It's over."

"How could it be over?" I protested. "Minnesota was just one game. Those things happen in the NBA. This is not fair. It isn't the right thing to do. We had a great year last year. Things aren't that bad here."

"It's done," Steve said. "You've been very loyal to the coach and to the team. But now we've got a problem. Where do we go from here?" Steve turned to Carroll, who had suffered some health problems in recent years. He had lost sight in one eye and his blood pressure had to be carefully monitored.

"Carroll, no one has worked as hard as you have," Steve said. "You deserve a shot at this job. But with the physical problems you've had, with the eye and the blood pressure, I couldn't live with myself if something happened to you."

Steve then turned and looked me in the eye. "In San Antonio, their general manager, Bob Bass, just took over as head coach of the Spurs. I'm not Bob Bass. Rudy, you're the guy. We want you to take over the team for the rest of the year."

I was shocked. I had thought there might be a small possibility that Don would get fired, but I never thought of it in terms of my being his replacement. I thought I would always be a part of the Rockets, but as a helper; all of a sudden, the man said: "It's you."

Steve left the room for a while, and Carroll and I talked it over. "Carroll, now dammit, I don't want to be a head coach. I haven't even thought about it. I'm not even a first assistant yet and suddenly I'm getting into this deal?"

Some of the reasons for my reluctance were family issues. I

remembered how it was when Del Harris was the Rockets head coach in the early 1980s. Del did a great job and he's a great coach, but we had a bad year in 1983, the year before we got Ralph Sampson. Even in a rebuilding situation, the losing takes so much out of you. Some of the things Del said—how it bothered his children and how other kids were taunting them—made a huge impression on me. I felt that proving myself or striving for something that I wanted to do wasn't important enough to make up for hurting my family. The ego part—I didn't have that. I was happy to be an assistant for many, many years as long as I got to work in basketball and help young players.

"Jesus Christ, I don't want to get into this," I told Carroll. "I haven't had time to prepare myself at all."

"Rudy," he said, "if you don't take the job, we might not *have* a job. They might bring in somebody else as head coach who will hire his own staff of assistants."

That usually is the case when there's a head-coaching change. Bottom line, we had to feed our families.

At that point Steve came back into the room.

"What do you say, Rudy?"

"I'll do it."

"That's good. You're going to do fine. The media will be here in half an hour. Why don't you freshen up? You don't look so good."

My mind was racing. I was in a daze. I ambled through the Summit hallway back to the locker room and looked in the mirror. Steve was right. I looked terrible. I hadn't shaved and there were bags under my bloodshot eyes.

I stood there for a while when equipment manager David Nordstrom walked into the locker room. We called David "D.H." because he used to be a fixture at a Rockets gathering spot called The Dark Horse on Richmond Avenue.

D.H. had a puzzled look on his face.

"What's all the commotion?" he asked. "There's thirty people in the press room."

I told him, "Don's been fired." D.H.'s expression changed.

"No," he said, shaking his head. "That's terrible. I love Don."

"I do too," I said.

D.H. started to walk away, but he turned back to me. "Who's going to coach the team?"

I had a hard time getting the words out. "I am."

A sudden wave of guilt came over me. I had heard how survivors of catastrophies feel this emotion, wishing they had perished instead of their loved ones. I felt I had failed. I felt I could have done something to prevent this—been a better assistant coach. And now they were making me the head coach. I felt awful.

D.H. had known me for a long time, and he read my expression.

"Rudy, most assistants would be happy as hell getting a shot at a head-coaching job. But you look like Sad Sack. Everyone knows how loyal you and C.D. were to Don. You guys did all you could. It's part of the business. Coaches come and go. You've worked hard for three coaches. You've paid your dues. I knew you would eventually be a coach here. I have to admit I didn't think it would happen today, but I believe you'll be a good head coach. Let me get you some shaving stuff and a towel. You look like shit."

When David came back, I said, "Thanks, D.H. . . . I mean for the talk."

I appreciated his attempt to make me feel better, but I couldn't suppress the sorrow I felt for Don. When I got to the media room, it was packed. I made my way to the center of the room and I was swarmed.

It was too much. I hadn't had any sleep. My mind was a blur. And here were all these people with microphones and cameras. Understand, I basically hadn't done interviews since I was a player; as an assistant coach, I'd maybe do one or two in an entire year.

So there I was, in my red, white, green, and blue warm-up suit getting ready to go on the 5-P.M. news with reporters yelling, "How do you feel? What changes will you make? Are you ready for this?"

Unfortunately, this was the first view the public would have of the Rockets' new head coach: a confused, worn-out man who looked like a wreck. I know the people out there in television land had to be scratching their heads and saying, "How the hell is this guy ever going to lead the team? He's mumbling, he's out of it."

What a first impression I must have made. I was, in a word, numb.

I went home that night and discussed the events of the day with my family. My wife, Sophie, had so much confidence in me. She didn't grasp what being a head coach can do to you and your family.

I told Sophie about my reluctance. "Rudy, don't worry. You'll be fine and I think you'll do a great job," she said.

The concern came from my oldest daughter, Nichole, who was a student at Southern Methodist University in Dallas. A few days after accepting the head-coaching job, I got a letter from her that said, "All the kids are running up and down the halls of the dorm because they're so happy you got the job. But Dad, I don't think it's the right thing for you. I know how much you cared and suffered when times were tough when you were just an assistant coach. I just don't want it to hurt your life and hurt who you are. Because now you're the guy who has the responsibility."

It was touching. And as I tried to gather myself for the task ahead, my main consideration was, Don't embarrass your family; if you lose, lose with dignity. When you're a head coach in pro sports, people can be cruel. I knew I could take whatever criticism there might be, but I didn't know if my family would understand everything that came with this job.

Again, this was my main reluctance—my family. I wasn't concerned about whether I could do the job; I didn't know, but I wasn't afraid to find out. I had always had my ideas about basketball—every coach does. And now I was going to find out whether my ideas had merit.

After I talked with Sophie, Carroll came over to my house for a work session. It wasn't easy to get this thing off the ground, because I had always been the guy who did the preparation and helped to carry out the philosophy that the head coach wanted to use. I had to start saying to myself, What is *your* philosophy? What do you want to accomplish with *your* team? The mind-set is completely different.

Carroll and I talked about what course we should take. We didn't need to make a lot of changes; the things that Don had put in were very solid in terms of percentage basketball. We had a great year in '91 when we won 29 of 34 at one stretch and finished with a franchise-record 52 wins using Don's system. This year, it was erratic play that was keeping us around the .500 level.

Carroll was an experienced coach, and his help was invaluable. He suggested that we keep the foundation that Don had built because the players were familiar with it and it was sound. But we needed to spend some time refining it in practice, really stressing the fundamentals. Carroll also thought it was important that we add something new, so the players would realize that the new coach had some different ideas. I had a headful of plays from my many years as an advance scout, but I didn't want the first thing I put in to be too complicated. That would frustrate the players and get me off to a shaky start; I needed them to trust my instincts. I didn't want to start overcoaching in my first practice.

I liked a play that Hubie Brown used to run in Atlanta; Carroll said he had run it, too, as a head coach at Baylor. It featured the big guard cutting off of the power forward and then swinging the ball to the opposite side for a post-up for the center. You had options on both sides of the floor, which would keep the defense honest. We decided to call it the "four-set."

This set had different options for every position. By using a second number, we could designate which position would be the primary focus on the play. For instance, "42" meant we would be looking to set up the "two" man, the big guard. A "43" play would exploit the curl by the "three" man, or small forward. Our "44" was a post-up for the "four" man, the power forward. And "45" was a pick across the lane for the "five" man, our center.

I thought this play fit our personnel well. I hoped the players would like it, too.

The next morning, Steve Patterson addressed the team at practice. He explained the situation and ended his talk by expressing disappointment with the team. "A good man has lost his job because of lack of production," Steve said. "Rudy will be taking over for now. The owner and I think he can do the job. A lot depends on how you guys respond."

Now it was my turn. I didn't have a speech prepared. I got right to the point.

I told the players I thought they were still a very good team, but that we needed to work on some things. We were a good running team, but we needed to become better in the halfcourt when teams got back on defense and made us set up. I emphasized that we needed to develop a sense of security late in games when things got tight. The only way we could accomplish this would be through a lot of hard work against pressure. It would take some time, but I truly believed we could get it done.

"We start getting better today," I said in conclusion.

When my first practice ended, I had a feeling of satisfaction. I thought the players had been receptive, and I gave a deep sigh and said, "Whew, the first day is done." And then the doors opened and here came the press again. I had completely forgotten about that element: Not only do you have to put in the energy for practice, you've got to talk about it later. Little by little, I was learning about this job.

My first game as an interim head coach came the next night against Philadelphia, and I'll always remember the pregame interview with Jack Ramsay, the former NBA coach who was working as a television analyst for the Sixers. Some of the questions that Jack asked, he asked as though he had a lot of respect for the way I had played the game. To get that feeling from another coach is just an unbelievable boost to your confidence.

After the interview, Jack took me aside. I still hadn't slept much. I was nervous about my first game and noticeably wobbly.

"Rudy, let me give you some advice," Ramsay said. "You want to do a good job. Work hard at it. But you have to understand that you can't do it all by yourself. The players have the biggest role. Don't put too much of a burden on yourself. Don't let this job hinder your health."

In that first game, the opening quarter was amazing. Everything we did was like clockwork. Of course, part of it was due to the fact that the Sixers didn't have a report on us, because a lot of what we were doing was new. We won that first game, 110–101, and I was especially pleased with how comfortable our players were with the new plays after only one day of practice.

Everybody was in high spirits after the game, but things were a lot different the next night in a back-to-back against the tough Utah Jazz in Salt Lake City. They murdered us right from the jump ball. Their pick-and-roll with John Stockton and Karl Malone was unstoppable. By the end of the third quarter, Jerry Sloan had taken out his starters and was playing all reserves. The smoothness we had displayed the night before was now replaced with uncertainty. We couldn't complete even simple plays. What a contrast. Back-to-backs can bring out the worst in a team.

We got past San Antonio, 90–83, in my third game at home, and the next one was against Golden State at the Summit. The Warriors were coached by Don Nelson, a master at putting unique lineups on the floor and creating mismatches. Don would force a big, slow defender to guard a smaller, quicker man, or he could exploit a size advantage by posting up. Nelson also frequently ran a passing-game offense, which is an offense with no set pattern featuring a lot of movement of players without the ball. The ball can be passed five or six times before a shot is taken, or sometimes a player can find an opening quickly and exploit it for an easy, early shot. It's unpredictable and tough to defend.

Chris Mullin, their 6-7 small forward, is one of the best passing-game players I've ever seen. He's in constant motion, cutting to the basket or using a screen. If you try to overplay him and deny him the ball, he reads it and breaks to the basket for an easy layup. He handles the ball well, and sometimes Nellie would use him to direct the offense like a point guard. In fact, they even came up with a term to describe his position as "point forward." Mullin was a tremendous passer, especially off the dribble. To make matters worse, he had a great outside shot with three-point range.

A defender's nightmare.

Tim Hardaway, their stocky point guard, was known for his killer crossover dribble. He'd use the crossover to get his defender moving in one direction and then quickly change hands and speed by him in the other direction. Hardaway was fearless in taking the ball to the basket and had a knack for finishing off a play in a forest of big men. Hardaway also could stick the three-pointer; he'd pull up behind the three-point line five or six times a game because the defenders had so much respect for his driving ability and couldn't play him tight out there.

These were just two of the many Warriors who put on a clinic against us in the first half. We were a step behind on every play. They did whatever they wanted against us. The lead grew to more than 20 points. On the bench, after calling several timeouts to try to get us going and to get them stopped, I was wondering what the hell I had gotten myself into. A few nights earlier, we got our butts beat by 27 in Utah and now we were getting trounced by Golden State. How hard was this job going to be?

Mercifully, the buzzer sounded to end the half. I now had to give my first forceful talk to the team in the locker room. I don't know if I sounded like a coach or not, but I said, "To win in this league, you have to play defense. I didn't see any defense out there. We didn't have a hand in their face. We were afraid to make contact. We're playing passive basketball. We've got to make them feel uncomfortable. Get in their face. Put a body on someone. Get their attention. Let them know we're here to fight for this game. If we're going down, let's go down fighting."

As I walked back to the bench talking to Carroll, I didn't know if my message hit home or how believable I was.

"Rudy, you've made your point loud and clear," Carroll said.

We were soon to see.

The third quarter began with a different Rockets team. We had energy right from the start. Our guards, Kenny Smith and Vernon Maxwell, were pressuring in the backcourt. Otis Thorpe was being physical inside and fighting his man for position. Nellie liked to play his center away from the basket to bring Hakeem Olajuwon out of the lane so he couldn't block shots. When Hakeem's man, Victor Alexander, got the ball out beyond the three-point line, Hakeem was chest-to-chest with him, using his hands to knock the ball loose.

Hakeem got two steals in a row to start fast breaks. Buck Johnson hit the floor for a loose ball and passed it to Maxwell, who hit Kenny in the corner for a three-pointer. The tide had changed. Timeout, Golden State.

When we got into the huddle, I excitedly said, "That's what I'm talking about. Defense will get us back in the game. Don't ease up."

The Warriors had another spurt with Mullin hitting a three and Sarunas Marciulionis getting a layup. But we kept our intensity level high, really putting out effort at both ends of the floor. The crowd showed its appreciation by getting behind the team. We chipped away at the lead. In the fourth quarter, we narrowed the deficit to four points with two minutes to go.

We needed a stop and the crowd urged us on, chanting, "Defense, defense." Maxwell made a great play on Marciulionis. He was beaten on the play but didn't give up; Max kept pursuing from behind and got his hand in Marciulionis's face just enough to make him miss a short jumper. We took it down and got it inside to Hakeem. He shot a fadeaway, and that brought us within two.

Both teams failed to score on their next possession. We brought it down and missed a shot. But Otis Thorpe, working the offensive board, scored on a putback to leave us in a tie game. Golden State called timeout. On their next possession, the Warriors ran a pick-and-roll with Hardaway and Alexander. Hardaway dribbled into the lane. He drew all five of our defenders and, spotting Mullin open outside, snapped a quick pass to him. Buck Johnson ran out quickly to try to cover him. It was a great effort by Buck, but Mullin faked a shot, took a dribble to his right and released the ball. I cringed on the sidelines. The rotation on the ball was perfect.

It hit the back of the rim, then bounced off the front part of the rim and popped into the air. Bodies collided and Thorpe grabbed the ball with two hands. Before hitting the ground, Otis called timeout.

Two seconds were left on the clock. Because of the timeout, we could pass the ball in from halfcourt and get a quick shot. In the huddle, I asked the team if it felt comfortable with a new last-second inbounds play we called "quick." We had been working on it the day before in practice.

The players nodded. The play called for Thorpe to throw the ball in. This was an important role. He had to read the defense, then make a perfect pass. Smith was to cut off Olajuwon and then Buck Johnson, who were both positioned on the three-point line.

Then Maxwell would set a backpick on Hakeem's man. Hakeem would break to the basket looking for the lob. If that wasn't open, Max would be the next option at the top of the key for an outside shot.

The referee handed the ball to Otis and he slapped it to signal the start of the play. Our players ran their routes and the Warriors covered it well. The five-second count to get the ball in was winding down. When Hakeem saw he wasn't open for the lob, he didn't stop. He ran toward Otis, who passed in to Hakeem with Hakeem's man trailing. Olajuwon caught the ball and shot in one motion. It was in the air for what seemed like a minute. It swished through the net as the buzzer sounded. We won, 118–116.

As the ball was in the air, my nervous energy had me moving down the sidelines toward the opponents' basket. As the shot went in, I exploded with emotion and ran from under their basket down the middle of the court looking for any of our players to hug.

They had all run toward Hakeem and pounced on him. I joined them.

What an emotional roller coaster this game had been—the doubt early in the game, the pride of the team responding in the second half. In the locker room, as the team was still celebrating, I got their attention for a few postgame comments.

"Guys, I'm very proud of the way you hung in there and didn't give up," I said. "There's an important lesson to be learned, and the sooner we get it, the better our chances for success. We're just an average team if we don't play defense. If we want to be contenders, we have to become a defensive team every game."

As the interim process continued—and at that point I had been given no indication I was anything other than an interim head coach—there were other little hints that maybe I was having a positive influence on the team. One night we were playing the Lakers and starting to struggle a little bit. During a timeout, Vernon Maxwell said to me, "Coach, I think we need to get back to running some of that new stuff. Let's run some of that four-set that you put in."

Boy, what a feeling. I was starting to see a different look in the players' eyes. In the fourth quarters, I saw more confidence, more security. The fourth quarter of an NBA game is always really tough. Say you've got a 10-point lead. It's almost inevitable that the other team is going to make a run at you. You have to come back with something really solid in order to hold them off.

We were doing that. We went 11-4 in my first 15 games and were evolving into a consistently good team. That's when I got my next lesson in how difficult this job is. After 15 games, Hakeem went down with an injury and we went into a five-game losing streak. When we got Hakeem back, something was missing. In a crazy scenario, we were 42-38 and needed a win over Dallas in the next-to-last game to get a playoff spot. Dallas, 21-60, would get an extra Ping-Pong ball in the NBA draft lottery, which might be Shaquille O'Neal if they lost the game.

The Mavericks beat us.

Now, we went home needing to beat Phoenix in the season finale. The Suns already had their playoff spot locked up, and their coach, Cotton Fitzsimmons, made his intentions well known as we conversed before the game.

"You know I've got to go after this game. I've got to try and beat you because it's the right thing to do," Cotton said.

I agreed with Cotton. You don't want anybody giving you anything. It's not fair to the other teams competing for playoff spots. I respected him for saying that. That's the way the league should be.

Phoenix was playing free and easy, and we were playing tight. In the end, we just couldn't get it done. I'll tell you, it was very depressing sitting in the back office of our locker room that day. We had gone 16-14 since I took over as head coach, with no playoff berth. I was starting to understand that luck and staying injury-free are such a big part of a coach's livelihood. Until Hakeem went out, I kept seeing that look I liked in our players' eyes. I knew we were better than 16-14, but people judge you by your record. Consequently, my future was still very much up in the air.

The day after that Phoenix game, something happened that compounded the situation. Our veteran center, Tree Rollins, made some comments about a lack of discipline on the ballclub. It was true that the team had had a problem with tardiness. The Phoenix game was a rare 5-P.M. start and a couple of guys showed up late.

Once it got into the media, that one screw-up brought back whispers that the team was out of control and I wasn't a disciplinarian. It wasn't a true picture of what had happened, and it really hurt me—just another example of how one incident can wipe out two months of good work. Another commentary on how anything can happen in the wacky world of coaching.

During my 30 games as interim head coach, I had refused to throw my hat in the ring for the permanent head-coaching position publicly because I didn't want it to seem as if I was campaigning. Privately, I felt I had been a positive influence on the team, but in a very humble way, not a cocky way. Nobody knew this team as well as I did. Yeah, you could bring in somebody else, and I'm not saying somebody else couldn't have done a better job, but he would have had to start over from zero in understanding who the players were, what our weaknesses were, what our strengths were.

While I felt that I was probably the best guy at the time for the job, I didn't want to make public statements about it and pressure our owner, Charlie Thomas. The decision-making process went on for a while, and I have to admit I was wondering why it went on so long.

But Charlie did the right thing. He had an opportunity, because he didn't have a guy locked up, to explore all the candidates and make a very careful, calculated decision.

Finally, in late May of 1992, Charlie and I got together for a meeting. "I think you're the guy for the job," he said.

Because I hadn't talked about my feelings a lot, I wanted Charlie to know what was going on inside of me. I wanted him to know that this assignment would be more than a job to me and that he couldn't get a more sincere, hard effort than I was going to give him, simply because of my love for the Houston Rockets.

I probably care about the Rockets more than anybody around. I was here when the team moved to Houston and endured all the bumpy times in the 1970s. I've been here for all of it.

To have spent an entire career with one organization is a privilege that very few people have. I told Charlie, "No matter what,

I'll work as hard as I can to do what's right for the Rockets, to present the best possible team and a team that people will be proud of."

On that steamy May afternoon in 1992, as I left that meeting with Charlie, there's no way I could have envisioned the tremendous success the Houston Rockets would achieve in the first three years of my head-coaching career. In that span, there were two division championships, two conference championships, and two world championships.

I used to drive around Houston and see the kids in our community wearing Michael Jordan jerseys. That always irked me, but I understood it. Jordan was a champion and a very good role model. People across the nation and the world looked up to that, and I yearned for the day when people would be just as proud of the Houston Rockets.

Now they are, because the Rockets became true champions. When I drive around my city today, I see kids everywhere with Rockets caps and shirts. It really warms my heart.

How did the Rockets go from being a team with a reputation for consistently letting its opponents back into the game to repeat champions who showed as much character in 1994 and 1995 as any team in league history?

Well, it was a long process in getting to the mountaintop. It's not something that can easily be explained, because there's no direct, surefire way to that mountaintop. It's an everyday, hands-on, development-and-growing process that gets you there.

What I've experienced in coaching our great Rockets teams the last few years is in keeping with the values I've learned and held since childhood. It has always been my experience that the best things in life don't come easily. You struggle and struggle. You put in the work. You conduct yourself with class. You see things through.

The Rockets did all those things in becoming champions. They've made me feel like the proudest man in the world.

On a personal level, my life now is certainly different from before we won those championships. Back then, I could do everyday things. I could go to the grocery store, the drugstore. Once or twice a month, somebody might say, "Yeah, aren't you the guy who coaches the Rockets?"

But now, when I'm in my car and stopped at a red light, I'll start hearing a horn beep. I'll think I'm daydreaming and that the light has turned green, but it's still red. I'll look around, and somebody in the next car is giving me the thumbs-up.

I think about Jordan, I think about Hakeem, guys who are so recognizable. And now it's happening to me, not only in Houston but in other cities, too.

The fame, the notoriety is something I know comes with the territory, but I'm not really comfortable with it. You work hard, you do your job well, and then you just want to live your life. With all the success the Rockets have had, it's been hard for me to live a normal life. Again, I understand it, but I don't really think it's healthy for your ego when you are so recognizable that you no longer have a private life.

I just try to keep everything in balance and to go on with my normal routine, realizing that adulation certainly beats the alternative. When a coach loses too much, the fans might grab a rope and form a posse, saying "Let's drag this guy out of town."

Our world championships have meant so much to so many people. When I ran my basketball camp in the 1970s, we had some kids attending who loved the game. But Texas has long been known as a football state. Those kids would go back to their schools and be ridiculed by the football coach. "Why would you want to play *that* sport?" the coaches would wonder.

To be able to say we've had *basketball* champions deep in the heart of Texas—to know that kids in Houston were able to share closely in that experience—is a real thrill.

And how about all of our players who've lived those championship moments? I think about where I began as a basketball player: out in the alley, shooting baskets, dreaming about the championship game. You're always envisioning that last-second shot that you make to win the title. When you start out with a ball in your hand, that's the pinnacle.

Our players have been able to live that dream. Twice.

There's no way that I could ever rank one championship over

another. I was asked that question by NBC's Bob Costas on the floor of the Summit after our second championship. Was the second one sweeter?

As good as I felt at the time, I couldn't take that approach. To get there in any year takes so much work and sacrifice; picking one over the other would be like telling one of your children, "I like you better than the other one." Each is special to you in his or her own way.

When we won the championship in 1994, everybody thought we were going to tease 'em and then fall flat on our faces. Our city was conditioned for that, because Houston had never won a major pro sports title. We broke that barrier, and I think it numbed us all for a while.

I know I literally had to wind up in another state before it sank in. To get away from all the craziness in town, my family and I took a little trip to South Carolina. I was sitting there watching television when an ad came on for the 1994 championship video. I was looking at all these highlights, as if I was some guy from South Carolina watching another team.

Finally I said, "That's us. We're the champions." The feeling just came over me, and what an amazing feeling it was.

The next year, we faced a lot of doubt. When we didn't successfully defend our division title, it hurt. But there was still a feeling of pride within our team, a conviction that we were still the champions until somebody showed they could beat us in a playoff series.

We were backed into a corner time and time again in those '95 playoffs, but the heart of a champion was not to be denied. When you've been through as many crisis situations as we have, you develop a sense of calm, that you'll be able to get it done in the pressure moments. Everybody we faced had the homecourt advantage on us, but when the dust settled we were the champions again.

I want to savor our championships, but I also want to go forward. My coaching career isn't over, and there's still a lot to accomplish; we've set our standards high, but that's the only way to achieve everything that's worthwhile.

Along the way, I've thought a lot about how differently my life could have turned out and how much the Rockets and basketball mean to me.

To have stayed in one place as a player, scout, assistant coach, and head coach . . . to have been a part of championship celebrations in the city I love . . . it's like a fairy tale. My life couldn't have turned out any better if I had written the script.

2

MY FATHER had a variety of jobs when I was growing up in the blue-collar town of Hamtramck, Michigan, which is within the Detroit city limits. The job I remember most—and the one he was most known for—was when he was a shoemaker.

"You're the shoemaker's son," the adults would say to me.

I was proud of my father and the work that he did. His little white shoe-repair shop was right on the route to my elementary school. After I finished safety-patrol duty and all the other kids left, I liked to walk up there and spend time with him. The smell of the leather, the smell of the shoe polish . . . it was such a warm, pleasant place.

We weren't exactly raking in money like the Rockefellers, though. It didn't take me long to figure that out.

One day before school, I was sitting at the kitchen table watching my father scribbling away in his little three-by-five spiral tablet.

"What are you doing?" I asked.

"I'm figuring out my profits," my father said.

I looked over his shoulder and saw some of the figures. He received $.75 for a heel and $1.00 for a sole. A complete repair on a set of shoes was $3.50.

"How many pairs of shoes do you do in a week?"

"About ten."

At that time in school, we were doing story problems. I started figuring: If my Dad averaged fixing 10 pairs of shoes a week at $3.50, I knew we had about $35.00 coming into the house. I also used to go shopping with my mother, and I knew that her three bags of groceries usually came to about $10.

At first I felt pretty good. There was $35 coming in and only $10 going out. Great.

But then I started thinking about all the other things that go into living. As each item came up, I started getting an uneasy feeling. We lived in my grandmother's house, so we didn't have rent. We didn't have a telephone or a car. But I knew there was clothing and other necessities that had to be paid for.

My father had a bad back and some other health problems that intermittently forced him to go to Veterans' Hospital. At times we would have to go on welfare. The welfare program offered parceled food; you'd go to their building, pick it up, and take it home. My father would ask me to come along to help him load it on a wagon. As we wheeled it through the neighborhood, people could see the generic labeling on the packages. It was humiliating.

If your buddies saw you, they would joke about it. "Heard you're on relief," they would say. But if they later found out you were cooking those commodity beans, they would surely come over to the house looking for some.

No, there wasn't a lot of money in our home, but there was always love. My mother was probably one of the most loving, gentle people who ever lived. To describe her best, I would say she's very much like Edith Bunker on *All in the Family*, only nicer.

Like my father, she didn't finish high school. But what she lacked in knowledge, she made up for with her warm heart and caring ways. "Rudy, why don't you put on a sweater?" she would say. "Rudy, fix your collar."

My line coming back was always, "Mom, I'm not going to the senior prom."

My father, Rudy Tomjanovich I, was of Croatian descent. He was born in the Upper Peninsula of Michigan, in the city of Calumet, and came to Detroit to work in the factories. When he got there, he heard there was a Croatian girl working on the other side of the factory. After a brief courtship, Catherine Modich became Mrs. Tomjanovich.

My father didn't express himself openly like my mother. But I knew how much he loved me and my sister, Frances. Even when he'd yell at me for doing something foolish, I mostly felt his concern for me, not anger. And I learned about the goodness of my father's heart from the way he treated others.

There was an older man living next door named Mr. Novak. He became something of a legend. If you've ever seen the movie *The Sandlot*, Mr. Novak was a lot like that. His whole yard was like a farm, with strawberries, corn, and vegetables. He even had chickens and he had two big dogs.

Over the years, if any kid knocked a ball into the yard, he wouldn't give it back. Everyone was afraid of him. He had white hair and was always crouched over. Just seeing him gave us all an eerie feeling. It hurt us to lose the footballs and baseballs, but there was no way we wanted to deal with Mr. Novak.

One night I came home and was shocked to see Mr. Novak sitting in our living room. He was eating off one of our TV trays and watching *Bigtime Wrestling*. I learned that he had taken ill; my father hadn't really talked to him much before this, but he took it upon himself to help nurse this man back to health. He would take him soup and sit with him awhile.

The day after our neighbor came over for dinner and *Bigtime Wrestling*, he called me over to his yard and handed me a big box of balls. There must have been a hundred balls of all sizes in there. My father had treated him kindly, and he was responding to the gesture. I admired my father for what he had done for Mr. Novak. It made an impression on me that he cared for a cantankerous old guy.

Overall, I look back on my childhood days with extremely fond memories. My house looked like all the other houses in the neighborhood, but it was special to me; I had heard about how my mother's father had built it, and I felt it had history.

We had a big maple tree in the front, flowers in the front yard, a vegetable garden in the backyard, and behind that a big two-car garage. Most of the people who lived on our street were Polish. They took great care of their small lawns, and every yard had flowers.

There were a lot of older people on the block and also some young couples with children, but there was no one in my age category. It was just me and my sister, Frances. We did everything together. When I was old enough to venture out and find friends, I didn't do it on my street; I went out the back gate into the alley and found a group of boys my age. They lived on the next street, Dequindre, a much busier street than mine. About seventy percent of the people who lived on Dequindre were black. I had a lot of white friends from school, but none of them lived in the neighborhood.

Four of us—James McCier, William Odom (we called him Hawk because he had a widow's peak in the front of his hair and looked like a hawk), Robert Crockett, and myself—were almost inseparable from elementary school through high school.

James and Hawk were a couple of years older than I, and Robert was the youngest. We started a club, using my garage as a clubhouse. We played all the neighborhood sports—pickup games in which we used our creativity.

One of the games was Strikeout. It was a game we played up against the wall; you drew a rectangle for a strike zone and used a rubber ball. We played Home Run Derby, street hockey with brooms, and basketball using a tennis ball and a drain pipe.

The game we really thrived at was two-hand touch football. We'd venture out to the different school yards and take on all comers. We were the Dequindre Jets and we rarely lost. But as good as we were in touch football, we were terrible in tackle football. One day, after we beat some older guys in touch football, one of them said, "Why don't you guys come to the park and play some *real* football."

When we got to the park, we found out they had brought in a ringer—an older, muscle-bound guy with a big scar on his face. On his first carry, he ran up the middle. Hawk went for the tackle, but this bruiser, instead of trying to avoid Hawk, let out a yell and ran right over him. Then he proceeded to chase us right off the field, calling us punks and cowards.

We got a big laugh out of that. We were all athletic, but we were skinny kids and it didn't make much sense to us to get pounded by some big frustrated guy who had a chip on his shoulder.

My friends and I would even do some camping, if you can believe that, right in the middle of the city. On Dequindre, next to the housing projects and behind the Chrysler plant, a large field of undeveloped land was overgrown with a lot of bushes, which made it seem like we were in the middle of the country when in fact we were in the middle of the city.

Since we weren't in the Boy Scouts, we used that field to get our outdoor adventures. We would start a campfire and each of us would bring a little potato. When the coals burned down and the embers were red hot, we'd toss the potatoes on the fire and tell stories. We thought that was the best feeling you could ever have.

We were good kids and most of what we did was clean fun. About the only thing we did that was bad was to raid people's fruit trees. If somebody had a nice cherry tree, we would climb it and eat our fill. We got in trouble a little bit in the neighborhood, so we took our adventures out on the road.

We rode our bikes a couple of miles into Detroit and found a street that had a bunch of peach trees. We made a big raid and came up with a great idea about how we were going to transport our loot. We pulled our belts tight and tucked our shirts into our pants. Then we threw the peaches down our collars. But all the peach fuzz irritated our skin; after about one-half mile, we all wound up getting so itchy that we threw those peaches away.

James was an excellent musician. He played the drums in the high school marching band and invented some very creative street beats. Those were the rhythms that our marching band would use. A lot of those band members took pride in the way they marched on the street because of James's different rhythms.

Mainly because of James, our group became interested in music. When we got a little older, we formed a garage band with electric guitars and generally played the blues.

Hawk was the group member who always talked about culture. He wanted us to expand our horizons through reading. He taught us to play chess, and when a new coffeehouse opened in Hamtramck, he would take us there and we'd observe all the different-looking people.

One night, we were in a coffeehouse when Hawk went to the jukebox and pushed some number.

"Guys, you've got to hear this," Hawk said.

The Beatles came on.

We looked at him like he was crazy, because we were all soul men. To us, the number-one singing group in the world was the Temptations.

Robert was the youngest. He was influenced by all of us and did pretty well in school and in sports. After the older guys graduated and got jobs, it was just Robert and I—until, that is, our neighborhood was torn down so they could put in Interstate 75. People began to scatter and the old gang lost touch.

I did hear years later that James got married and wound up playing the drums professionally on tour for some soul performers. But the guy I often thought about was Hawk. There will be days when I'm out on the road and I'll get a thought that this guy is going to come up to me and I'll know him right away by his hairline.

A couple of years after we moved across the street to a house on the I-75 freeway service drive, I was in downtown Detroit. I saw Robert walking down the street. He had a sad expression. He told me he had just gotten out of jail for punching a teacher; I couldn't believe it, because he had been such a good kid.

These guys were such a big part of my growing up, and race was never an issue. We were truly friends deep down inside.

Who could have forseen the way our lives would unfold? Wherever I've gone, whatever I've done, I feel those childhood experiences were a great foundation for what was to come.

Though my parents were very caring people, they weren't very ambitious. I wish I could say there was an easy explanation for my success in life—that my parents said things or trained me in a certain way. But it wasn't like that at all. Yes, they instilled in me a desire for achievement. But they didn't preach the work ethic and say you've got to succeed. My mother would tell me late in life that it almost scared her and my dad that I was successful. They might have preferred it if I'd stayed around Hamtramck and worked in the factories. I thought that was the wrong attitude to have, and my mother and I had a pretty good debate about it.

The world is tough, yet it isn't a bad place, a scary place. But I understand my parents' sentiments. They spent a lot of years in a big city, and that can wear on you and knock you down. So I didn't get that aggressive push from my folks; it was more a caring, supportive upbringing. But somehow I gained the self-confidence to go on in a world outside Hamtramck, and basketball became my outlet for doing that.

When I was nine, I played my first basketball game. A buddy and I had just watched a Celtics–Hawks game at his house. He had a bongo on a wood floor, and it reminded us of the famous parquet floor at Boston Garden. We flipped the bongo over and it had a hole in it; we got a tennis ball and played a little basketball right there in the house. Shooting that ball into the basket simply gave me a great, great feeling.

For a few years, though, it was baseball rather than basketball that captured my attention.

When I was ten, I started playing Little League, and I was a pretty good player. During that time, the twelve-year-olds in our town were phenomenal. My cousin, Mark Modich, was an all-star second baseman. There was another great twelve-year-old named Art "Pinkie" Deras; when you batted against him, it was an awesome situation. I could barely see the ball, it was so fast. If you struck out, but managed to get a foul tip during your at-bat, you came back to the dugout feeling that you had really accomplished something.

As a hitter, Deras was just as impressive. I remember him knocking one to left field as our guy kept going back and back and disappeared into the darkness. After about ten seconds, he came back with his arms up, saying, "I can't find it."

As that team of all-stars advanced through the Michigan districts, I would go along with my Uncle Joe, my mother, and my sister. It was like watching pro players. They wound up winning the Little League World Series in Williamsport, Pennsylvania, and becoming celebrities. They were on *Lawrence Welk*, which was very big in Hamtramck because of the polkas. They were on *The Ed Sullivan Show*. They had a parade down our main street in Hamtramck. They were our heroes.

My cousin Mark was just a couple of years older than I, but he had such a positive effect on me through the type of person he was. Kids at that age can be cruel. Mark was a star on the championship team and it would have been easy to look down on another kid who wasn't a star, yet he was the best role model anybody could have. If I asked him about one of his experiences, he shared it with me openly. It was as though I lived that Little League World Series championship right along with him.

Looking back, I would have to say that my relationship with Mark was instrumental in my development. And his father, my Uncle Joe, was a special person, too.

Uncle Joe was my mother's younger brother. He was a factory worker, but he knew there was a world of opportunity outside Hamtramck, and he took it upon himself to be very supportive of me and my sister. He was a soft-spoken guy, but he had a way of doing things that let you know there were horizons to explore beyond our modest, tree-lined neighborhood.

On Sundays, Uncle Joe would come over and pick up my mother, Fran, and me. Mark was usually with Uncle Joe, and we would all take a ride in his car. He would take us to some of the more affluent neighborhoods around Detroit—through Grosse Pointe and St. Clair Shores where there were nicer homes. And then we'd go around the northern suburbs.

I have great memories of the parks in the countryside north of town. One of my favorite spots was an apple cider mill, which was located just about where the Palace of Auburn Hills, home of the Detroit Pistons, stands today.

On some of those tranquil outings, Uncle Joe would talk to me about my future. He had a plan.

"To make it in the world, you have to get to college," Uncle Joe said.

With our family's financial situation, there was no way my folks could afford to pay my way through school. But from the beginning, I had been a bright student, getting mostly As and Bs.

Uncle Joe saw the potential in me.

"You've really got something going there with the good grades," he said. "Keep hitting those books, but also find yourself a sport. If you're good enough in that sport, you may be able to go to school on an athletic scholarship."

We were always going to athletic fields. Uncle Joe taught me things in baseball, soccer, even basketball. But it was usually baseball, because that was the identity for kids in Hamtramck. Everybody knew us as the best Little Leaguers in the world.

When I was twelve, I made the all-stars in baseball. I was a pitcher–first baseman–outfielder. Pretty good player, but nothing really special.

As we moved up to Pony League, I found baseball losing its appeal. I just didn't have a deep passion for the game. I was better than average, but I lacked the love for it. Still, I kept playing, for a while anyway.

Uncle Joe had bought me a really good glove that probably cost about $30 back then. He got me a shiny pair of spikes. And the truth is that I felt obligated. It was almost like a job: You go to the ballpark because that's what we do in Hamtramck. But as time went on, it became more and more of a burden to go there. I would actually look up in the sky for rainclouds, hoping I didn't have to go play baseball.

When I was fourteen, they made a coaching change and things got even worse. The new coach had a sharpness to him and sometimes wound up insulting the kids. I dreaded it, but I still would go. When it got to be too much, I knew I had to have a talk with Uncle Joe about this situation. It was a hard conversation, because I didn't want him to think I was a quitter.

"Try to make it through the season," he said. "Maybe if you were on another team it would be better."

"It probably would be an improvement," I responded. "But I have to be honest with you. I'm losing my love for this game. I just don't enjoy it."

As the conversation ended, I promised I wouldn't quit on the team. But then something happened that brought the situation to a head. One day I didn't even get in the game. I wound up coaching third base. Afterward, the coach was talking about the mistakes we'd made, and his attention suddenly turned to me.

"Rudy, at least *you* didn't make any mistakes."

I was really dejected. As I was leaving the ballpark with my head down, my uncle came up to me. I hadn't even known he was there. He had watched the game and had heard the sarcastic comment from the coach.

"This is a tough situation," Uncle Joe said. "I see how miserable you are, but I still think you should stick with it."

"What if I tried another sport?" I suggested.

"What sport?"

"I really like basketball."

Uncle Joe was surprised. I had been on the basketball team through junior high, but I had never gotten into a game.

"Rudy, you've been an all-star in baseball and you haven't really played in this other sport."

"I really love it," I insisted. "I think I'll get better at it."

Uncle Joe looked me in the eye and saw the sincerity. At that point he gave in.

"Rudy," he said, "you've got a long way to go in basketball."

It was Uncle Joe's way of telling me it was okay to give up baseball for basketball. When he gave in, it was like the weight of the world had dropped off my shoulders.

I just started running. "Uncle Joe, I will. I will work hard," I yelled.

I ran right across the city, about three-quarters of a mile, and went right to the basketball courts, where I got into a pickup game. I would wind up at those courts almost every day. It was me and basketball, and nothing was going to separate us.

The next year, when I went to high school, I naturally tried out for the freshman team. They had a new teacher coming in named Mr. Hall. He was an ex–football player from the University of Michigan, but he got the job as freshman basketball coach.

Before the season started, a good friend of mine who happened to be in Mr. Hall's homeroom found out I wasn't on the list of guys who survived the cut.

I went into a panic and wound up asking Mr. Hall if he wanted to play me one-on-one after practice. He wasn't a very good basketball player; he played as if every time the ball bounced he thought it was a fumble. He kept lunging at me and knocking me down, but I kept bouncing up. I think he could see the desperation in me, because when the team was announced the next day I was on it.

Our freshman team wound up being one of the worst in school history. One game, against River Rouge in the Twin Valley Conference, we went into the locker room at halftime down 50–4. Suffice it to say, my commitment to basketball didn't get off to a quick start.

After my freshman year, it became a way of life that I would go to "The Courts." That's what we called it.

"Where you goin'?"

"The Courts."

The Courts were at Copernicus Junior High School. There were five full-length courts. The first two courts had L-shaped supports, and the others were just on straight poles. Why people, most of them black, came from all over the city to play at Copernicus, which was a white neighborhood, was a mystery to me. But it was always busy there, and people from all walks of life would congregate because of their love for the sport.

On the straight-pole baskets were the youngsters who were just beginning to play. You'd see fathers there teaching their sons how to shoot layups. The recessed poles were for the advanced group. This wasn't official; there wasn't someone there who would supervise. It was just understood. You knew where you belonged.

After I left baseball and committed myself to basketball, I began to get into games on the straight baskets. A monumental time for me was when some high school player was injured one day and I was selected to move to the higher court as a fill-in.

That felt like graduation day and basketball heaven all rolled into one. I was so damned excited that I stayed at The Courts until everybody left and shot hoops in the dark.

You never knew what kind of excitement would be in store during those pickup games. Occasionally, a Piston like Reggie Harding, Eddie Miles, Jimmy Walker, or John Tresvant would even show up to spice up the competition.

With each passing day, I was getting better. I had gained some strength, and instead of shooting the old set shot from the hip, I could now shoot a jump shot. And I could dunk the ball. The first time I did that, I stayed out there for long hours to work on the timing and strengthen my jumping muscles.

For a lot of guys, The Courts were a way of life. Men in their thirties would come and play after working in the factories. Some of the guys would even play in their work boots, which had the reinforced toe. You don't know what pain is until you've been kicked in the shin with one of those boots.

I was just a high school kid, but The Courts were a part of my life, just as they were for those thirty-year-olds. You sleep, you eat, you work, and you play basketball all summer long. Some of the older guys were legendary out there. Since we played halfcourt basketball, being in great physical condition wasn't a necessity.

The older guys had their unique styles. I remember one guy who played the whole game without ever jumping. He would out-rebound you by using position, then back his man in and get layups by scooping the ball. There were guys who were expert at reading the wind and could consistently make 25-footers.

One of these playground legends was Walt McCier, James's older brother. Walt was in his early twenties, about 6-3. What was unique about him was his array of fakes. He would put his whole body into it, get the defender to react, and beat him. He would use a combination of exaggerated fakes, like making a jab step to get you back on your heels and then faking a shot. You'd go flying in the air, feeling foolish. But Walt might not do anything at that point. He'd wait for you to come down and make one more move to embarrass you. He just had complete control of his defender, like having a puppet on a string.

"Rudy, you're way too stiff with your moves," Walt would tell me. "Get some rhythm in your game. Dance with your man. Lead for a while, then get him to follow you. And then change your dance step."

"Thanks, Walt," I said. "But I don't know how to dance."

Walt sort of resembled Jimi Hendrix. He had similar facial features, the same skin tone and long, unruly hair. But there the resemblance ended. Walt had no front teeth and he usually had a sneer on his face. In the neighborhood, Walt would be smiling, telling stories. But when he went to The Courts, he'd wear that sneer and look very intimidating. His appearance put fear in a lot of people. He knew it and he wanted it that way.

But I knew that Walt was a big teddy bear. We started hanging around together because we both loved basketball. He was proud that someone from his neighborhood was getting good at his game.

Unfortunately, Walt never played high school basketball. He quit school after the eleventh grade but he kept telling me, "One day, you're going to play for Hamtramck. But to do that, you always have to go against good competition."

If the competition wasn't good at The Courts, we'd find some form of transportation and go to a playground somewhere in Detroit. We never had any problem when I was with Walt; they'd take one look at him and say, "You want next game? You can have it. And that little skinny white kid can play, too."

We played all over Detroit for a couple of summers, against all types of competition. We would face inner-city fast-break players and the passing game from players out in the suburbs. Because of the age difference, Walt and I eventually grew apart, but I'll always be grateful for his tutelage and advice.

One of my most memorable days at The Courts was when Reggie Harding paid us a visit. Reggie was one of the first players in the pros who never went to college. He drove up in a convertible Thunderbird with a couple of his friends, and there happened to be a long line to get into a pickup game.

Reggie announced that he played for the Pistons and he wasn't waiting. He would *have* next game.

There were some protests, but Reggie stared toward the chatter and it quieted down quickly. I was on the team that happened to win the game in progress, so two friends and I took on Reggie and two of his buddies. I had to guard Harding. He was a seven-footer and must have outweighed me by about seventy pounds.

But Reggie started off just clowning around. He'd pass up shots to give the ball to his buddies. Meanwhile, we were busting our butts. We wanted to beat the pro, and we were holding our own, a couple of points up. Reggie continued to clown around, grabbing rebounds with one hand and posing for the gallery. The next shot we missed, he did the same thing. I came running in, snatched the ball out of his hand and dunked it in one motion. It was one of the best plays I ever made and the crowd responded—not only for the play, but to razz Reggie for getting burned.

Reggie didn't see it like everybody else. He said the basket was his, that he had tipped it in. We started to protest, but Reggie gave us that stare and we didn't know what to do. Hey, I didn't want to lose one of the greatest plays I had ever made.

At that point an older spectator walked onto the court and got right in Reggie's face.

"It can't be your basket," the man said. "They shot the ball and you have to rebound and get it out past the free-throw line to score. The fact is, the young boy dunked on you."

The crowd yelled "Yeah," and we were all looking at Reggie, wondering how he would respond. He started slowly shaking his head up and down.

"Yeah, you're right. That was their basket," Reggie said.

We all breathed a sigh of relief and the game resumed. The next time Reggie got the ball, the playful, clowning expression was gone. He was at the post and he turned and slammed a dunk right over me.

"Whose was that?" Reggie yelled.

The next time he did the same thing. "Whose was that?"

On the third possession, my teammates tried to help me hold off Reggie, but it didn't matter. His team needed one point to win and Reggie started backing in. We all jumped on him, trying to take a foul, but he carried us all to the basket and dunked one last time.

"Who's got next game?" he demanded.

As proud as I was of my dunk on Reggie, it wasn't the best dunk of that summer. That happened a couple of weeks later when a young man named Spencer Haywood paid us a visit. Spencer had just come up from Mississippi and enrolled at Pershing High School. We were going at each other one day when "The Dunk" happened. A guard on his team drove in for a layup. I left Spencer to protect the basket and knocked the ball off the backboard. As it started floating out toward the foul line, Spencer was well behind me. He took off for the rebound, even though the ball was well over his head.

Everybody was sure the ball was going past him, but Spencer's arms were spread-eagled. As the ball was moving away, he palmed it like a grapefruit with his right hand and grabbed the rim with his left hand. Then came a thunderous, windmill dunk.

For a moment, everybody stopped in shock. People started running around in a frenzy, trying to understand what had happened.

We were in the middle of a game, but we didn't finish it. We all went to the corner store and bought sodas. Then we came back to The Courts to talk about the greatest dunk we had ever seen.

Spencer was a modest guy. He wanted to know why we couldn't play anymore. "Why should we?" we said. "How can you top that?"

It was almost like a religious phenomenon, and we wanted to give that playground dunk the respect it deserved.

When I tried out for the freshman team, I was about 6-1 and very scrawny. The growth spurt came after my sophomore year. I went from about 6-3 to 6-6 as a junior. In the summer after my sophomore year, I was growing so fast you could almost see my pants crawling up my leg.

My father was 6-3 and my mother was 5-7. I would eventually top out at 6-8, which meant I was destined to be a frontcourt player. They didn't have 6-8 guards in those days.

When I went back to school for my sophomore year, I worked my way up to the junior-varsity starting lineup. We were running the offense that the varsity coach was using, and I was able to master some of the little techniques that he liked. I was the kind of guy who had trouble immediately picking up what the coach was showing me, but I would go home, work on it, and the next day I would have it down.

The varsity coach was a guy named John Radwanski. One time I made a backdoor cut for a layup, that brought a positive response from him. To get a positive comment from Radwanski was like the voice of God speaking to you. When he praised me, I felt like I was on top of the world.

After that season was over, I got my class schedule changed so I could be in gym class with the varsity guys. They would have great pickup games, and my game was improving to the point where I started outjumping and outrebounding the varsity center.

Here I was, a tenth-grader doing that. I was proud of how far I had come.

But one day Coach Radwanski called me over. I was really nervous as I went up to talk to him.

"What are you doing in this class?" he asked.

"I just wanted to be in here because the best players are here."

"Are you planning on coming out for varsity?"

"Yes, coach, I'd like to give it a try."

"Well, I've been watching you and let me tell you this: You don't have what it takes. The stuff I see you do out there . . . you'd be wasting your time and my time," Radwanski said.

I was devastated, absolutely devastated.

I never asked Radwanski why he said that and I don't even know if he really believed it. It might have been his way of motivating me.

I had looked up to those varsity players and was starting to compete on their level. To get a critique that negative just totally deflated me.

I was depressed for a couple of days, but then it hit me: I just said to myself, I love this game. If I can't play on his team, I'll play recreational ball or whatever. But I'm going to play basketball.

I enjoyed everything about the game. You could do so many things on the basketball court. In football, the position dictates that you do certain things. In basketball, you can shoot, rebound, pass, play defense; all of the elements of the sport are there for every player.

My fascination with the game was such that I even scratched into the little metal headboard on my bed I LOVE BASKETBALL. When I went to bed at night, I would hold on to it.

By the end of that junior-varsity year, to my surprise, Coach Radwanski advanced me to the varsity basically to watch and learn. We had a high school All-American named Ralph Brisker, who went on to play at the University of Detroit and had some tryouts in the pros. By the end of the year I had become friends with all the players on that team. They accepted me as one of the group.

Most of those guys were black and lived in the projects. The best player coming back was John Brisker, Ralph's younger brother. John was a big personality guy who would go on to the ABA and later to the Seattle SuperSonics. John took a liking to me. In the summer, we went to different playgrounds around Detroit and he would make sure the five Hamtramck starters all went together.

Some of those "road trips" that summer were tough. There weren't a lot of gangs back then, but people had their turf. If you went to the wrong neighborhood, you could get in some threatening situations where you had to get out of Dodge—quickly.

That was an adventure, because the car that John had didn't always start the first try. And the brakes didn't work very well, either.

In my junior year, we were rated No. 2 in the state. We won two games in the state tournament and then lost to Pontiac Central.

In my last year of high school, I was the only returning senior on the team. All of the guys who had played in front of me in the previous years had one way or another gotten out of basketball. With some, it was grades; with others, it was getting in trouble with the law. And some just lost interest in playing the game.

With John Brisker and my other teammates having graduated and gone off to college, I became the leader of the team. My skills had improved. I was a center, but I didn't always stay close to the basket. I was now about 6-6 and 195 pounds. I could shoot the ball out to 20 feet, but I really loved to rebound and block shots. We had a very athletic team. We were a quick, fast-breaking team. One of our guards, Isaiah Blessitt, who later was drafted by the Detroit Tigers and played in their farm system, was exceptionally fast. We had a play that "Ike" (that was his nickname) and I worked out ourselves. When I got a defensive rebound—while still in the air— Ike would give a yell and I'd just throw the ball toward our basket. Ike would just run by the other team, grab the ball, and put it in the basket.

Coach Radwanski was tough on all of us, but we respected him. We thought he was a little crazy sometimes because he would get

physical with his players. He would grab a guy and shake him, trying to fire him up. Once, when I was a junior, we were playing an
early-season game against a Catholic school. The first half was
winding down, and the man I was guarding—a pudgy player who
looked like he belonged on a football field—got the ball in the
backcourt. I knew the time was short. I got in front of him, playing position defense. He wasn't even over halfcourt when he threw
the ball over my head. I thought he had passed the ball, but it went
in the basket.

As I was making my way to the bench, I heard something
behind me, like footsteps. Then all of a sudden, I felt a blow to my
backside. Coach Radwanski had kicked me in the butt. He was
ranting and raving about my not having my hands up. I was in a
daze. I thought I was playing good defense and it was a lucky shot.
I realize now that Coach Radwanski felt he had to be this kind of
monster to handle these guys from the inner city.

No one ever questioned any of the things he said. Coach Radwanski was the boss. He rode me hard my senior year.

"Rudy, you've got to be involved in every play," he said. "If
you're not shooting, you've got to get the offensive rebound. When
you get a defensive rebound, bust your butt and get into the fast
break."

"Even when I throw the long pass to Ike?" I asked.

"Yeah, he might miss it," Coach Radwanski replied. "Be there
to tip it in."

I had a good senior year, averaging over 30 points and 20
rebounds. I began to appreciate what Coach Radwanski was doing
for me. His constant motivation was helping me reach my potential.

Coach Radwanski had a softer side to him. He and his wife
never had children. I felt he sort of looked at me as a son. He'd ask
me how things were going at home and in class. He knew I was
short on money, so he created a job for me: I was a hall monitor,
making sure students wouldn't pass my post.

For what reason, I never could figure out.

In exchange for this duty, I'd get a free, hot lunch.

My father began to take an interest in my ballplaying. He had heard the men at work talking about me. My father didn't know much about sports. I knew he didn't know the rules of basketball. The first time he came to the gym, the junior-varsity game was still in progress; we were to play later.

My father saw a seat he liked on the other side of the court and he walked directly to it. The problem was, he cut right across the court. The players were shocked. Who was this extra guy on the floor in street clothes? The referees blew the whistle, stopping play. My father never knew he disrupted the game. He was just happy he got a good seat.

In my senior year we battled our perennial rivals, River Rouge, for the conference title. We looked forward to the state tournament, hoping to do better than the previous year. We won our first game, but lost our second to the University of Detroit High School. It was a tremendous disappointment to all of us.

By this time, I was receiving letters from colleges all over the country. It started to get mind-boggling. West Coast. East Coast. The South.

I'll always remember the day that Guy Lewis, the head coach at the University of Houston, came to our gym. He was dressed in a pinstripe suit and looked like a movie star. As it came down to decision time, Coach Radwanski called me to his office to discuss my future. We decided to focus on four schools: the University of Detroit, Toledo (where John Brisker was playing), Michigan State, and Michigan.

I didn't want to go too far from home and I was really a fan of the University of Michigan team. Cazzie Russell and Bill Buntin had turned Michigan into a contender for the NCAA championship. I watched them every time they were on television, and I liked their coach, Dave Strack, when I made my visit up to Ann Arbor.

I was also impressed by John Bennington, the coach at Michigan State. The students at State were middle-of-the-road, All-American types. At Michigan, it was a little different. Remember, it was the mid-sixties, and there were a lot of hippies at Michigan. I had nothing against them; I just hadn't seen many in Hamtramck.

Coach Radwanski and several other teachers were in favor of

Michigan. They touted it as a great academic institution. My parents were just happy I was getting an opportunity to go to college.

"Rudy, what do you think is best?" my mother said. "Don't let someone else make the decision for you."

I finally chose Michigan. There were a lot of logical reasons for that decision—the location, only forty miles from Hamtramck. The academics. But the deciding factor was basketball. I had always fantasized about wearing the maize-and-blue uniform. When I signed a letter of intent to become a Wolverine, I thought of all the people who had helped me along the way.

Most of all, I thought of Uncle Joe.

His advice had been true. Now I had a chance to receive a college education. It had taken a tremendous amount of hard work to get to this point, and I knew there was a lot more ahead of me.

From Hamtramck to Ann Arbor. The journey was just beginning.

3

GOING OFF TO COLLEGE was a big adjustment for me, especially in terms of meeting different types of people. The changes going on in the world in the mid-sixties were reflected in Ann Arbor. It was all new to me—the sites, the freshman mixers, the music. It seemed like there was a different adventure in my life every day. But through it all, basketball remained my primary focus.

My freshman year, we only played three regular-season games. Freshmen couldn't play varsity sports back then, so it was more of a training period, with a lot of practice and a lot of dreams. We were in Yost Field House that first year, and it was typical of the arenas in the Midwest, almost like a big barn. The lighting was perfect for shooting, and I would spend many hours alone shooting baskets and dreaming of the day I would put on a varsity uniform. Each day I would look around and think about how I was in a place where my heroes had played—the Cazzie Russells, the Bill Buntins, the Oliver Dardens.

I kept practicing and improving, and by my sophomore year I was a varsity starter for the Wolverines. We were opening up a brand-new building—Crisler Arena—and our first opponent was a very good Kentucky team coached by the legendary Adolph Rupp. The Wildcats had a great young sophomore, Dan Issel, and we were anxious to find out how we could do against a quality opponent.

Well, it didn't take long for us to find out how far we had to go. Kentucky completely dominated us to the point where Rupp finally had to tell his players not to shoot on the first or second option, just so it wouldn't get to be completely humiliating experience. What a rude welcome to big-time college competition.

I was so hyper in that first game that I wound up doing something kind of crazy: I got 27 rebounds because I was running all over the place, overdoing everything. When I shot the ball, I was jumping so high that I completely lost my touch. The next morning I woke up and couldn't even walk. I had strained an arch in my foot from overuse. I figured there was no way I'd be ready to play in our next game at the University of Detroit, but I made the 42-mile trip back home.

My high school coach had sent a message that he wanted to see me before the game, and I told him I thought it was doubtful that I would play. As we stood talking by an entrance, it seemed that everybody who came through the door was from Hamtramck. They were all fired up and offering encouragement.

"Rudy, are you sure you can't give it a go?" Radwanski said. "I think you should try it."

So I did.

The first time I touched the ball I shot a long jumper. It went in and the adrenaline started pumping. I lost the pain and wound up having a great shooting night, finishing with 30 points. Because I couldn't jump that high from the soreness in my arch, I learned a valuable lesson about shooting. You can't use all your energy on the jump. If you're going to shoot from 18 to 20 feet, you don't need to jump over your opponent; if you're doing that, you're not open and probably taking the wrong shot.

It was something I had never thought about. I had always been an instinctive player, but I learned that my touch was so much better when I didn't burn up all that energy.

I was learning, but our team absorbed more tough lumps the rest of my sophomore season. We went down to play a great Houston team led by Elvin Hayes, Don Chaney, and Ken Spain.

The game was at Delmar Fieldhouse, and again we were over-matched. Chaney put on a defensive clinic, stealing the ball from our guards on three consecutive possessions. Walking off the floor, we were really embarrassed, and I happened to cross paths with a little gentleman who had an unlit cigar in his mouth.

The little man grabbed me by the elbow and said, "Good game, kid."

I was so down, I sort of told him to buzz off. The next day, as we were on our way back to Ann Arbor, we were at the airport and I was talking to a teammate.

"Did you know the great Red Auerbach was at our game?" he said.

It hit me like a thunderbolt. The man I had brushed off was the king of the Celtics. Sure enough, we later saw Red walking through the airport and I had this sinking sensation. How could I have done that? Even though he got the snub from me, it was a profitable trip for Auerbach. He went on to make Chaney his first-round draft pick that year.

The next two years, Michigan was in the middle of the pack in the rugged Big Ten. Iowa was led by John Johnson and Fred Brown. Purdue had Rick Mount, a legendary outside shooter from rural Indiana. Mount's running mate at guard was Herman Gilliam. Ohio State had Dave Sorensen, who would become a second-round NBA pick, and Northwestern had Don Adams, who would go on to play for the Rockets.

Nobody could say we dodged the big boys. *Basketball Weekly* did a rating of schedules and concluded we had the toughest schedule in the country my junior year. In my senior year, our schedule was voted second-toughest. Even though we didn't have great teams, that exposure really helped me when it came time to be drafted by the NBA.

I had been recruited by Dave Strack, a good man and a good basketball coach. Dave had coached those great Cazzie Russell teams, but he left after my sophomore season to become athletic director at Arizona. Assistant Johnny Orr took over. Johnny was like nothing we had ever seen. He was a very excitable guy who had a different way of talking, and his sense of humor always stood out. At every banquet, he'd break people up. The women would be laughing so hard they'd have to go to the bathroom.

I'll always remember Johnny's defensive lecture to us: "Guys, you've got the wrong idea out here," he would say. "When the other team scores, I see you put your head down. I want one of you guys to grab that ball out of the net, get your head up, and we'll have Bird Carter streaking downcourt. He'll get the basket right back. I don't want you guys to get your daubers down."

Basically, Johnny was telling us we were just going to try to outscore people. As his coaching career unfolded, he came a long way from that philosophy; a couple of years after I left school, I went back for a banquet and had a great talk with Johnny.

"Rudy, we've really advanced what we're doing here," he said. "We really teach and work on the fundamentals."

That was reflected in Orr's teams. I watched them play good defense and a disciplined game. He was telling me that he had grown as a coach.

We all grew from the Michigan experience. I got to be close friends with several of the guys who played on the team: Bill Lyle, Steve Fishman, Bill Fraumann, Rick Bloodworth, and Dan Fife. We all came from different backgrounds, and sharing our experiences helped me see the world as a much bigger place than my old neighborhood.

Moving out of the dorm and into an apartment was another educational step. I had to learn to balance a checkbook and pay the rent. I also had to learn to cook, because I couldn't afford to eat out every day.

For a guy with my background, being at Michigan was a mind-expanding experience. Hamtramck was basically blue-collar, and now I was being exposed to a liberal outlook. There were protests on campus and a lot of students questioned authority. Ideas about the way things had been done—the old conservative beliefs—were being challenged.

I still had strong ties back in Hamtramck. I'd make the short trip home on the Greyhound bus to see my parents and the group of guys I had become friendly with my senior year in high school.

They were a bunch of fun-loving people, all Polish, with last names like Jaworski, Milewski, Stahovich, and Romanski. Most of my high school friends weren't going to college and were eventually drafted into the Armed Forces. About once every two months, we'd have a big party to send one of the fellows off to the war in Vietnam. Fortunately, all of my buddies made it back.

There was another reason I was spending weekends in Hamtramck: I had met a wonderful girl. She was a dark-haired beauty with big, brown eyes and the best pair of legs I had ever seen. Her name was Sophie Migas. I first met her when a friend was taking me back to Ann Arbor. As we were driving through Hamtramck to the freeway, we passed her house. Sophie and a friend were sitting on the porch. My friend asked them to come along for the ride.

I had seen Sophie before. She was a cheerleader for St. Florian High School, a Catholic school a few blocks away from Hamtramck High. I'll always remember our first conversation.

"You cheered for St. Florian?"

"Yeah."

"Were you at the Hamtramck game?"

"Of course."

"Don't you remember me?"

"No. Why should I remember you?"

"Never mind."

We had played St. Florian my senior year and I had scored 54 points, my career high. I was the tallest player on the floor and the only white guy on our team who played a lot. How could she not remember me?

Prior to meeting Sophie, I hadn't dated any other girls at Michigan. I told a buddy from Hamtramck to get a date and bring Sophie up to Ann Arbor for the football weekends, so I could see her in a double-date situation. The problem was that each time he would come up, he'd tell everybody in Hamtramck what he was doing. And those people didn't need an excuse for a party. So I'd get to the apartment and the whole gang would be there. It got to be sort of frustrating because a friend of Sophie's was giving me all her attention and became a barrier between Sophie and me. I didn't have the finesse to tell her to leave me alone without hurting her feelings.

One weekend the gang was all together when Sophie finally said to the other girl, "Why don't you get off Rudy's lap?" Then Sophie got on my lap. It was what I wanted, but panic set in because I didn't know what in the world I was going to say to her. I had all these things in my mind, but nothing would come out of my mouth.

Right at that moment, a fight broke out in the apartment. The television was pushed over and bodies were rolling around on the floor. I was almost relieved by the ruckus, because I needed time to compose myself.

Later we took a walk through Ann Arbor. Snow had fallen that night and it was beautiful around 2 A.M. As we were walking, the sky turned completely bright for several seconds. I thought, Hey, this is the kind of thing you see in the movies, with the bells ringing and all that stuff. I found out later it was the northern lights. But at that time, as I looked at Sophie in the bright light at 2 A.M., it truly seemed like an omen. I was thinking this was really it, the start of a lifelong commitment.

My relationship with Sophie grew stronger and stronger. She would come up for the games and I would spend a lot of weekends back in Hamtramck. It wasn't easy because I didn't have a car. I bought a lot of $7 Greyhound bus tickets.

As a college student, I was good to fair. When I was really motivated, I could get the job done. The one class I really got fired up for was anatomy. There I was, dissecting a cadaver. I really got into learning about the body, because I felt that was something I could use the rest of my life. I got one of the highest grades among the athletes—a B-plus—and it took hours and hours of study to accomplish that. When we needed help, there were tutors, but mostly we were on our own and had to make classes. There was no cruising up there at all. I was very proud to be at a great university. I didn't know how my basketball career was going to go, and I felt a degree from Michigan would help me later. Books and basketball filled my days.

It was during my junior year that I developed the midrange

bank shot, which became a trademark of my game. One of my activity classes that year was with assistant coach Fred Snowden, who later went on to coach at Arizona. Snowden had been a great high school coach and was an assistant under Johnny Orr. In class, we had a lot of time to talk about basketball. At that time, my game consisted of being a long-range shooter or offensive rebounder.

"You should try shooting the bank shot when you're at a forty-five-degree angle," Snowden suggested.

I went out and shot a few in his class and it felt good, so I decided to try the bank shot in our next game. It was amazing. I could see the spot on the backboard so clearly. It didn't matter how hard I shot the ball, as long as I hit that spot.

I wound up scoring a career-high 48 points against Indiana, which tied Cazzie Russell's school record. The bank shot became an integral part of my game. From then on, whenever I had the midrange shot at an angle, I used that board.

One of my most memorable games at Michigan was against Marquette in Ann Arbor. Marquette was coached by the flamboyant Al McGuire. He used a ploy I hadn't seen before: When his starters were introduced, instead of running straight out to the free-throw line, they first came to our bench, shook my hand, and glared in my face.

I guess Coach McGuire felt this would intimidate me, but it had the opposite effect. As the last couple of starters were approaching, it hit me: He must think I'm pretty good to go through all this.

When the game started, my confidence was soaring. Marquette had a great team, led by point guard Dean "The Dream" Meminger, who later played on the New York Knicks' 1973 championship team. Marquette's forwards, Rick Cobb and Joe Thomas, were physical rebounders, and the supporting cast was strong.

I started out hot, making a couple of outside shots in the first couple of minutes. Then I got a couple of offensive-rebound baskets. McGuire made a substitution. In came Gary Brell, a gangly 6-7 forward with a head of shaggy blond hair. Gary had been given the assignment of putting the clamps on me. I knew this because he told me, "I'm going to shut you down. You're not that good."

I had learned on the playgrounds how to deal with trash talk. You ignore it, filter it out. This frustrates the talker. He's trying to break your concentration, but you're going about your business, doing your job. He's not getting to you. He starts thinking of other things to say. Now, he's lost *his* focus on the game. This is what happened with Brell.

He started playing me aggressively, chest to chest and face to face. He was constantly jabbering. I began moving without the ball and making sudden stops. Brell would be trailing and couldn't stop fast enough without fouling me. He fouled me twice before I even got the ball, and I continued to have a good first half despite his antics.

As the first half was coming to an end, I wound up with the ball with only five seconds to go. I had to get a shot off quickly. I dribbled to my left with Brell playing me closely. I pump-faked and Brell went up high to block the shot. I was still on the floor. As he was coming down, I began my jump shot. He raked me across the arm, but it didn't affect my shot. I continued to follow through. The ball banked off the board and into the hoop as the referee blew the whistle for the foul. It was Brell's fifth foul. He was out of the game before the half.

Brell stomped off the court. As I took my free throw, I glanced at their bench. Brell was sitting there with his shoes off, and he was still talking. Only now he was talking to himself.

It was a close game until midway in the second half when we started to pull away. Mark Henry, a player from Fort Wayne, Indiana, who had made our team as a walk-on, did a great job defending Meminger. Then McGuire did another thing I had never seen before: I grabbed a defensive rebound and spotted Mark Henry, who was all alone downcourt; I threw a baseball pass, leading him a little. Mark had a clear path to the basket. All of a sudden, McGuire came off the bench and tried to get in Henry's way. He scared the hell out of Mark, but Mark avoided McGuire and put the ball in the basket.

The referees were stunned. They didn't know what to call.

"If you're going to screw me, you've got to kiss me first," McGuire told the officials.

It was that kind of bizarre game.

The next day in the paper, Coach McGuire was extremely complimentary. "We threw everything we had at Tomjanovich and he handled it all," McGuire said. "He's a true All-America and I think he'll be a great pro."

I ran into McGuire a couple of months later at the National Invitational Tournament in New York.

"Hey, kid, that was a great game you played against us," McGuire told me. "Those things I said in the paper . . . I wasn't just blowing smoke. I think you'll have a great career in the NBA."

During my senior year, I averaged 30.1 points and 15 rebounds per game. But I still didn't really know *how* to play the game. I wanted to win, yes, but I didn't have any patience. At times I played selfishly, but not in a deliberate way; it was more a lack of understanding. I'd play hard, but my thought always was, Get the ball and get it in the basket. If the ball was on the right side, I'd run to the right side. I didn't have a concept of spacing or letting the play develop.

If Rudy the coach was evaluating Rudy the Michigan Wolverine, I'd say this guy could shoot and jump, but boy, does he have a long way to go.

Still, I wound up being the No. 2 overall pick in the 1970 draft behind Bob Lanier. I thought I'd be drafted high, but not No. 2. A lot of it had to do with the fact that I had already signed an NBA contract before the draft. Whoever took me knew exactly what they were getting from a financial standpoint. The NBA–ABA war was going on, and it was a hectic time to be a college senior. Agents would call every day, and I had no idea whom to believe. My father had always been suspicious of strangers, and I guess I inherited some of that.

At one juncture, I went down to Detroit to watch a Pistons game and meet an agent. When we sat down in a hotel lobby, the agent said, "There's going to be an NBA–ABA merger. If you don't sign in the next couple of days, you aren't going to get full value."

That kind of pressure to sign really troubled me. I went home and told my father, and it really got to him. I went to bed confused, and when I woke up the next morning my father said, "Call Johnny Orr. He wants you to meet somebody."

Johnny arranged for me to meet with a group of attorneys from Ann Arbor. I explained the situation to them and they, in turn, explained the situation to me. They felt this particular agent was angling to get a group of guys and deliver them to the NBA. I didn't trust this agent. It was a gut feeling. While I didn't know this particular group of attorneys from Ann Arbor either, they had a completely different approach. It wasn't the big-city, fast-talk approach.

I eventually decided to go with the Ann Arbor group. Phil Fichera and a partner, Allan Price, accompanied me to New York, where we had scheduled separate meetings with the NBA and ABA. At NBA headquarters, on the top floor of Madison Square Garden Tower, we were led into a posh office where Eddie Gottlieb, one of the founders of the NBA, was sitting behind a desk.

Eddie was a jolly man who told a couple of NBA stories that I really enjoyed. When it came time to talk business, I waited in another room. The NBA proposed a deal, and my people said they would have to check with the ABA first before making a final decision. We got in a cab and drove out of the skyscraper district toward the New York apartment district. It seemed like we were lost, but finally we located the ABA headquarters in the basement of an apartment house. What a contrast.

I met Vince Boryla, general manager of the Utah Stars, who had drafted me. The ABA had just signed Rick Mount and Dan Issel. The Mount deal was reported to be worth $1 million, and Boryla suggested that I sign with the Stars for a similar amount.

I'm thinking, Oh, man, I always dreamed of being in the NBA. But I can't turn down a million dollars. I have to do this for my family.

Then I heard my attorney say, "We don't want that deal. Just give us a hundred thousand dollars per year."

I looked at these guys like they were crazy. Why did I get mixed up with these people? I asked myself.

Then Boryla, who had given me high praise, said, "We can't do that."

Now I was completely confused. It turned pretty negative after a while, and Boryla was right in front of me when he made a comment that he didn't want me that much anyway. I had been on a roller-coaster ride listening to all this stuff. We went outside and my attorneys could see I was completely bewildered.

They explained that the "million-dollar deal" was an annuity and not worth much at all. We retired to a hotel that night and the next day we got an early call that the commissioner of the ABA, Jack Dolph, wanted to meet with us.

Commissioner Dolph proposed a deal that would have allowed me to play for any team in the ABA that I chose. My attorneys asked Dolph if the ABA could deliver the cash. "No, it has to be the annuity," he said.

We went back to the NBA and signed the deal: three years, no cut, $100,000 annual salary. "In a couple of years, I'll see you at the All-Star Game," Gottlieb said. That was a wonderful way to leave it. A couple of years later, I did see him at the All-Star Game, and he reminded me of his prediction.

Had I not been safely under contract, I'm not sure I would have gone No. 2 in the draft. As it was, San Diego general manager Pete Newell called me the night before the draft and said they were thinking strongly about taking me. I knew San Diego was in California, but I had no idea what part of the state it was in. We had a globe in my house, and I found San Diego tucked way off in the southern part of an extremely large state. Going in that direction, you couldn't have an NBA destination farther from Detroit.

I didn't know much about the team, either. I knew they had Elvin Hayes, but that was about it. Today, you can get all the coverage on *SportsCenter*, but you didn't hear about a lot of teams back then.

Of course, a part of me had wanted to be a Piston, since Detroit was my hometown team. I had watched them play for a dollar when I was a kid: a quarter for a bus ride to the game, a quarter for the ride back, and fifty cents for a seat in the rafters.

Still, people had cautioned me that it's not always best to play at home. I was up for the challenge of going west to play a game I loved for big dollars.

I thought back to my father's little financial tablet, and I thought about pulling the welfare commodities on a wagon through the neighborhood. A six-figure salary to play basketball?

I was in shock.

4

LATE ONE NIGHT, after spending an evening at Sophie's house watching television, we were sitting in her car, half a block from my house. I still didn't have a car. I usually walked home. But on this night I had asked her to drive me home.

I wanted some private time with her. I had a lot of things on my mind. We sat there in silence for several minutes before I slowly began to talk.

"This is a very exciting time in my life," I said. "I've got a lot of new adventures in front of me. San Diego is on the other side of the world. I hear it's beautiful. I've spent a lot of time imagining how my life is going to be. Everytime I do that, you're a part of it. I can't see going to San Diego without you. Will you come with me?"

"Are you asking me to marry you?"

"Yeah, I am."

"Of course I will," Sophie said.

We embraced each other. It was a beautiful night.

We only had a couple of weeks to get our wedding invitations out and arrange all the details. Things were pretty hectic, but we got it done. We were married on May 29, 1970, in St. Florian Church. It was a beautiful ceremony. The church is one of the biggest in Michigan. You can see the steeple from miles away. What made the church extra special was that it was right across the street from Sophie's house.

The bride and her bridesmaids walked to the church, which gave the ceremony a homey, personal feeling. The reception was a typical Polish celebration; there was plenty of food, featuring some Polish dishes like kielbasa sausage and sauerkraut. The band played polkas and everyone danced. Even me.

Of course, we had an open bar. Everyone had a great time.

Leaving Michigan was a gigantic step for Sophie and me. We were very young, just married, and about to move all the way across the country. Her family was extremely close; she had lost her father when she was eight and her mother, Stella Migas, was truly a great lady. Stella raised four daughters all by herself—Wanda, Sophie, Irene, and Rita.

Stella was a proud woman who understood how tough life could be but never let it knock her down. She had even spent time in a work camp in Germany when she was a young married woman. You talk about resiliency—during that time she never knew if she would see her husband again. Stella was strict in teaching her daughters manners, how to handle themselves in social situations. When the five raven-haired Migas ladies entered a room, you couldn't help noticing that they carried themselves with an air of dignity.

It wasn't easy for Stella to say goodbye to Sophie. Things got very emotional, and we promised we would stop by the cemetery on the way out of town to pay respects to Sophie's father.

At my house, my mother had sad eyes that I just couldn't meet. I knew that if I looked in her eyes, I was going to break down. As we prepared to leave, she was her usual caring self.

"Do you have a sweater?" she asked.

And then my usual response: "Mom, I'm not going to the senior prom."

Right there, the floodgates broke and the tears came bursting forth. "I'm going to miss you," my mother sobbed.

It took Sophie and me some time to compose ourselves. I think we cried all the way across the state of Michigan. But once we settled down, our sadness turned to excitement. We decided we would try to enjoy the trip out west.

Since we hadn't had a honeymoon, we said we were going to

live it up. We decided we would eat lobster all along the way as we crossed the country. But it didn't take long for us to find out that lobster isn't the easiest thing to find around the interstates near Joplin, Missouri, or Gallup, New Mexico.

When we finally made it out to San Diego in our little green Camaro, it was like being on another planet. We had left an industrial city and we were now in a resort town that was like paradise. The days were always sunny, in the seventies and eighties, and the nights were cool and romantic, especially for a young married couple.

We found an apartment five minutes from the Sports Arena, ten minutes from the beach, and fifteen minutes from the airport. I quickly found out where the pickup basketball games were and started tuning my game for my rookie year. I also found out that the fans in San Diego were disappointed the Rockets had drafted me instead of Pete Maravich, who had led the NCAA in scoring three years in a row.

The headline in the local paper read ROCKETS DRAFT RUDY WHO.

Two months before rookie camp was due to begin, I contracted the mumps, which is usually a childhood illness and can be very dangerous if you get it as an adult. The danger is that you can become sterile if the swelling drops. The prescribed treatment was to stay off my feet for a couple of weeks. I got through that, but I wound up totally out of shape.

Gradually, I worked my way back to about seventy-five percent of where I should have been. I had a lackluster rookie camp; my timing was off and my shot never came around. Not exactly the type of first impression I wanted to make.

The rest of the summer was spent working with the Rockets' veterans and going to Los Angeles to play in summer-league games. By the time training camp started, I was in much better shape and felt I had gained some respect from the veterans on our team.

Alex Hannum was the coach of the San Diego Rockets. He had won a championship in Philadelphia, coaching great players like Wilt Chamberlain, Chet Walker, and Hal Greer. I was really looking forward to playing for Alex. He was an imposing man—about 6-8, 250 pounds, and solid as a rock. Really a tough guy. He was into fitness, and surfing was his hobby.

Alex didn't have an assistant; it was a one-man coaching show. He would gather the team for practice, explain what we were going to do that day, and then give us his battle cry: "They got 'em, we want 'em, let's get 'em, hum diddy-diddy."

Then practice could begin. As we were taking our warm-up laps, Alex would sometimes do isometric exercises on the sideline. When the bleachers were folded against the wall, he would put his hand into one of the slots, grip it tightly, and start flexing. As he flexed, he would begin to shiver and then the bleachers would vibrate. A rumbling noise would come over us. The first time he did it, we thought we were in a California earthquake.

The 1970–71 Rockets had point guard Larry Siegfried, who had played many years for the Boston Celtics; Stu Lantz, a rapidly improving athlete who could score and rebound, was our shooting guard. John Block, at 6-10, played one of the forward spots; he had a deceptively quick first step and was one of the nicest people I've ever met in sports—a gentle giant. Toby Kimball was a good front-line role player for that team, and Elvin Hayes was the center. Elvin was a remarkable athlete. He never lifted weights, but he was exceptionally strong. And at 6-9, he had the speed of a greyhound.

Elvin could really score. He could play inside or face up from the outside. He had a solid shot and could rebound; he was a quick jumper with a sneaky way of blocking shots. Sometimes Elvin would look the other way when someone was driving toward the basket. The driver would get a false sense of security and leave the floor for his layup, but once Elvin saw the shooter commit, he would quickly come over and leap to block the shot. Elvin didn't just swat the ball out of bounds like a lot of shot-blockers do. He would merely flick his wrist, tapping it to a teammate, much like a jump ball.

John Q. Trapp was a reserve forward, and the rest of the players were rookies. I was the first-round pick and Calvin Murphy, the tremendous scorer from Niagara, was our second-round pick. Our third-round pick was Curtis Perry from Southwest Missouri State, a 220-pound rebounder. Don Adams, my old competitor from the Big Ten, was an eighth-round pick who did a great job in training camp of impressing Hannum with his feel for the game.

As the season began, I played sparingly. But in mid-November, I got a chance to show what I could do. We were playing Detroit, which had gotten off to a 10-0 start. Butch van Breda Kolff was the Pistons' coach, and he had so much quality depth that he was using a platoon system so that ten guys could get minutes. The Pistons had All-Stars such as Dave Bing and Jimmy Walker, as well as Bob Lanier, who had been the No. 1 overall pick in the draft.

Lanier weighed about three hundred pounds and happened to fall on our starting forward, John Block, causing John to leave with an injury. I came in and had my best minutes as a pro.

Though I had been a big scorer in college, my role with this team was to rebound. Soon after I got in the game, I helped spark the team with a tip dunk on an offensive rebound. That really got the fans into the game. We wound up winning, and I got 19 points and pulled down 12 rebounds.

I felt bad for John Block, who would miss some games with the injury, but I was excited about helping us beat a good team. Would I now get on the floor more often? In the back of my mind, I even thought about starting. Yeah, I was really fired up. The next game, I came off the bench again and immediately started working the boards. I got three offensive-rebound baskets quickly and really thought I was helping the team. The key was that I didn't need plays run for me; I was doing a lot of the dirty work and getting hustle points. The top scorers were still getting their shots, and I was putting back some of their misses, so our offensive efficiency was on the rise.

But for some reason, I didn't get much playing time the rest of that game, even after giving us an early lift. The next game in Portland, I got even less time, and afterward Alex said he wanted to talk with me. We stayed at a hotel across the street, and Alex and I walked back together. I was anxious to hear what he was going to say because I was really confused.

Alex explained that it was hard to break into the NBA as a

rookie. There are so many things to learn. "Some players learn while playing and other players learn by watching," Hannum said. "You will have to learn by watching."

"Coach, I'll do whatever it takes. I just want to help."

"Watch," Alex repeated.

I never questioned the coach in more detail. I simply wasn't into questioning authority. I thought I deserved to play, but maybe I was doing something wrong out there and didn't realize it. My spirits were low and my confidence was fading. Thank goodness I had Sophie, because she was my support. She was always there to pick me up. Sometimes at night she would come along to the gym and pass me the ball while I was practicing my shooting. She'd even demonstrate some basketball maneuvers that would really get me laughing.

I was grateful for her support. I just wanted a chance to play so I could make her proud of me.

As my rookie year moved on, playing time continued to be sparse. It reached rock bottom one night in Cincinnati. We were having a great game against the Royals. By the second quarter, we were up 30 points. Everyone on the team had played except me. In the fourth quarter, we were still up by 30, and our reserves were on the floor. Still no call from the coach. When Alex substituted for the reserves, he put the starters back in.

Now my mind was racing. What was going on here? I figured this was a great opportunity for him to get me some experience. I couldn't lose the game; we were too far ahead. The Rockets had invested a high draft pick and good money in me. Why wouldn't the coach try to see if I was improving?

It didn't make sense. Something was wrong. In my mind, this was not about basketball. I had done nothing so terrible to deserve this. I was the hardest-working player in practice. I had a lot of energy, which was natural since I didn't play much. But I was always hustling and trying. All I could think was, Why me?

A couple of years later, I think I got the answer to what was going on in my rookie year. Well after the fact, I learned that Alex had had a conflict with management concerning Elvin Hayes. Alex wanted to trade Elvin, but management refused. So Alex was using me as leverage.

You won't trade Elvin? Okay, I won't play your No. 1 draft choice.

At the time I had no way of knowing this was going on. I started to doubt myself because I believed the coach always played the players who could help him.

The final blow came at our postseason banquet. During the season, I had grown a mustache and not a good one, I might add. I wore it for a couple of months and decided it wasn't me. At that banquet, they gave out various awards. There was MVP, Most Improved Player, and so on. My award was a fake mustache. That's all I had to show for my rookie year.

It was totally humiliating. I drove Sophie home in silence, changed into my basketball gear, drove to a gym, and started working on my game.

I had been in these situations before—being cut as a freshman in high school, having my high school coach say I didn't have what it takes. I made a vow with myself that I wouldn't stop believing in Rudy Tomjanovich. But believing wasn't enough. I would have to work harder than ever.

That summer, two important events came to pass. Alex Hannum was relieved of his duties, and a group of Houston businessmen bought the team and announced the Rockets were headed to Texas.

We had heard there was a significant problem with the San Diego arena. A couple of players had gone down to a city-council meeting to show support, but when push came to shove they couldn't guarantee a playing site for the following season. We were getting ready to leave the apartment one day when a news bulletin came on television that the Rockets were moving to Houston.

Sophie and I didn't know what to think. Texas was foreign to us. I had visions of tumbleweed, cattle, and oil wells.

From the ballclub's perspective, Houston made sense because the team's young star, Elvin Hayes, had been a big name at the University of Houston. He was the guy they would initially count on to lure the crowds. We knew it would be tough because Texas was a football state, but the hope was that the Rockets would eventually be able to cultivate new NBA territory.

How appropriate that in our first season in Texas, the new coach was named Tex. After a successful career in college basketball, Tex Winter came in with a sound plan. He believed in an offense that reacted to the defense. Through Tex, I would learn what spacing and movement of the ball can do for you.

It would be a clean slate in Houston after a tough rookie year. We were packing and moving again, but I had a feeling things were going to work out.

5

ANOTHER YEAR, another move. From industrial Detroit, to the resort town of San Diego, to this big city of Houston—deep in the heart of Texas. I have to admit I was a little apprehensive about living in the South. I had never known anybody who spoke with a Southern accent or would say *y'all*. Where I came from, people from my neighborhood would use the term *you's guys*.

My apprehension about the South was overcome by my excitement about jump-starting my pro career in a new environment under Tex Winter. When we got to Houston, Sophie and I found a townhouse on the southwest side of the city. The complex was built around a square that featured many restaurants and shopping facilities. Basically, anything we needed was in walking distance—and that was nice, because at the time we only owned one car. If I had to take the car to the airport or practice, at least Sophie wasn't trapped in the house.

Right away, we found the people of Houston to be friendly and warm. The weather was warm, too. More than warm. We came down in August, and for the first month we were here, it rained every day in the afternoon. It was also sunny every day, so we got to know what humidity was all about. Temperatures in the nineties and hundreds. Sweat, sweat, and more sweat.

If we went outside even for a few minutes, a film of perspiration would come over you. Then you'd go in a place of business and get hit with a blast of air conditioning.

Everybody we knew who was new to Houston got sick early on, just as Sophie and I did. But we eventually got used to the humidity and settled in as happy, transplanted Houstonians.

On the court, I was making the transition from seldom-used rookie to the starting small-forward spot. We were pioneers for NBA basketball in Houston in 1971–72, and the season started at the AstroHall against Philadelphia. Sophie drove me to the arena that night. She knew I was nervous and excited. Before I got out of the car, she pointed to five pennies that were on the console. As she pointed to each one, she gave me advice on a different phase of the game.

"This penny is for rebounds. You've really got to go up and snatch them," she said. "The second penny is for the bank shot. You've got to find your spot. The third penny is for defense. Go up and block that shot."

And so it went. My wife was being very professional about it, and it really broke the tension. I began to laugh, and as I walked away from the car I turned back and said, "Thanks for the great advice, coach."

Although we lost that Houston premiere, 105–94, I was able to get a career-high 28 points. Poor Sophie didn't know what she was getting into with the coaching lecture. From then on, whether we were at home or on the road, I would ask her to tell me about the pennies.

There were times when getting that advice from Sophie wasn't easy. Suffice it to say, I was willing to pay *more* than a penny for her thoughts. But I had to contend with different time zones and the fact that she was sometimes away from home when I'd call in from the road.

Once I couldn't get her all day, and it made me antsy. By the time we had to catch the bus to the arena, I still hadn't talked to her. We had our pregame meeting and were on our way to the court when I saw a pay phone. I dashed over, made a collect call, and was told the line was busy.

"It's an emergency," I told the operator. "Can you please break in on the line?"

When I finally got through, I said, "Sophie, I don't have much time. Quick, tell me about the pennies."

She did, and I breathed a huge sigh of relief. It wasn't the most conventional way to get ready for a game, but it was mine.

We got off to a terrible 2-16 start, and it could have been even worse if we hadn't gotten a break from the officials in our seventh game. We were 0-6 and playing at Detroit in a tight game. With a few seconds left and the Rockets down one, we had a shot bounce around the rim for what seemed like an eternity.

Suddenly, a hand came out of a crowd of rebounders, touched the ball, and knocked it off the rim. The ref blew his whistle right before the final buzzer, and everybody stopped and waited for the call. Goaltending, basket good.

It felt great to get that 104–103 win, the first triumph in Houston Rockets history. But it never should have been. In the locker room afterward, Elvin Hayes quietly told me it was *his* hand that had touched the ball. It should have been called offensive goaltending, which would have given the game to the Pistons.

We really needed a break like that because we were up against incredibly tough odds that first year in Houston. The new owners—Wayne Duddleston, Billy Goldberg, and a handful of investors—wanted the team to do well, and their hearts were certainly in the right place. But I don't know how any team could have been successful under the conditions we faced.

First of all, we didn't have a permanent home court. We played in the makeshift AstroHall and the cavernous Astrodome until January, when we moved into Hofheinz Pavilion on the University of Houston campus. Hofheinz featured a rubberized floor that really took a toll on a player's legs. I was just a young guy, but the floor aggravated my Achilles tendons right away. The older players? They were feeling the effects even more than I was.

As if all this weren't enough, we also played thirteen "home games" in San Antonio, about two hundred miles to the west of Houston. The good news was that we drew large crowds at HemisFair Arena. The bad news was that those crowds generally cheered for the other team. If we were playing the Knicks or the Lakers in San Antonio, forget it; we were made to feel like the road team, right from the starting lineup introductions. It was depressing and deflating.

We also had a home-away-from-home way out in El Paso. Never mind that this "homecourt" site was located halfway between Houston and Los Angeles. Even though we had a long day of travel to get to the game site, it went down in the books as a home game.

One night we were in El Paso when a windstorm blew through town. When we arrived at the gym, there was sand all over the court. No matter how much they mopped, they couldn't get the sand removed. But the show went on. You couldn't change directions without sliding, so the referees decided not to call traveling. I couldn't believe they allowed us to play—it was that dangerous. Guys were doing the splits as if we were on ice. It was a minor miracle that nobody got hurt.

Our homecourt travels took us to Waco. Usually, when we played a designated "home" game in another Texas city, it was promoted well and people came out. One of our most memorable Waco games came in the '71–72 season when we managed to beat that great 69-13 Lakers team that had a 33-game winning streak.

But one night in Waco we drew a crowd of seven hundred. It was like having a practice. Those few fans who did show up heard the thump of the ball and everything the coaches and players were saying.

Basically, the 1971–72 season was the "Have Rockets Will Travel" show. You've got to start somewhere, and we were blazing a trail for that first world championship that would come 23 years to the day after Duddleston, Goldberg, and Mickey Herskowitz went to San Diego with a group of lawyers to hash out the details of the sale and the move of the Rockets. (The Houston group had been told by Commissioner Walter Kennedy in the spring of '71 that three teams were available for purchase—the Milwaukee Bucks, the Cincinnati Royals, and the San Diego Rockets. The Royals were available for a reported $3 million, but the Houston group decided to pay $5 million for the Rockets because they had Elvin Hayes. Ironically, Hayes was traded just one season after returning to the scene of his collegiate glory.)

After our woeful 2-16 start, there was a turning point that made us a fair team as the season wore on. At the start of the year, we didn't have a legitimate small forward. I was playing that spot, and I just didn't match up from a speed standpoint. Finally, we made a trade for Greg Smith, who had been on the Bucks' championship team of '71. Just getting a guy who could chase a John Havlicek represented a major improvement. We had been starting Dick Cunningham, who had been the backup center to Lew Alcindor the previous year, with Hayes at power forward and me at small forward. Imagine me chasing Havlicek; the one thing I did learn that year was how to spell Havlicek's name because all I did was chase the guy all over the place from the rear.

Players were coming and going that first year. We even had a 6-10 guy—Jim Davis—who was here and gone before his furniture arrived in Houston. By the time his stuff came in from Atlanta, we had already traded him. Jim was a guy from a different era. One night at halftime, Tex came in and began his speech, only to look up and see Jim lighting a cigarette.

"We don't do that here," Tex snapped.

I had never seen a player smoking in the locker room, but that was how it was in the old NBA. For the record, Jim Davis played 12 games with the Houston Rockets, starting once.

The powerhouse team in the West during that era was the Los Angeles Lakers. They were led by Jerry West, one of the greatest shooting guards to ever play the game. The Lakers had lost in the '69–70 finals to New York when Willis Reed made a courageous appearance while still limping badly from a leg injury. But the Lakers were still a remarkable team, with West, Wilt Chamberlain, Elgin Baylor, Happy Hairston, and a youngster from Columbia University, Jim McMillian.

The Phoenix Suns had a solid team with steady Dick Van Arsdale and Connie Hawkins, a legend from the playgrounds of New York. "The Hawk" had a style all his own. He was graceful and smooth on the floor. He had gigantic hands and loved to palm the ball. It looked like a grapefruit in his hand. Hawkins was a superb one-on-one player with exceptional leaping ability. Connie was a crowd favorite and also a player favorite. When he made a spectacular move, the players on the bench—although not openly —would express their respect for his special abilities.

"Man, the Hawk is flying tonight," someone would inevitably say.

In the East, the New York Knicks were the epitome of team play. They played together so well and had a knack for reading each other's moves. Willis Reed, Dave DeBusschere, Bill Bradley, Dick Barnett, and Walt Frazier comprised the starting unit, with Phil Jackson and Cazzie Russell coming off the bench. The Knicks weren't the biggest team or the fastest team, but they played tough defense and executed their plays to perfection. They knew how to win.

The Baltimore Bullets were New York's big rivals. Earl "The Pearl" Monroe was a premier scorer. He came from tiny Winston-Salem State College to take the league by storm. Earl was the master of the pump fake. He always had his defender on a string. Gus Johnson, a powerfully built man, was one of the toughest players in the league. He did everything well. Gus could run, jump, and defend. He dunked the ball with such force the arena would rumble. Johnson and DeBusschere had some classic battles.

The other Bullets forward was Jack Marin, a sharpshooting left-hander who complemented the other scorers well. In the middle, Baltimore had Wes Unseld, who had been Rookie of the Year. He was a total team player. Wes set the best pick in the league and also had the strongest outlet pass. After grabbing a defensive rebound, he'd snap bullet passes to Monroe around the halfcourt line, making their fast break hard to stop.

The team that won it all in my rookie season of '71 was the Milwaukee Bucks. They had acquired Oscar Robertson, one of the best players of all time. He had been a longtime member of the Cincinnati Royals, but they had never contended for the title, even though they had two great scorers—Robertson and Jack Twyman. Oscar was 6-5 and a floor general, always in control. One year, 1961–62, he *averaged* a triple-double per game, but they didn't refer to the stat that way at the time. There wasn't anything on the floor Oscar couldn't do. He was a perfect complement to their great young center Lew Alcindor, who would later change his name to Kareem Abdul-Jabbar.

Abdul-Jabbar had played on John Wooden's great UCLA teams in the late sixties. He had perfected an unstoppable shot, the "sky hook." He would position himself on the left post-up spot, take a dribble and a giant step, and shoot the hook over his defender. He kept his body between the ball and the man trying to stop him.

Once Kareem got to the middle, you had no chance; it was up to him to make it or miss it. Teams would try to take away that step in the middle, forcing Kareem to turn to the baseline, and this would cut his percentage somewhat. But when you tried to double-team him, he was ready for it. At 7-2 he could see over the defense and find the open man. He was a fundamentally sound player. The years under John Wooden really paid off for him.

The Bucks also had Bobby Dandridge, another young player who was starting to make a name for himself. Greg Smith was a strong runner on that Bucks team and later was a great addition to our Rockets team. The top outside shooter was Jon McGlocklin, and they had solid forward reserves in Bob Boozer and McCoy McLemore.

The Boston Celtics, in the aftermath of the Bill Russell era, were on their way back to the top. They had the incomparable John Havlicek, a player who never stopped moving on the court. Boston also had a tough defender in Tom "Satch" Sanders and an explosive streak shooter in JoJo White; Don Chaney anchored the backcourt defense.

Don Nelson was a key bench contributor for Boston. He was a guy who most noticeably used stickum, a gooey substance some players used to help them grip the ball. Most players were discreet about using it, but you could usually see Nellie reaching under the hem of his shorts to get a dab. I didn't like to use it; the ball would sometimes get stuck in your hand, and I preferred to have the ball roll off my fingertips when I shot.

The Celtics drafted Dave Cowens from Florida State in 1975. He was only about 6-9, but he played the center position with such aggressiveness that lack of height never became a negative factor;

in fact, Dave made it work for him. He could outrun any center in the league. No one played harder than Dave.

We finished 34-48 in '71-72, which wasn't bad considering the 2-16 start. We were starting to do some good things under Tex. Alex Hannum was an ex-player and had kept things very simple. We had maybe four or five plays my rookie year, as well as some sound rules. One of them was that any time a defender turned and watched the ball, it was our cue to cut to the basket.

Tex Winter really covered more of the fundamentals. He actually got down to the proper techniques in making a chest pass or an over-the-head pass. He also stressed a lot of footwork drills that taught players to catch the ball while looking away from the basket and then using various pivots to square up. His offense—the triple post— was based on reading the defense; if the defense took away an option that was always a release pass, you would have a way to exploit what the defense was giving you. Tex always had a man at the top of the key to swing the ball. If that pass was denied, the opposite forward would cut into an area beneath him toward the ball. The man at the top of the key would read this, and as the ball went to the forward, he would cut backdoor, usually getting free for a layup or short jumper.

On June 23, 1972, the Rockets made a shocker of a trade: Hayes was dealt to Baltimore for Jack Marin. As players, we looked at that deal and thought there had to be something more coming to us. That was no knock against Marin, who was a pure shooter and a very good player. But Elvin was a real star in the league and, as I said, the primary reason why the NBA had come to Houston.

There was a lot of debate about the Hayes trade, but the team itself just had to move on. In '72-73, we had only one less win than we had had with Elvin. We had some good offensive talent, as shown by our 112.8 scoring average. But unfortunately, we didn't present much of a defense: our opponents averaged 114.5 points.

The losing in those early years didn't deflate our spirit. There's always hope and a positive feeling that you have young players and you're going to turn it around. We felt we deserved some credit for hanging in there that second season, especially after starting 2-16.

Off the court, we were continuing to try to cultivate Houston as an NBA town. It was a battle, to say the least. I had received my first clue about this the previous year when the Rockets first set up shop in Houston. We were doing a lot of things to try to promote the Houston Rockets, and one day there was a players'-appearance session at the Sharpstown mall. Not many people were coming by, just a few kids here and there. After one of the lulls, a nice elderly lady came up and said, "Gosh, I just love you guys. I have so much respect for you. Can I take a picture with you?"

As I was getting up from behind the desk, the lady continued to speak. "I never knew you were that big," she marveled. "How do you fit in the spaceship?"

She thought the Houston Rockets were the astronauts from NASA. The NBA? What NBA?

My scoring average zoomed to 19.3 in '72–73, but I continued to view myself primarily as a rebounder. I averaged a team-high 11.6 rebounds and had several 20-rebound games. But my rebounding style got me in trouble one night against none other than Wilt Chamberlain.

I had a habit of getting a running start toward the boards on every shot. Wilt used to zone it up and he'd be standing under the basket on most possessions. After I had run up his back a couple of times on made shots, Wilt gave me an ultimatum with that deep, deep voice.

"Tomjanovich, don't come in here anymore."

"Wilt, I've got to do my job," I responded.

Let me just say that I didn't make that statement with a lot of conviction. After all, I happened to be talking to one of the strongest men in the world.

Late in the game, I went barreling in to grab a loose ball. Wilt grabbed my arm and was called for a foul. As I was starting down-court, Wilt wouldn't let my arm go. He spun me around and said, "I told you not to come in here anymore."

At that tenuous juncture, I threw a finger up into Wilt's face and he let me go. When I got back to the bench, everybody was saying how great it was that I had stood up to Wilt.

But what I was really saying—and I never told my teammates this—was, "Please give me one more chance."

IN 1973-74, we continued to be stuck in a sub-.500 mode. We finished 32-50 and simply weren't ready to take that next step up to playoff level. While our team wasn't too exciting that year, there was some excitement around the Tomjanovich household.

In early December 1973, Sophie and I were expecting our first child. We knew from the ultrasound that it was going to be a girl. I was just hoping to be in town on Sophie's due date, which was the first week of the month.

Sophie was so full of energy. I remember leaving for a road trip out East as she was stapling fabrics in the baby's room. I wanted her to get off her feet, but she was eager to stay busy. I did have to go on the road trip, and I was in Philadelphia when Jean Gibbs, the wife of my teammate Dick Gibbs, called me and said Sophie was having labor pains and had been rushed to the hospital.

We played the Philadelphia 76ers that night. It was a close game throughout, and I kept having visions of getting the game over and finding out about my new baby daughter, whom we planned on calling Nichole. Late in that game, inside one minute to go, I wound up with an open shot. I nailed it, putting us up by one with a few seconds remaining. As I ran off the court, I thought, This is a wonderful omen. This will be just like a fairy tale. The headlines will read, DAD HITS WINNING BASKET THE DAY HIS DAUGHTER IS BORN. The Sixers got the ball in and Fred Carter went up for a jumper. At the last instant, he spotted Leroy Ellis open under the basket and fired a hard pass. Ellis, almost in a defensive position, never really got control of it, but the ball hit his hands and popped up into the basket at the buzzer.

I started thinking, Forget about omens. This *couldn't* be an omen.

When I finally got home, Sophie was at Hermann Hospital. I had come during feeding time. I was behind a little barrier, the kind you see in movie theaters. I watched the nurse take babies to and from their mothers, and a lot of things went through my head: Would the baby be healthy? I prayed to God that it had ten fingers and ten toes. One of the babies had caught my eye. The hair was dark, and the baby looked a little darker than the others. I thought,

If my baby looks anywhere near as cute as that healthy little Mexican baby, I'd be very happy.

It wound up that the healthy little "Mexican" baby turned out to be Nichole. Later, her hair turned blonde and her skin turned lighter. It was funny that I had seen her go by, admiring her healthiness and good looks even as an infant. And I didn't even know she was mine.

My first full season as a father proved to be fruitful. Finally, we broke that barrier under Coach Johnny Egan to give Houston its first NBA playoff team in 1974–75.

Johnny was a guy I had always respected when he was with the Rockets as a player. I took every word he said as gospel when I was a young player, because Johnny didn't bullshit you. Everything he said was on the money and made sense. When he took over as coach midway through the '72–73 season, I really felt a closeness. My thought was, Do good not only for yourself, but do good for Johnny. I really liked his approach to the game.

When we beat New York 2-1 in the opening round of the '75 playoffs, we felt we had finally gained some respectability. Granted, the Knicks weren't the same team that had won two championships earlier in the decade, but just beating New York—the city renowned for being the hotbed of basketball—was a tremendous source of pride. Boston was too good and too smart for us in the second round, but we had a lot to look forward to as our first playoff season came to an end. We were hoping to build on the 41-41 season and two playoff rounds. Furthermore, we were about to move into the Summit, a great facility that was being constructed through the vision of new Rockets owner and real-estate developer Kenneth Schnitzer.

Despite the new building, we didn't make an immediate leap in '75–76. We finished a disappointing 40-42 and missed the playoffs. But we were acquiring some assets that would help us make a major breakthrough the following year. Small forward John Johnson was coming on for us, and Joe Meriweather was a big man we wound up trading to secure the No. 1 pick in the 1976 draft. We also had Kevin Kunnert, a seven-footer with a great shooting touch from 15 feet and in.

The keys for us would come in the summer of '76. On June 7 that year, Meriweather and Gus Bailey went to Atlanta for Dwight Jones and an exchange of first-round picks. We got the No. 1 pick, and it turned out to be John Lucas.

On October 25, we acquired a young man named Moses Malone from Buffalo for our 1977 and 1978 first-round picks. Tom Nissalke would be replacing Egan as head coach, and the trio of myself, Calvin Murphy, and Mike Newlin remained intact. It had been a long, bumpy ride to get in position for the Houston Rockets to challenge the heavyweights of the NBA.

Now the fun was about to begin.

6

EARLY IN MY CAREER, the players didn't have individual rooms on the road. My eventual rooming buddy turned out to be Calvin Murphy, a guy I had first seen on the basketball floor during my college days at Michigan.

I remember talking with a couple of Wolverines players about an article we had seen in *Sports Illustrated*. It was about this player from Niagara who was only 5-9, but was one of the top scorers in college basketball. It just so happened that Niagara was scheduled to play in a holiday festival at the University of Detroit, so we got a carload of guys together and went to see the man they called "Million Moves Murf." We got to the game in time to see the teams warm up, and I kept my eyes on Murphy as they went through the pregame routine. Right away I noticed the great form on his shot. In fact, if you wanted to demonstrate perfect technique, this was the guy you would use for a model: elbow in, ball on the fingertips, great rotation, always in balance. He made about ninety percent of his warm-up shots and then finished with a dunk when a teammate lobbed the ball toward the basket.

Niagara's opponent that night was Valparaiso. As Valparaiso went through its pregame drills, there was a player who didn't take layups with the rest of the team. Instead, this guy was practicing defensive slides. I had never seen a player do this before, and we surmised he was the guy assigned to guard Murphy. This Valparaiso player was about 6-3 and very athletic. By the way he carried himself, you could tell he was confident and cocky about his upcoming assignment against one of the top scorers in the country.

Valparaiso came out in a box-and-one against Murphy—one man shadowed him all over the floor and each of the other four guys protected an area. The guy on Murphy would try to funnel him into an area where one of the zoners could help double-team.

What we saw that night was truly amazing. Because of his speed and ballhandling ability, Murphy still got any shot he wanted. He would make a quick move, leave his original defender behind, and suddenly go straight up for a jumper with a soft, feathery touch. When most players make a move this quick, their momentum causes them to lose balance, but Murf was different; he could stop on a dime and go straight up. When Valparaiso adjusted its defense and became more aggressive, and the zoners left their area to attack him out on the floor, Murphy countered by making sharp passes to teammates for layups.

He was fearless. He challenged bigger people and would loft shots over them. He'd take a blow from the big people, hit the floor, tumble, and pop up before heading to the free-throw line. On the way back to Ann Arbor we raved about what we had seen. One of my teammates summed it up best: "Most of us athletes are like tennis balls," he said. "But this Murphy guy is like a golf ball. He's a little smaller, but he's tougher and he has a heck of a lot more bounce."

The San Diego Rockets drafted Calvin in the second round in 1970. I couldn't believe it. I felt we got a steal. All I could figure was that the other NBA teams must have been apprehensive about Calvin's size, or else someone would have snatched him quickly in the first round. That snub would be the fuel that would push him through his great thirteen-year pro career. I mentioned how I had a poor showing in rookie camp. Calvin didn't; he excelled. The differences between NBA ball and college ball were perfect for Calvin's game: There were few double-teams, no zone defenses, and the open-style, fast-break game fit him to a T. Calvin worked his way into the rotation, and Alex Hannum particularly liked to have Calvin on the court when the opponents were over the foul limit. Calvin would quickly push the ball downcourt, causing more fouls or getting a high-percentage shot. Sometimes I'd be in the game in these situations, primarily to hit the boards and make outlet passes. But on some possessions I wouldn't even make it to the offensive end by the time the ball was pushed up the floor. Murphy was that quick.

In San Diego, we had a racially balanced team—seven black players, five white players. Alex wanted white players to room with black players, and the only two black players to room together were our stars, Elvin Hayes and Stu Lantz.

My first roommate was John Q. Trapp. He had asked Alex to let him room with me because we were homeboys. John grew up in Highland Park, Michigan, which is right across the railroad tracks from Hamtramck. John was a reserve forward who had pretty good skills. He was a fair runner and jumper, fair shooter and fair rebounder. He made it on his tough-guy image; he had a sinister look and would try to intimidate, especially when he felt he was facing someone weak. It worked in his favor, and he was getting more playing time than I was.

John Q. liked me and was supportive, but at times he made me nervous. When we'd be in a room watching television, I'd get that strange feeling you get when you feel someone is watching you. I'd look over at Q. and, sure enough, he would be staring at me. I'd ignore it a little while, check again, and he'd still be staring.

"What, John?" I would ask.

"Homey," John Q. once said in that situation, "did you see that move I made in the third quarter last night? Maybe one of these days you'll be able to do that."

"Thanks, Q., I'll be watching you," I said, turning back to the television.

Trapp had been around the league a couple of years and had friends on other teams. After certain games, he would tell me, "Rookie, I'm going out. Don't wait up for me."

John Q. and his friends would do the town. After one of these paint-the-town-red excursions, I woke up around 5 A.M. to what I thought was a thunderstorm. It turned out to be John Q. snoring. The snow was on the television, so I could see him in the light. He was completely naked, sleeping on top of the covers. He had his arms folded across his chest like a mummy and his eyes were wide open. I got up and tried to converse with him, then I had this eerie feeling his eyes were following me around the room. I think John was even scarier asleep than he was when awake.

As it turned out, Murphy wasn't exactly having the most harmonious experience with his Rockets roommate, either. On an off-day in Atlanta, I was walking down the hotel hallway when a door opened. Out popped Calvin in his underwear. He was always hyper, but even more so on this day. He asked me what I was doing, and I told him a couple of players were planning on catching a movie.

"Can I please come?" Calvin inquired with urgency. "I've got to get out of this room."

"Of course you can come," I said. "I've never seen you this way. What's wrong?"

Calvin said he wanted to get dressed and then he would fill me in on the problem. A few minutes later he explained the situation in detail. Murphy was rooming with Larry Siegfried, a veteran guard who had been on championship teams in Boston. Larry was a leader, and he relished being able to break in a rookie to the ways of the NBA.

"I want to do well," Calvin said. "I get my rest, I don't run the streets. But 'Siggy' expects too much. We don't have a game for two days, but Larry comes in while I'm watching TV and shuts it off, saying we've got to get some rest.

"I slept ten hours last night. Here it is, two o'clock in the afternoon, and I'm pretending to sleep. I'm so restless. I move in the bed and he tells me to stop rustling."

Murphy went on to tell me that Siegfried finally fell asleep, but Murf had to go to the bathroom. He eased out from under the covers and tiptoed into the bathroom. As Murf was turning to leave, he bumped into a fuming Siegfried.

"Rook, when are you going to learn respect for your roommate?" Siegfried yelled. "You don't pee *in* the water. You pee around the edge."

Murphy said that bathroom episode was the final straw. He was going to ask Alex to switch roommates.

"Would you room with me?" Murphy asked.

I said fine, and The Odd Couple moved in together. There have never been two people more opposite. One white, one black. One tall, one short. One reserved and shy, one loud and boisterous.

But there were similarities, too. We were both offensive-minded, and usually that's an unlikely match. Our first night as roommates after a game—about 2 A.M.—Calvin and I were both still hyped up and trying to wind down. The national anthem was being played on the television as they were signing off. Calvin asked me if I was ready to go to sleep. I explained that I was a night person and always stayed up late; after a game, I said, it's even harder for me to fall asleep.

Calvin suggested that he play some music on his portable stereo; I thought that was a great idea. I figured he would put on something like Smokey Robinson and the Miracles or Curtis Mayfield and the Impressions. Maybe some Stylistics, something nice and soft. But to my surprise, I heard James Brown roaring, "I feel good, I knew that I would."

I started to wonder what I had gotten myself into with this new roommate.

But the relationship grew closer and we began to spend more time together off the court. Calvin was married to a wonderful young lady, Vernetta, whom he called "Little Mama." She was quiet and shy, and Sophie and Vernetta became close friends. They had a lot in common. Both came up in the Catholic schools, both were raised by strong mothers who had to do it without a father around. Being away from home in a strange city, it was comforting to have friends who were experiencing the same feelings. We would visit each other's places or go out to dinner and really enjoy each other's company.

The Murphys and the Tomjanoviches did a lot of laughing in those days. As the years went by, we became like a family. Calvin bought the house next door to us and, as our families grew, we considered their children, Tiffani, Tracy, and Calvin Jr., to be our children.

The Murphy's first child, Tiffani, couldn't pronounce "Rudy." She wound up calling me "Whitey." This would make Calvin very nervous around a group of Southerners.

When I think about Calvin Murphy, I think about one of the fiercest competitors I've ever been around. It was his natural makeup, but I believe a big factor was the "too small" tag that was always hung on him. Because of his explosiveness and ability to change the pace of a game, some coaches would choose to bring him off the bench. It was a special talent, and Calvin understood that, but he still wondered why he should be penalized by not being allowed to start.

Consequently Calvin never, ever relaxed. Not even in practice. When Calvin was a starter, he would use practice to make sure his backup never got the upper hand. When Calvin was a reserve, he would do his best to prove to the coach he could outplay the starter. He pushed himself to the limit, even if he was ill or hurt. I'll never forget the time in Atlanta when he had the flu and spent most of the day vomiting. Calvin didn't want to let the team down by staying in his hotel room. He decided to give it a try, and wound up being our leading scorer and making the game-winning shot at the buzzer.

One year Calvin played half the season with torn cartilage in his knee. Every night he was in a lot of pain and he constantly had to ice the knee. But by doing numerous leg lifts, he built up his quad muscles so that he could make it through the year even with the cartilage problem, delaying surgery until after the season.

In all the years Calvin and I roomed together, I never picked up the phone to answer a wake-up call. I was a heavy sleeper and Calvin was an extremely light sleeper. He'd jump out of bed and grab the phone before the first ring ended.

One night I was engrossed in a great book as Calvin slept. I happened to cough, and Calvin jumped out of bed half-asleep and answered the phone, thinking it was the wake-up call. A couple of minutes later, I coughed again and the same thing happened. Then again. And again. I wasn't coughing on purpose, but it was one of the most entertaining nights I ever had.

As hyper as Calvin was, he showed amazing patience when it came to practicing free throws. He had textbook form, no wasted motion, and great concentration. Because of these sound fundamentals, he could have easily shot around eighty percent with little practice. But he wanted to be the best, and no one put in more time shooting free throws. The result was an .892 career foul-shooting percentage, including an NBA record streak of 78 that stood for more than a decade.

If one game defined Calvin's career, it was Game Seven of the 1981 Western Conference Semifinals at San Antonio. He had been a reserve most of the year, but he got the start in a do-or-die situation. I had seen Calvin get hot before, but he was in a different zone that night. I don't think he was even conscious of our being around him. I didn't play in that game, but I was right there in the huddle, and there was something noticeably different about his eyes and his approach. He finished with 42 points in one of the great clutch performances you'll ever see.

The final playing tribute to Calvin was his induction into the Basketball Hall of Fame. It was extra special for him to be recognized not just as a great little player, but as a guy who could take his place among the true giants of the game.

Today, my No. 45 jersey is in the rafters of the Summit, and I'm tremendously proud that it is hanging beside Calvin Murphy's No. 23.

Nobody ever had a greater will to succeed than my ex-roommate.

7

THE ROCKETS FRANCHISE had made the playoffs twice before the 1976–77 season, but we never had the feeling that we were a legitimate championship contender. Then Ray Patterson, our general manager since 1972, made two moves prior to that '76–77 season that propelled us to a different level.

Thanks to a June trade, we wound up with the top pick in the draft, and it turned out to be John Lucas, a 6-3 point guard from Maryland. I had never played with a distributor like Lucas, the point guard of our dreams.

Lucas was what they call a "true" point guard. He had a floor general's mentality. Here was a guy who thought "pass" first, and we had plenty of shooters who knew how to finish once they received one of Luke's set-up feeds. Mike Newlin, Calvin Murphy, John Johnson, Kevin Kunnert, and I were all in that category.

Luke was a catalyst for enthusiasm, always talking and pumping up his teammates. He was just what our team needed at the time. On and off the court, he made us into a cohesive unit.

The second move that the club made was monumental. We figured something was up when, in late October, just after the regular season started, our head coach, Tom Nissalke, was absent from practice for a couple of days. It's extremely rare for a head coach to venture away at that time, and the players kept asking assistant coach Del Harris what was up.

"Hopefully, something big," Harris hinted.

A few days later Nissalke returned, and an announcement was made that Moses Malone was a Houston Rocket. Tom had left in order to get the Malone deal finalized. We had to give up our 1977 and 1978 first-round draft picks and cash to the Buffalo Braves for Moses, but it was destined to be one of the great deals in Rockets history.

Moses was 6-10, very slender, and wore a big Afro. He was only twenty-two, a quiet kid who had to adjust to teammates who were five to ten years older. When he first came to our club, Moses was undisciplined on offense—understandable, since he missed the four developmental years he would have had in college. Instead, Moses had chosen to go right from Petersburg (Virginia) High School to the ABA. He would try things like dribbling between his legs in a crowd or shooting layups from his hip instead of extending and using his size and jumping ability. He was so young and had a lot of catching up to do.

But right from the start, we could see the tremendous potential of this young man. He had surprising quickness for a man his size. He could run like a guard and had unlimited energy. For a 6-10 player, he had unusually small hands, but those small hands gave him a better feel for shooting the ball from midrange spots. Malone's touch from 15 feet was another shooting dimension for our ballclub.

What really set Moses apart was his amazing instinct for rebounding. Some people call it a nose for the ball. Moses always seemed to wind up where the rebound was coming off. He would study the shot in the air, judge how it would hit the rim, and maneuver himself into the likely area of retrieval. This whole process would only take a fraction of a second. Moses would simply react quicker than the other guys on the floor, especially the man guarding him. But the most important factor was Malone's desire. He was relentless. He went hard to the boards on every shot. The man guarding him could hold him off for a while, but eventually his opponent would wear out. Moses never quit on a rebound. If he grabbed it and put it back up for a miss, he would stay with it for a second and third effort. He'd do whatever it took to finally get that ball in the basket.

It has often been said that the point guard and center are the two most important positions on a basketball team. With Lucas and Malone, we were getting two youngsters who had star potential at those key positions.

This was exciting stuff, because the '76–77 Rockets finally had a great passer and rebounder to go with the stable of shooters we had collected over the years. It was time for us to go to work and take our place among the better clubs in the league.

ON THE HOMEFRONT, the Tomjanovich family was expanding. On the evening of December 6, 1976, I was fortunate that our team was on a homestand and I was able to be in Houston for the birth of our second daughter. I hadn't taken the Lamaze classes, but it was late at night when Sophie went into labor and the doctor said I could come into the delivery room. It was an experience I'll never forget. I had been on the road and missed Nichole's birth three years earlier. Now, I was numbed as I watched the miracle of my baby being born.

When I got out of the delivery room to make phone calls to our close friends and relatives, I couldn't unball my hands right away to dial the numbers. That's how emotional I was.

There were a lot of ideas on names, but we didn't have one picked out while Sophie was in the hospital. I had heard a song by the Allman Brothers Band called "Melissa." As soon as I mentioned it, Sophie said, "That's it. Melissa is a great name."

IT WAS DESTINED to be a wonderful year on and off the court. We started the season 6-5 as Moses adjusted to our system on the fly. An eight-game winning streak took us to 14-5, and we managed to stay well over .500 the rest of the year. If there was one regular-season game that served as a barometer, it was our February 17 road game at San Antonio. Until that time, we really hadn't established ourselves as a road club, but when we marched into San

90

Antonio and beat an excellent Spurs team by 14, we had the feeling we could win anytime and anywhere.

While we had diverse talent among our top rung of players, it takes a lot more than that to become an elite NBA club. There were a lot of quality people on that '77 team, and the result was a feeling of unity. We liked each other and sacrificed for each other. Everybody did his job, from Moses right down to the last man on the bench.

Midway through the season, Tom could see that Moses had a great future. The organization wanted to do anything that would help the young Malone along in his development and there was a feeling that Moses might relish seeing a friend. So, in order to make sure Moses was comfortable in his new environment, the club acquired Eugene "Goo" Kennedy, who had played against Moses in the ABA.

Goo helped us on the court. He was a tough defensive player who would really battle on the boards. He was also the happiest person I've ever met.

This was a guy who simply never stopped laughing. Goo would begin every sentence with a little laugh and only then would he speak.

"Ha, ha . . . how you doin' today?" Goo would laugh his way through conversations even when the mood was serious.

"Ha, ha, ha . . . I heard your dog died . . . ha, ha, ha. It's really sad, isn't it?"

One morning on the road, I happened to be in the room next to Goo. Only a wall separated our beds. I heard his clock radio go off, and Goo immediately broke out laughing. What a happy way to start a new day. His first waking moment was worth a prolonged chuckle.

While Kennedy represented the happy spirit of the '77 club, Mike Newlin was symbolic of the team's true grit.

Mike was an outstanding player. He could shoot from outside and he was fearless driving the ball to the basket. At 6-4, he was one of the more physical backcourt guys in the league. Newlin was also a unique person. He graduated with academic honors from the University of Utah and was a Rhodes Scholar candidate.

Because he was such a private person, none of the players got to know him that well right away. But as the season wore on and the pressure built, I learned a lot about Mike's tenacity and commitment to the Rockets organization.

We wound up capturing Houston's first division title with a 49-33 record, and that gave us a bye through the first round of the playoffs. In the second round against Washington, we would win the last three games of a 4–2 series, and Mike was the hero of the finale.

After we wrapped it up in Game Six at the Capital Centre, I had a conversation with Newlin on the team bus. He told me that the Rockets had wanted to trade him earlier in the year. But Mike had a clause in his contract stipulating that he had to approve any deal. Mike vetoed the trade by telling management, "You might not need me now, but before the season is over, you will."

Mike was right on the money with that statement, and after we won that Washington series I felt great for him in particular. What inner strength it must have taken to battle through something like that. I don't know if I could have handled it nearly as well as Mike did. When most players hear that a team wants to move them, they say, "Okay, get me out of here."

In that Washington series, we truly began to see the form that would eventually turn Malone into an MVP. Moses had shown flashes through the regular season, but now he was, at times, dominating the likes of Elvin Hayes and Wes Unseld. The maturity Moses gained in that first year with the Rockets was amazing. We all had the feeling this was indeed a Moses who could take us to the promised land.

When we defeated the Bullets to reach the Eastern Conference Finals, we were starting to get major-league respect around the city of Houston. "We've finally got a winner in town," people were saying on the streets. The Oilers were still the big sports story of Houston under popular coach Bum Phillips and quarterback Dan Pastorini, but the Rockets were coming on strong.

We had four days of preparation for the Eastern Conference Finals, but we could have used forty days. When it was time for Game One, we quickly found that it was going to take a herculean

A ROCKET AT HEART

effort to handle the abundance of offensive talent that we would see from the Philadelphia 76ers.

Julius Erving was right in his prime. Doug Collins, George McGinnis, Lloyd Free, Darryl Dawkins—as a team, we were wondering how to stop all those weapons.

The Sixers rang up 128 points on us in Game One and beat us by 11. We did a better defensive job in Game Two, but lost, 106–97. Now we were down 0–2, and a lot of people on the outside were expecting us to go down quietly. Instead, we came out with a great effort in Game Three at the Summit and won 118–94 behind Malone's 30 points. But Collins came back with a clutch offensive performance two nights later to burst our bubble temporarily. Doug scored 36 points and the Sixers beat us 107–95 to take a 3–1 series lead.

We were right at the edge of the cliff, but we weren't about to take that plunge without a struggle. Back at the Spectrum for Game Five, we fell way behind in the second half, but Newlin got hot with his shooting to bring us back. Mike also made a spectacular diving save on a Sixers fast break, totally sacrificing his body and getting everyone fired up in the process.

Somehow we rallied to win 118–115, forcing a Game Six back in Houston. By now, there was a supercharged atmosphere in our community and you could feel it in the Summit as we battled the Sixers through three tight, tense quarters. In the final period, there were two controversial charging fouls on our team that could forever be debated.

On the first sequence, Newlin had a fast-break opportunity with Caldwell Jones retreating for the Sixers. As Newlin laid the ball in, there was contact. Was it a three-point opportunity or a charge? The official ruled it an offensive foul, and I remember running back on defense, looking at the replay on the big screen, and watching the official look at the replay, too.

In the final seconds, trailing by two, it came down to a do-or-die possession for us. Lucas drove and laid the ball in as Collins hit the floor.

Charging foul. Again.

The Rockets players just stood there, and it was as though we were suspended in time. The fans were on their feet, but nobody moved. It seemed like everything was frozen.

Then we just slowly moved off the floor as total quiet cast a pall over the Summit.

On the make-or-break drive by Lucas, we felt Collins was too far under the basket and that it should have been a no-call. Had John's basket counted, we would have gone into overtime. Who knows what would have happened?

But I give Collins credit for using his head and doing his job. He made the official make a call, and he got the benefit of the doubt. Consequently, the Sixers were headed to the NBA Finals.

Our initial shock was soon replaced by keen disappointment. We had won the last three games of the Washington series and we felt we could have done the same thing to the Sixers. We had just won Game Five in Philadelphia, so going back there for Game Seven was an opportunity we really wanted.

The "what if" game continued through the NBA Finals, as Portland beat Philadelphia, 4–2. We had gone 3–1 against the Blazers during the regular season. Moses matched up well against Bill Walton in the middle, and we really felt we would have had a good chance against those guys.

It took a few weeks for our emotions to simmer down and for us to reflect with pride on what had been a breakthrough year in Rockets history.

From those struggling early years when we were fighting for respectability, we had made it to the NBA's version of the Final Four. Now we wanted to build on that success and go all the way in 1977–78. The sky was the limit for Moses. Lucas was just a rookie. We had a nice blend of youth and experience, and we were hungry to take that next bold step.

Personally, I felt rejuvenated to have Moses around to shoulder the rebounding load and Lucas around to deliver the ball.

Everybody was working hard in the off-season, and I fully expected 1977–78 to be the best year of my professional life. It turned out to be the worst.

8

WHEN TRAINING CAMP OPENED in September, we definitely had visions of grandeur. Winning the Central Division, beating a quality team like the Washington Bullets, and then giving Philadelphia a serious threat in the Eastern Finals had left our entire organization with a feeling of genuine confidence. We felt we had the right combination of experience and youth to contend again for the title.

After a slow 6-12 start, Coach Nissalke put in some new plays that we really liked. Those plays had the forwards setting backpicks for the guards, which gave us some nice scoring opportunities. The man guarding me, for instance, had to help cover the cutting guard for a second or else the guard would get a layup; while that defender was helping, I would move away from him for an open shot. If my man switched to the guard, our guard would then take him to the other side of the floor. At 6-8, I would be left with a smaller man on me and immediately take him inside for a postup.

We were having a lot of success with this particular offensive maneuver because Lucas read the defense so well and delivered perfect passes. We won three of four, and then we headed for the Los Angeles Forum on December 9 to face the Lakers.

We were on an offensive roll early in that game, and at the half I had already scored 19 points. Early in the third quarter, we had a fast break going and I ran the right lane, looking for an easy opportunity basket.

Suddenly whistles blew, and I looked around to see what was going on.

In the backcourt I saw that a skirmish had broken out. What I witnessed sent chills through me. Our center, Kevin Kunnert, was trying to avoid punches being thrown by their power forward, Kermit Washington. Kareem Abdul-Jabbar grabbed Kevin from behind and turned him away, but Washington was still going after Kunnert. The thought that ran through my mind was, Kevin's hurt. I instinctively ran back toward them, and the next thing I knew I was lying on the floor looking into the concerned face of our trainer, Dick Vandervoort. Dick had a towel in his hand and told me to put it on my nose. I then noticed my nose was bleeding. The stuff was coming out like water out of a faucet.

I didn't feel any pain and I didn't know what had happened. While still prostrate on the court, I started to look around. The crowd was on its feet and I happened to notice actor Walter Matthau staring at me.

As I turned my head, I caught the eyes of Lakers coach Jerry West. Jerry had an odd expression on his face that made me feel uneasy.

I finally got to my feet, and Dick kept asking me questions that I didn't hear.

I was thoroughly confused. I kept asking him, "What happened? Why am I bleeding? Why is everyone looking at me?"

"Kermit punched you," Dick said.

"He punched me?" I said, puzzled. "But I wasn't in the fight. He was punching Kevin."

"Rudy, let's just go to the locker room."

As strange as this may seem, I felt fine at that moment.

"Dick, just put some gauze on my nose," I suggested. "I don't want to leave the game. I want to play."

Vandervoort kept insisting that we go to the locker room. I gave in, and as we were making our way off the court, I looked into the stands and saw the sad face of a teenaged boy named Bud, who used to live in Houston.

Bud had attended my summer basketball camp. He was the smallest kid in camp, and everyone's favorite. He used to lead us in calisthenics each morning. Bud's parents later told me his week in camp was one of the most positive experiences of his life. As Bud looked at me walking off the floor at the Forum, there were tears in his eyes.

The spectator behind Bud was ranting and raving. He kept pointing his finger at me. "Tomjanovich, he should have knocked your head right off."

I felt terrible that the kid had to hear something so cruel. The basketball camp may have been one of the most positive experiences of Bud's life, but this certainly wasn't.

I now really wanted to get back in the game. "Let's hurry this thing up," I told Vandervoort.

As I entered the corridor leading to the locker room, I saw Kermit pacing back and forth. He looked upset.

I was wondering what the hell he was upset about. I was the one with the bloody nose, and I never saw it coming. My temper started to boil as I looked at Kermit.

"Why'd you sucker-punch me?" I yelled. "If you wanted to fight, we could have just squared off."

At that point Kermit and I charged each other. Security guards pulled us apart before any contact was made.

I've always felt that fighting is a senseless act. There are better ways to settle differences. Growing up in a big city, I had learned that sometimes fights are unavoidable. I had been in a handful of fights, but they were always a last resort and a matter of survival.

I wouldn't, by any means, call myself a good fighter. But I am a survivor. I've been hit with a lead pipe, and I've had a broom handle broken over my shoulders. During that broom incident, I defended myself well enough for my opponent to feel it wasn't worth the pain to pursue it any further.

Even as I roared toward Kermit, I knew he was a lot stronger than I was. In fact, he was one of the strongest guys in the NBA. It was common knowledge that he was an avid weight lifter. You could look at his well-sculpted body and figure that out. Furthermore, he had better boxing technique, because I had none.

In all probability, had we gone at it in the corridor, he would have won the fight.

Still, I was willing to give it a go. I felt in my heart I couldn't let him get away with what he had done without doing something. My heart was pounding, I was breathing hard, and I had this awful, bitter taste in my mouth. Once the security guards pulled us in opposite directions, I was led to the locker room.

I lay down on the training table; a doctor was waiting to examine me. I asked him if he could fix me up quick so I could get back in the game.

The doctor told me just to relax so that he could accurately assess my injury. He asked me to open my mouth. As I did, I felt something strange. My upper and lower back teeth were still touching. He asked me to open wider. Still, the teeth were touching.

"Oh, man, my caps must have been knocked loose," I said. I figured the caps were probably hanging from my upper teeth, touching the bottom.

Then I panicked. I realized I didn't *have* caps on my upper teeth. Something was wrong. Something was definitely wrong.

"We have to get you to the hospital," the doctor said.

I was quickly put in a wheelchair and taken to a waiting ambulance. I couldn't believe what was happening. Within minutes, I was in the emergency room at Centinela Hospital. My eyes were swelling shut as a Dr. Paul Toffel introduced himself.

My mind was racing wildly. What the hell was I doing in an emergency room? I'm a basketball player. I'm supposed to be in a game right now. I wanted to be back on the court so I could help my teammates finish the job of beating the Lakers.

I was mumbling to myself when Dr. Toffel said, "Let me explain what kind of injury you have. The doctor at the arena told me what happened to you. I'm a plastic surgeon who specializes in facial injuries. Usually, my patients are people who have been in automobile accidents and have hit the windshield. Or people who have been hit in the face with an object like a baseball bat. You have that type of injury."

I went numb.

"What about basketball?" I asked.

"You won't be playing for a while. You'll be out the rest of the season."

My heart sank. Then I became angry. I didn't deserve this. Why'd the guy punch me? I did nothing to him. It wasn't fair.

I got madder and madder. My thoughts turned to revenge, and I started to get off the examining table.

"Doc, you've got to get me out of here. I've got to go back to the Forum. I've got to do something about this."

Truth is, I had no idea *what* I would do. My mind was in disarray. Everything had happened so fast. I was angry, sad, scared, and frustrated all at the same time.

Dr. Toffel then spoke to me in a tone that really got my attention.

"I don't think you understand the seriousness of this," he said. "You have a major injury. Your face has been broken away from your skull. It has caused cracks in your brain cavity and you are leaking spinal fluid. Did you have a funny taste in your mouth?"

I remembered the bitter taste I had experienced walking down the hall.

"What you tasted was not blood, it was spinal fluid," Dr. Toffel said. "This is a very dangerous condition. We'll have to monitor you closely the next couple of days. We're sending you up to our intensive-care unit."

"Intensive care? Are you telling me I could . . ."

I couldn't say the word *die*.

"This is a very dangerous condition," Dr. Toffel reiterated. "The next few days will tell."

All the rage left my body and was replaced with outright fear.

"Let me give you some advice," Dr. Toffel continued. "You can waste a lot of energy thinking negative thoughts. Revenge or feeling sorry for yourself—that won't help you get through this. In fact, it will probably hurt the healing process. You must accept the reality of what has happened to you. Take each improvement you make along the road back to be a special event—a celebration. It can make you appreciate the little things in life a lot more. There are so many things that we take for granted."

Dr. Toffel's advice made sense and I cleared my mind of negative thoughts. I became determined that I would conserve all my energy to get through this.

Before I went to intensive care, I made two telephone calls. One was to Sophie, and the other was to Calvin Murphy.

By the time I talked to Sophie, she had already heard from Vandervoort. Dick simply told her I had a broken nose, but I would be okay. I really appreciated that he contacted her quickly and provided some reassurance. When I spoke to Sophie, I recommended that she remain at home, but Sophie was determined to come out to Los Angeles. She said that as soon as she could get her mother to come down from Detroit to watch the kids, she would be on the next plane out.

When I talked to Calvin, he was extremely emotional. It was a touching conversation.

"I can't believe that happened to you," Calvin seethed.

Calvin's emotions had spilled over to the court. His great play had helped us beat the Lakers, 116–105, after I left the arena.

By the time I got to my room in intensive care, my eyes were swollen shut. I had to use my fingers to pry open my eyes, which I did often to take a peek at the clock on the wall. Minutes seemed like hours. There was no way I was going to fall asleep. I felt that if I were to fall asleep, I would never wake up.

As I lay there wide awake in the darkness, I was cognizant of what was going on in the room next to mine. A baby girl who had been injured in a car accident was in a coma. I could hear the mother constantly talking to the baby, encouraging the infant to wake up.

It was the saddest thing I had ever heard. When I talked to God, which I was doing frequently, I asked Him to give both me and that baby the strength to get through our ordeals. I didn't beg; it was very personal, one-on-one, and I knew it was the real thing.

After a sleepless night, I was happy to see Dr. Toffel the next morning. He was all smiles and had a positive attitude. He introduced me to a colleague who would be assisting him in the surgery to put my face back together.

When his colleague looked at me, he had the same expression

that Jerry West had while I was down on the floor of the Forum. I assumed the expression was concern. I was getting another expression from people when they saw me for the first time since the injury. I assumed this impression was shock.

I had not yet seen my face. A nurse took it upon herself to cover the small mirror in the bathroom with a towel. When she asked me if that was okay, I told her, "Thanks for the concern. I must look horrible."

Using my hands, I could feel how much my face had swollen. It was about the size of a basketball. I got confirmation about my looks when the maintenance man came in to put an extension on my bed.

He took one look at me and said, "Damn, man, did you get the number of that truck? A car accident, huh?"

"No, basketball."

"Basketball? Did the scoreboard fall on you? Man, your face is messed up."

Nice tact, I thought.

At that tenuous time, I didn't really care how I looked. I just wanted to live. I could take looking like the Elephant Man. All I wanted was to be with Sophie and my little girls, Nichole and Melissa. They could keep me locked away from people. That would be okay. Just let me live and be with my family.

The next major hurdle was to make it through a second night. I was willing to make any compromise just to be alive the following morning.

By the grace of God, I again made it through those dark hours. The next morning, Dr. Toffel had good news: The brain cavity had sealed and the leaking had stopped. I was out of danger.

A decision was made to move me to a regular room, but they had to wait until the swelling went down before they could do the surgery. Mercifully, the life-threatening crisis had passed.

From the time I had entered intensive care, I hadn't eaten or even thought about food. My nourishment came through intravenous feeding. When I got to my regular room, the first order of business was a celebration meal. The food had to be soft, but it all tasted fantastic.

In the bathroom of my new room was a large mirror. The nurse asked me if I wanted to cover it, and I declined. I already had agreed I would accept any appearance. So why not see what was actually shocking people?

I walked into the bathroom and slowly turned to the mirror. I was astonished at what I saw. My head was the shape of a pumpkin. My normal face was long and narrow, but now it was wide. My cheeks were about two inches puffier, and the discoloration was like a rainbow: black, blue, yellow, red.

My eyes were blood red. Gravity had pulled the internal bleeding downward, causing a black pigment to show in my upper chest.

That maintenance man had been right: I *was* messed up.

I stood there for several minutes and stared at a face I couldn't believe was mine. Hollywood couldn't have done a better job of making a human monster.

Sophie finally arrived, and she looked great. I was so happy to see her. She gave me a long, warm hug and said, "Let me take a look at you."

She took a moment to appraise me.

"Rudy, I think this is an improvement. Really, it's a big improvement on how you usually look."

I knew what she really thought. I loved her for trying to humor me, and I admired her for her strength.

Over the next couple of days, I spent time with Sophie and either read or watched television late into the night. While I was watching the second half of a UCLA–San Jose State basketball game one evening, something caught my eye in the lower right-hand corner of the screen. I could have sworn I saw a San Jose player turn and punch a UCLA player. The announcers never mentioned it, and I thought I was hallucinating.

I read the sports page the next day and there was no mention of the punch. I started to think I was losing my mind.

I read a lot of magazines while I was in the hospital. In one article that dealt with my incident, they quoted some players as saying that what Kermit had done was right. The line of thinking was that Washington had to protect himself when I attacked him.

Another article had Hall of Famer Bob Cousy saying he would not only have punched me, he would have kneed me in the groin, too.

I was in a state of complete confusion. It sounded like I was the attacker.

Suddenly I wasn't completely sure what I had done. Was I suffering from amnesia? I had been told I was briefly unconscious as I lay there on the floor. I don't remember ever seeing the punch. Could I have actually attacked Kermit? I didn't remember that ever entering my mind. My last thought was being concerned for Kevin Kunnert.

Shortly thereafter, they started running replays of the incident on television. It was the first time I actually saw the punch, and what a punch it was. As I was running downcourt, Kermit caught me with full extension square in the upper jaw. My head snapped back, my feet left the floor, and then my head bounced off the floor as I curled into the fetal position.

My hands were not in an offensive position, as though I was going to hit someone. I started to bring my hands up to protect my face, but they were too late. At the very last second, I must have seen the punch, but the memory of it was lost somewhere in my subconscious.

It was an ugly incident to see on a television screen. But I was glad I had seen it because it confirmed my original feelings about what had actually taken place.

Kermit never was the focus of my actions; if he had been, I would have been watching him and seen the punch coming earlier. If I had been thinking of attacking Kermit, I wouldn't have been surprised when our trainer told me he had hit me.

After being holed up in the hospital, after staying up days and nights and worrying continuously, after seeing the punch in the college game and seeing the negative articles, my mind was in shambles.

But now my conscience was clear.

The following day, I did find an article about the San Jose player who punched the Bruin. He was suspended for his action, and it made me feel a little saner. I was relieved that I wasn't really going crazy; I wasn't seeing things that didn't exist.

I spent some of my time wondering how they were going to clamp my face back to my skull. Dr. Toffel spent time with me every day. He offered a lot of encouragement and carefully outlined the procedures so I knew what to expect.

I asked the doctor about my eventual appearance, and Dr. Toffel smiled before giving his response.

"They gave me some photos of you before this happened," Dr. Toffel said. "To be honest with you, Rudy, no great loss. You'll probably look better."

"I guess everybody around here is a comedian," I said.

The surgery was successful. They wired my jaw together, and I finally felt the pain. Hoses had to be placed in my nose so I could breathe.

A couple of days after surgery, Dr. Toffel escorted me on a plane back to Houston. He carried shears with him. If I had gotten sick on the way home, the shears would have enabled him to cut the wires. That would have been the only way to get the vomit out; otherwise I could have wound up choking.

It was good to be home finally and see my daughters. My appearance shocked them. When I picked up Melissa and gave her a hug, she looked at me and asked, "Daddy, are you okay?"

There was still a lot of discoloration on my face, and Sophie said Nichole had asked a lot of questions about "why the man hit Daddy."

I rested, got my bearings, and gradually began to see other specialists. One doctor took care of my teeth. Another doctor had to repair a hole in the back of my eye with laser surgery.

I also had to have tear-duct surgery because of all the scar tissue. The tear duct was dammed up, and tears wouldn't flow through my eyes. Water would well up in my eyes, and the view would be like it is when you're underwater.

It was a long, slow process of making my way back to becoming a basketball player.

I had plenty of time for reflection in the long convalescence period after I got home. Basketball had been so important to me, and then it was taken away. When Dr. Toffel brought up the question of my life, I started to think differently.

While in the hospital, I had come to the conclusion that if I never played basketball again or could never see people because I was the Elephant Man, I would still be thankful for what I had. That was the approach I took, and it sustained me as the days and weeks went on.

There were little victories along the way. For a while, I had to suck food through my teeth because they were wired shut. But then one day I was surprised that the wires came off and I was allowed to eat some real food.

On the way home, I stopped for cheese enchiladas and that was, as Dr. Toffel said, a celebration. Best cheese enchiladas I've ever had.

As the winter of 1978 turned to spring, I was determined not to let an incident like this stop my basketball career. Really, at that point, I never even thought about the possibility of *not* coming back. I was so strong-willed that I was going to get through this and be a good player again.

Kermit Washington wasn't playing, either. He had been assessed a record $10,000 fine and 60-day suspension without pay that cost him an additional $50,000 as the NBA took a landmark stance against violence on the court. But I didn't really stay on top of that story.

After what the doctor had said, Kermit simply wasn't on my mind. In terms of trying to figure out why it happened and what was going through his mind—it didn't matter. The thing had occurred. I had to deal with it and get my life back in order.

All through my life, I've tried to take a negative and turn it into a positive. There are always obstacles in people's lives that they have to overcome; this was one that I had to overcome, and what made it a little tougher was the fact that it happened in the public arena.

There was so much more emotion expressed by other people than by me. Some people tried to make it a racial thing. That never entered my mind. Not once.

I didn't feel hate toward Kermit. I just said to myself, Something terrible happened. I wish it hadn't, but it did.

Years later, I had a conversation with Kermit Washington about the incident. He said, "You have to understand that this ruined my life, too."

I just accepted what he had to say without comment. I don't know how much meaning came out of it. I imagine that this was what he was going to hear about for the rest of his life. And I was leery that this would be what I was known for the rest of *my* life—not as a good basketball player, but as the guy who got punched.

Traveling around to different basketball camps through the years, I would hear people say, "I don't think I've seen you play. Wait a minute! Aren't you the guy who got hit?"

The replay of that punch was used as much as any replay I've ever seen. Each time I would go home to Detroit, it seemed like my mother had to watch it fifteen times a day on every station.

It got to be a sad joke.

I don't know if *resentment* is the right word for how I felt about this. I understand how people react to this type of thing. I just say, "What a shame." I thought I had done some nice things on the basketball court, and I had to wonder if those things would all be forgotten. Not that I'm big on living in the past, but to have my playing career overshadowed by a negative incident was really unfair.

Even after we won a world championship in 1994, *Sports Illustrated*'s commemorative issue included a story about the Tomjanovich–Washington incident seventeen years earlier. What did that have to do with our championship?

I'm just so thankful that I was given an opportunity to be in this league long enough to do something else to overshadow that image of me. I think it *has* been overshadowed—finally.

Through the years, people have looked to me to be a spokesman against violence because of the Washington episode. I'm just not comfortable in that role.

Of course I think violence is terrible. The incident happened to me, and I had to live with it long enough. But to speak out publicly on this issue would draw me right back into it, and undo everything I've done to put it behind me. The NBA has taken a very strong stand against fighting, and I think the league has done the right thing.

But I just want to be a basketball coach at this stage of my life.

I believe in aggressive play, and I respect players who play tough and hard. If you cross the line, it's wrong. I think all of us in the league feel that way.

My incident spoke for itself. If that's what I had to give to help the crusade against violence, I gave that. Now I just want to go on and not be the lightning rod anymore.

THE WASHINGTON INCIDENT cast a shadow over the entire '77–78 season, and when Malone and Newlin were injured in the second half of the year, we plummeted to a 28-54 record.

After the season ended, I received clearance to have contact again. I joined the Rockets' summer-league team in Los Angeles and worked under Del Harris out there. When that session ended, I felt pretty good about my chances of having a strong comeback season.

Later that summer, there was a charity game at the University of Houston. It was a fun game, nothing serious, so you couldn't really draw conclusions one way or the other. One of the Houston newspapers said I looked like my old self, and the other paper said it seemed as though I was shying away from contact.

That just prepared me for the intense scrutiny that would come down the road when I would begin to play in meaningful games again.

The Washington saga didn't really end until the fall of 1979, when I was awarded a multimillion-dollar settlement following a court case in Houston.

This negative incident is a part of my life story. I understand that. But thankfully, with the help of God, my family, and so many friends, I was able to go forward with a bright outlook.

It could have been worse. I could have died on the court that December night at the Forum. So many people have so much more misfortune than what I experienced.

The right thing to do was count my blessings and go on, realizing just how precious life is.

9

IN THE SUMMER of 1978, I got an unexpected call from Tom Nissalke. He informed me that the Rockets were interested in signing celebrated free agent Rick Barry. Rick was a sure Hall of Famer who had won a championship at Golden State and been one of the premier scorers in both the NBA and ABA. Besides being able to put the ball in the basket, he was a great passer from the forward position.

The NBA rules at the time stipulated that the team losing a free agent would be compensated by the team signing him. Commissioner Larry O'Brien would make the final decision on what was supposed to be a player of similar value.

My initial reaction to the telephone call was that Tom was letting me know I would be the compensation for Rick. But Tom immediately assured me I wasn't leaving Houston.

My next thought was one of excitement over the prospect of playing with Rick. But who would be the compensation? Who was leaving our team? Would it be Murphy?

Tom said we would have to give up John Lucas. Hmmm. I didn't know what to think about that. Barry was still good, but he was on the downside of his career after twelve pro seasons. Rick had maybe a couple of good years left if he stayed healthy. Lucas, on the other hand, was entering his third pro season and had many good years left. Furthermore, true point guards are extremely hard to find.

"Is there any way we can keep Lucas and add Barry?" I asked Tom. What an awesome attack that would have been. But Tom quickly let me know there was no chance of that happening. I don't know if management suspected any drug use on Lucas's part; I know I didn't have any suspicions at that time.

But Barry was in, Lucas was out.

When the season rolled around, I was raring to go. I had completed a year's worth of doctor's appointments and I was pronounced one-hundred-percent fit. I had spent a lot of time running in Houston's Memorial Park and playing pickup basketball all over the city. I had even taken an elbow in the face from a big, strong college kid during one of those pickup games. The kid was really nervous when I bent down holding my face, but I quickly let him know I was fine.

"Thanks, I needed that," I said, hoping to relieve the tension. The guy breathed a sigh of relief and, to be honest, I did, too.

I knew this was a barrier that I would eventually have to break in my comeback season. I knew I was under the microscope. Everybody was watching how I would respond to the physical part of the game. I kept hearing that phrase *Gun-shy*.

I thought people were making too much out of it. I still had no conscious memory of the Washington punch. If the injury had occurred under the boards going for a rebound or setting a pick, I could see that "gun-shy" concern, but it had happened outside the realm of basketball, and now I was back inside that realm.

My teammates made me feel welcome. When I'd do something positive, I'd hear, "Good to have you back, Rudy."

It was clear to me that the Washington episode had had an effect on anyone who saw it. It had become something that was attached to me, sort of like a monkey on my back. "Oh, yeah, you're the guy who got nailed."

I learned to tolerate these kinds of comments. I realized it could have been worse: I could have been hearing these things and not have been able to play basketball. I felt fortunate. I was happy to be playing the game I loved, and I really didn't care *what* people were saying.

With Barry fitting in nicely, we got off to a 5-1 start in 1978–79. But losing a distributor like Lucas eventually had to take a toll. We lost nine of the next 13 to fall under the .500 mark, and the "quarterback" role became a major issue. To help fill the Lucas void, we acquired Slick Watts, a bald-headed point guard. Slick played the last 61 games and gave us a penetration lift. Even though he wasn't as creative as Lucas, he had a point guard's mentality in terms of setting up his teammates.

We started rolling again after Slick came over, and I was feeling pretty good about things. But I got a big scare two days after Christmas when we were in Detroit. With my mother and sister in the stands, I suffered a blow to my surgically repaired face. We were holding the ball for a last shot, and a teammate penetrated and hit me with a pass. I was being guarded by M.L. Carr, who had his hands up, as a good defender should. I spotted an open man under the basket and threw the pass; M.L. tried to deflect the ball and accidentally hit me in the nose.

This was a much sharper blow than the elbow in the face I had taken in the summer. I knew instantly my nose was broken. But what I didn't know was how the rest of my face would hold up.

I was rushed to the hospital for X rays. Fortunately, there was no damage other than the broken nose. Even though broken noses are no fun, it was reassuring to know that I had mended well from all the facial damage the previous year.

I was having a pretty good season as fall gave way to winter. All the analyzing and skepticism began to die down, and Rick and I developed some pretty good chemistry at the forward spots. On one particular play, where I came off a pick for a shot at the top of the key, Rick was unbelievable in reading the defense. If I made the outside shot, the defense would inevitably try to cheat and beat me over the pick the next time. So I would fake using the pick, cut back to the basket, and Rick would deliver the ball perfectly for what was usually an uncontested layup.

Rick had always been the No. 1 option on every team he played on. Rightfully so; he had tremendous offensive talent.

On our team, though, there would have to be some adjusting. We already had a lot of offensive-minded players, and Moses was becoming a force inside. We were all wondering if Rick would be willing to sacrifice some of his offense to accommodate everybody else.

We got the answer when Rick made the comment one day that he had never played on a team with so many good shooters. He said he didn't need to be the constant focus and could act like a point guard from the forward position. He could conserve some energy, then pick his spots to look for his shots.

Bottom line, I was extremely impressed with Rick's unselfish attitude. In the two years he was with the Rockets, he just wanted to win.

I was really surprised that the fans voted me an All-Star starter in 1978–79. It would have been a great honor, but I felt in my heart I didn't deserve it. I think I got a lot of sympathy votes because of what had happened to me the previous year. Initially, I didn't want to accept that starting spot on the Eastern Conference All-Stars because I felt I was depriving a more deserving player of that special recognition.

I felt guilty. I didn't want players around the league to think that just because I got hurt, I could start in the All-Star Game. I would have been perfectly happy if I had made it as I did four previous times—via the coaches' vote.

I talked with friends and a couple of sportswriters about the situation. They told me I would have made the team as a reserve anyway, so it wasn't as if I was taking a roster spot away from another player. That line of thinking made me feel a little better, but still, I wasn't particularly enthusiastic about going to that All-Star Game.

The only good part was the site: The '79 All-Star Game was in Detroit, and Sophie and the kids got to visit the family before we went out to the Silverdome in Pontiac for the game. I had never had a really good offensive showing in my four previous All-Star appearances; I usually wound up rebounding while the players more adept at freelance basketball did the scoring. I was more of a system player, scoring off plays I was accustomed to running.

But this All-Star Game would be different. Julius Erving was the other starting forward, and Doc really got me going. He'd drive the middle, draw the defense, and hit me for open jumpers. He didn't look to set me up on purpose; he was just playing his normal, unselfish game.

After I made a couple of shots, my confidence soared. I even made a running hook across the middle. In 24 minutes, I finished with 12 points and six rebounds.

It was ironic: The All-Star Game I felt I didn't belong in was the one in which I wound up having my best showing. Being in front of the hometown fans made it extra special, too.

We were involved in a tense race for the Central Division title, but San Antonio beat us out by one game. This meant we had to face the Atlanta Hawks in the opening best-two-out-of-three round of the playoffs, and we didn't match up well against their personnel. Eddie Johnson, John Drew, and Dan Roundfield were the Hawks' top players. They stole the first game at the Summit when our defense fell apart and allowed 39 points in the third quarter. Then the Hawks went home and beat us at the Omni. What had been a positive season for the most part ended on an 0–2 sour note.

In the off-season, the Rockets were sold to Albuquerque, New Mexico, businessman George Maloof, and Mr. Maloof wanted to make big changes right away. He let us know immediately that he intended to replace the coach and the general manager. George White, a Rockets beat writer for the *Houston Chronicle*, had some meetings with Mr. Maloof and suggested that he shouldn't make key decisions so quickly. Get to know the people before making an evaluation—that was George White's recommendation.

Maloof used that advice concerning general manager Ray Patterson, but he didn't change his mind about Nissalke. At first, the new owner wanted to hire a college coach. Norm Ellenberger from New Mexico was his man.

But Moses was developing into a star, and Del Harris was the guy who had been working with the big people. In my meeting with Mr. Maloof, I suggested that if Tom wasn't going to be here, it would be best for Del to take over. All the other veterans that Mr. Maloof talked to felt the same way.

Del got the head-coaching job, and his first team in 1979–80 turned out to be an interesting array of guys. Midway through that season, we acquired Billy Paultz, who was nicknamed "The Whopper." Billy was seven feet tall, close to three hundred pounds, and one of the funniest guys I've ever been around. He had that New Jersey wit and he kept us in stitches. Billy would throw quick verbal jabs. "I see you got a haircut today. Did you pay for that?" But when it came time to play, Billy was dead serious and a true pro. He set big, solid picks to free up teammates and was willing to do the dirty work so the team could be successful. In fifteen pro seasons, Billy's teams never missed the playoffs. That tells you something about his value.

Shortly after Billy joined us, Del brought the team together one day for a positive-imagery session. It consisted of visualizing an upcoming event with a successful result. Golfers use it a lot, seeing the perfect shot in their mind's eye before they actually take the swing.

Before one game, Del asked us to close our eyes and visualize ourselves playing tough defense, then grabbing rebounds in traffic. After that he told us to visualize making our shots. Then Del said, "We've had some problems lately. Now, see a bag. We're putting all the bad stuff in the bag and walking to a bridge with water below. Drop the bag over the side. It hits the water with a splash and disappears. Our problems are gone. You can open your eyes now, guys."

Billy called out, "Del, it didn't work. Rick Barry is still here."

Billy was just joking, of course. Paultz and Barry had been friends a long time, dating back to their ABA days together. We all got a good laugh out of that one, and it was typical of how Paultz kept the team loose.

Other quality people were arriving as well. Mike Dunleavy was a gutsy kid who gave 110 percent. He always seemed to have stitches in the head or a bruise here or there. When you're always doing a little bit extra, you get popped. Mike was a true tough competitor.

Robert Reid was a third-year guy with great athletic ability, and veteran Tom Henderson and rookie Allen Leavell formed the new tandem at point guard. We had high ambitions for making Del's first year a major success, but we could only manage a 41-41 record. For me, the injury bug was beginning to bite. I was starting to experience an inevitable process—aging. My body didn't recuperate from injuries as quickly as in my earlier years. I missed 20 games and started only 50.

Despite our .500 record, we managed to gain a homecourt advantage against San Antonio in the opening round of the playoffs. We had a solid defensive effort in Game One and gained a 95-85 victory. Holding San Antonio to 85 points was a major feat, because in those days George Gervin was a scorer the likes of which we had never seen. He was so smooth it seemed like he never sweated. He never got into a double-team situation he couldn't gracefully escape. George's body control and athletic ability always made it seem like he could navigate out of the toughest traps.

Gervin got 44 points in Game Two to help the Spurs even the series. But we went home and blew them out 141-120 in the deciding game as Malone soared for 37 points.

The good news was that we had escaped the first round. The bad news was that we ran smack into a Boston team that had been transformed by rookie Larry Bird. Even as a first-year player, Bird had a distinct presence about him. You knew right away he was going to be a great one. That '79–80 season will forever be remembered as the year that Bird and Magic Johnson came into the NBA, touching off an unprecedented golden era.

Magic was a 6-9 guy thriving at what was supposed to be the smallest position on the court. With his size and ballhandling skills, he changed the sport. We started to say, "Where's this game going? Are we going to have seven-footers playing guard?"

Magic and Bird. They fit their cities perfectly. Bird was the more conservative guy, which seems proper in a place like Boston. Fundamental basketball. He was what you thought a player in Boston should be. Magic, in a glitzy city like Los Angeles, had the smile that captivated everybody. He had the flashy style, but never put so much flash into it that it hurt the play.

With Bird leading the way, Boston took us apart 4–0 in the second round. We had a summer to contemplate how we were going to reach the next level. Barry retired after that '79–80 season, but we otherwise came back with virtually the same cast that had been swept by the Celtics.

Seventy-seven games into that '80–81 season, it looked like we were in for another disappointing conclusion. We were 36-41 and struggling just to make the playoffs. But what would happen from that point until Game Six of the NBA Finals represented an unbelievable Cinderella story.

I had a groin injury and other physical problems that knocked me down to 52 games played. Late in the season, Del decided to go with the big lineup of Malone, Paultz, Bill Willoughby, Dunleavy, and Henderson. Murphy was an instant-offense sixth man.

Me? I was out of the rotation for the first time in my career.

As much as it hurt not playing, I have to praise Del for envisioning something that he could get done with the Paultz-Malone lineup. When we were 36-41, everybody assumed we were out of it. And to be honest, there were some doubts in our locker room. But everybody just stuck with it and we won four of our last five to make the playoffs. It didn't matter how we got there; the main thing was that we had survived, and the slate was wiped clean. It was like being reborn.

We were matched up against a great Lakers team in another of those dangerous miniseries. The Lakers were a club that was used to running. They played fast-break basketball, with Magic creating. Our answer was to use slow-down tactics that broke their rhythm. We started to see an anxious, frustrated look on the faces of the Lakers. When they made a couple of runs, Del would simply call timeout and slow it down.

One of the strong characteristics we developed in the '81 playoffs was the ability to make a shot with less than five seconds left on the 24-second clock. This is a maddening experience for a team that's anxious to get the ball and go. They have to exert themselves on defense for nearly the full 24 seconds, and just when they think that effort is going to pay off in a stop, we beat the buzzer with a clutch shot.

We stunned the Lakers 111–107 in Game One at the Forum as Malone scored 38 points. Moses had developed from a skinny kid to a dominating force on the boards and as an inside scorer. This was a gigantic win for us. For a team that had barely made the playoffs, beating the Lakers in L.A. gave us a tremendous confidence boost.

But we knew they were a quality team and would come back strong in Game Two. Sure enough, they came to our place and won, 111–106. Many people assumed that normalcy had returned.

The decisive third game was a hard-fought battle by both teams. We trailed by one point with 30 seconds left. Del called timeout and set up a play to get the ball inside to Moses. When Mo received the ball, the Lakers quickly collapsed on him. Malone passed to Mike Dunleavy on the left wing, and Mike sank an 18-footer to put us up by one with 15 seconds remaining.

The Lakers predictably put the ball in Magic's hands. He drove the lane, but his shot came down well shy of the basket. Malone got the rebound and hit two free throws after being fouled. Lo and behold, the last-seeded Western Conference team had upset the favored Lakers, 89–86.

They called our style "uglyball," but how beautiful it was.

I learned a lesson there that would stay with me when I eventually made my way into coaching: Everybody has to find his way of being successful. For that particular team, Del Harris believed the slow, deliberate game was best. Del did an outstanding job of selling it to the team. With our personnel, that was the only way we could have reached the NBA Finals.

For me, it was a bittersweet time. I was a Rocket through and through and I was so happy for the team, but I was still deeply disappointed not to be a part of it. It took its toll.

The way I lived my life throughout my career was to expend energy competing, playing the game. But here I was, sitting around and not having any outlet for all this stored-up energy. All I could do was watch and cheer.

I had plenty of cheering to do in the second round, too. We played an unbelievable series against San Antonio, with the road team winning five of the seven games.

It was such a great rivalry. With Houston and San Antonio just two hundred miles apart on Interstate 10, their fans would show up in droves at our building and vice versa. The Spurs were again led by the explosive Gervin. His running mate at guard was James Silas, a guy whose clutch performances earned him the nickname "Captain Late" in the ABA. San Antonio had a high-scoring small forward, Larry "Mr. K" Kenon. And the Spurs were tough inside with a bulky group called "The Bruise Brothers." That inside trio consisted of Mark Olberding, Dave Corzine, and Paul Griffin.

It all came down to Game Seven in San Antonio. As I said earlier, Calvin Murphy's 42 points in that game was one of the best clutch performances ever in the NBA. Murphy's shooting propelled us to a 105–100 victory, and we were off to Kansas City for the Western Conference Finals.

The Kings were also a 40-42 team that year, but they found some chemistry at the right time and shocked Phoenix in the second round. That was a crazy situation; Kansas City's starting guards, Phil Ford and Otis Birdsong, were out with injuries, but the Kings played a courageous Game Seven against the Suns with a makeshift lineup.

Against us, however, the Kings were facing the definitive Cinderella. We got a split in the first two games and then won twice on our home floor, with Moses dominating the middle. In the opener of that series, Reggie King was setting strong picks for the Kings, and guys like Ernie Grunfeld and Scott Wedman were coming off these picks for open jumpers. When we called timeout, Del emphasized that we had to get that play covered. But our guys complained that they couldn't get over King's picks because he was moving and the officials weren't calling it.

When play resumed, Kansas City ran the same play. As Calvin came over the pick, King suddenly went down in a heap, clutching his groin. At the next timeout, Calvin said, "I don't think King will be setting any more moving picks on me."

On April 29 at Kansas City, we prevailed, 97–88, to give Houston its first finalist in an established professional sport. Who would have ever dreamed it? We had a party after the game in our hotel. Our owner, George Maloof, had died earlier in the year, and his twenty-four-year-old son Gavin had taken over. Gavin was comparing our team to the 1969 Miracle Mets.

"We're a team of destiny," Gavin yelled over and over.

It was hard to argue the point. We were headed to Boston Garden and felt we had a legitimate shot at the big trophy.

In Game One of the title series against the Celtics, we were in control most of the way, much to the surprise of the national media. But Larry Bird just wouldn't let his team lose. Bird went to the boards like a madman when we were on the verge of delivering a knockout punch. One play in particular got the Celtics rejuvenated and almost caused the ever-present cigar to fall out of Red Auerbach's mouth. After a missed shot, Bird's momentum was carrying him out of bounds. The rebound caromed right to him as he was about to cross the baseline and, in one motion, he put up a left-handed shot while falling over the end line. Nothing but net.

Auerbach would later say that play by Bird was the greatest play he had ever seen.

The Celtics had a 98–95 lead when we called timeout to set up a last-second three-point try. Del wanted as many three-point shooters as possible on the court, so I took off my warm-up suit after sitting the whole game.

Because I was so stiff, I told Del, "I'll be on the floor as another threat, but don't let me be the focal point."

The primary plan was for Mike Dunleavy to take the shot, but the Celtics covered him and I wound up getting the ball. My three-point attempt had a chance, but it hit the rim and the Celtics had dodged a bullet.

Bird had saved them with his 21 rebounds and deft passing. Our strategy had been for Robert Reid to shadow Bird all over the floor; Robert did a great job of staying on him and not letting him get hot, but Bird kept feeding other guys and hitting the glass. He found a way to win it.

Though we came out on the short end, our guys were more convinced than ever that we could steal a game at Boston Garden. We played great down the stretch in Game Two and were up by two when Tiny Archibald pulled up for a jumper that could have forced overtime. The shot hit the back iron, and we walked out of fabled Boston Garden with a 1–1 split and the homecourt edge in the finals.

Now the Celtics were focused. They came to Houston and thrashed us 94–71 in Game Three. We had to play Game Four the next afternoon after that drubbing, and it didn't look good for the home team. But Del made another gutsy decision: He played only six men in a back-to-back situation against a great running team. We slowed it down and somehow pulled out a 91–86 victory that evened the series 2–2. It was reminiscent of what we had seen in the Lakers series: The Celtics wanted to get up and down the court, but we cut the floor in half with our slow pace.

All things considered, it had to be one of the most unlikely wins in postseason history.

The only negative that day came after our victory. As the press was conducting interviews in our locker room, Moses Malone was quoted as saying, "I could take four guys off the streets of Petersburg, Virginia, and beat the Celtics."

I didn't hear Moses say it, but it made for a prominent headline when we showed up in Boston for Game Five. Boston coach Bill Fitch had used Malone's alleged comment as bulletin-board material, and the Celtics promptly came out and routed us. You never want to give an opponent any motivational edge, and I don't believe Moses would have seriously made that comment. Truth is, it didn't sound like Moses at all.

But sometimes the truth doesn't matter. If there's a seed of controversy, the media will build it up, twist it, and use it any way they can. Even without this bulletin-board material, the Celtics were such a great team that they might have blown us out anyway, just as they had in Game Three. Much was made of the Moses angle, but we'll never know if it really made a huge difference in the outcome of that 29-point Celtic win.

We were down 3–2 in the series and fell behind by 17 points in Game Six back in Houston. But we wouldn't go quietly. We cut it to three before Bird made a three-pointer from the left corner that finally nailed the coffin.

In retrospect, we felt that championship series was a lot closer than 4–2. A break here or there and, realistically, there was a chance we could have been champions. It was sort of a revelation. We weren't just there giving them competition. A 40-42 regular-season team had made a legitimate championship run.

It was an inspirational story that all teams should consider. No matter how much you struggle through the course of a year, never give in. If you stick together and develop solid chemistry, anything can happen. The '80–81 Rockets almost pulled off a miracle.

When I removed my uniform after Game Six, it never even crossed my mind that I might be taking off No. 45 for the final time. I believed that this was just another obstacle that I would have to get over, just like in my younger days when I was cut from the freshman team. I was ready to deal with the task of working my way back into prominence, and I looked forward to it. In the middle of my career, I had actually looked for negative things in articles just to give me that added spark. This time, I wouldn't have to go looking. I was out of the rotation and the team was successful. I figured they would probably stay with the big-lineup approach, so I had either to prove my worth to the Rockets or find someplace else to play.

Rumors were circulating that I might be moving on. Tom Nissalke had surfaced as the head coach in Utah, and there was speculation I might be traded to the Jazz. I don't know how much validity those Utah rumors had, but I certainly visualized playing a twelfth year of NBA basketball for somebody.

When I get into a situation where I have to fight my way back, I like to be alone. I went to Memorial Park to run or lifted weights at Nautilus. I was constantly pushing myself, getting ready to make a comeback. But that time alone triggered something in my mind. While I had no doubt I could overcome another obstacle and become a productive player again, the thought finally hit me: Why do I have to prove it again?

I had enjoyed a good playing career with the Rockets and I felt fortunate to have spent all eleven years with the same organization. Not many players in professional sports can say that. My children loved where they lived and had made great friends. My wife was very comfortable.

Why do this? Why uproot everybody and change my family's lives just to say I did it on the court one more time?

I had two years left on my guaranteed Rockets contract. I talked with my Ann Arbor attorney, Phil Fichera, and finally the decision crystallized in my mind. I had burned up a lot of energy with the mental anguish of not playing late in the '80–81 season; at some point, if I stayed in uniform, I would experience that anguish again. Father Time eventually catches up with every athlete.

I had survived the punch and hadn't had any other major injuries. It occurred to me that if I could get out of the business and still be healthy, it would be a big plus.

I brought up the retirement question with Sophie, and she was comfortable with whatever I wanted to do. I next went to Ray Patterson to see if we could work out a deal. I didn't want to sit on the bench and collect money for two years if the Rockets didn't trade me. I felt we were okay financially, and I was willing to compromise if the Rockets would meet me halfway.

That's exactly how it turned out. Ray was great about it. We agreed that I would be paid for one year and I would waive the second guaranteed season. Ray congratulated me on a great career and gave me an open invitation to be around the team and help out any way I wanted.

So that was it.

After a satisfying eleven-year pro career in which I had averaged 17.4 points and shot .501 from the floor, I was ready to hang up the sneakers and move in a different direction. I just didn't know right away where that new path would lead me.

10

NOW WHAT?

In the wake of my retirement as a player, I had a lot of time to contemplate a second career. The Rockets and basketball had been such a big part of my life that I knew I wanted to stay in Houston and continue to work with the team in some capacity. But it took me a while to carve out a new niche.

The initial plan was to have me go out into the Houston community and talk with groups about the team, but that role didn't appeal to me. I liked being around the game, not talking about it in front of large gatherings.

Through the years I had been fascinated with the intricacies of basketball. I always liked diagramming things—even as a kid—and I developed an appreciation for the preparations that went into helping my teams get ready for an opponent. So the answer for me was scouting.

After I talked with Del Harris and Carroll Dawson, we decided that I could help take some of the work load off Carroll by doing both advance and personnel scouting. That would be my assignment for six years, and what a valuable time it was in preparing me to become a head coach in the NBA someday.

Advance scouting consists of observing opponents and determining their strengths and weaknesses, then writing out a detailed report. Every team has a wide variety of plays or sets; it's the advance scout's job to diagram them on the report and explain what they're trying to accomplish. Some teams stick with four or five bread-and-butter plays. Others have a lot more, and that is a real test for the scout. You also have to determine what kind of defensive tactics they're using: How do they play the pick-and-roll? How do they handle the post-up plays? What is their double-teaming scheme? Do they use presses that are full-court, three-quarter-quart or half-court?

You also assess the strengths and weaknesses of the individual players. On offense, you note if a guy can shoot. Where does he get most of his shots? Which side of the floor is he better on? How does he get his shots—off the dribble or off picks? Is he better going left or right? Also, what kind of shots does he use when he's close to the basket and posting up?

You also note who the poor free-throw shooters are, and which players want the big shots. And then on defense you look for weak links: Who is the poor one-on-one defender? Who doesn't run back on defense? Which players have trouble avoiding picks? Who has poor lateral movement? Who is prone to fouling? Which players like to play the passing lanes? If they overplay, can you "backdoor" them? Who are the best shot-blockers?

All the individual characteristics go in your report. What plays a team runs when it needs a basket late in the game is very valuable information. The scout is looking for any advantage he can give his team. You look for who is playing well and who is struggling.

In a word, advance scouting is spying. You could call it counterintelligence.

But what you see in a game you scout is not always what you'll get when the scouted team goes up against you. I remember scouting the Boston Celtics one game before they were to play us. Larry Bird happened to have a rare poor performance. He couldn't make a shot. It was just one of those terrible nights that even the great players occasionally experience.

When I reported back to the team, I let the coach know we were in trouble. Players like Bird don't become great by having back-to-back poor games; they have too much pride. I expected him to come out very aggressively against us and to have a great game to make up for his last one.

I suggested that we double-team him early in the game so he wouldn't get good looks at the basket. I thought that was a solid game plan. Unfortunately, we didn't get to employ it much; the Celtics got us in a transition game and Bird got several layups, nailed his outside shots, and wound up with a big game. Sometimes our suggestions work and sometimes they don't.

On another occasion I was scouting Seattle, and when I talked to Bill Fitch on the phone, he asked me how Xavier McDaniel had played. McDaniel was a 20-point scorer and a rugged rebounder. He was a physical defender and was known for his toughness; he played with an air of confidence and was always a big concern for us whenever we played the Sonics.

In the game that I scouted, Xavier was his typical aggressive self. But something happened that was noteworthy: A player not known for his offense posted up on McDaniel twice in a row. McDaniel looked at him with an animated expression, as if to say, "How dare you?" McDaniel got overly aggressive and committed a foul. He was upset by the audacity of this player's thinking he could score on him inside. McDaniel's emotions didn't cool down on the offensive end, either; he wanted to post up in retaliation, and he was so anxious that he ran over the opponent for an offensive foul.

Fitch said this was very interesting information.

With this scouting tip, we opened the game by running four straight plays for Rodney McCray, who was being guarded by McDaniel. Xavier got two quick fouls, had to sit down, and was never a factor in the game.

As an advance scout, I really had an opportunity to focus on how teams and coaches operate. Longtime coach Gene Shue was very inventive and intricate with his plays. I had a chance to scout a young Pat Riley when he was just starting his coaching career with the Lakers. Pat had a great big man in Kareem Abdul-Jabbar and a great playmaker in Magic Johnson. You knew the ball would wind up in Kareem's hands because he had the sky hook, which was about an eighty-percent shot if you didn't double-team him.

At the time, Riley wasn't getting his due respect as the coach of the Lakers. People said he had all the great talent and that anybody could win with that caliber of players. But I saw how instrumental Riley was in making that Lakers team go. I saw how the Lakers would make four passes, cut players to keep defenders busy, and then get the ball in to Abdul-Jabbar—only now, because of all this movement, it was always a different guy who had to double down. Those things influenced me. You'd say, "Maybe we can't do it like the Lakers did back then, but let's do whatever we can to make the opponent have to make a decision."

While advance scouting would help me cultivate an offensive and defensive philosophy, the personnel scouting helped me prepare for decisions that I would make years later as a head coach.

The way I look at it, words can never fully describe what a player is. It's like talking about movie stars: She's blond, she's beautiful, she has a great body. Now, who is that? It could be Michelle Pfeiffer, Kim Basinger, or Jessica Lange. All are good-looking movie stars, but all are different.

I believe in really editing the tapes of college players and sorting out anything that's meaningful, whether it's positive or negative. You have to watch a guy's body language. You have to watch the way he walks back to the huddle when his team is down. By scrutinizing the tapes, you may pick up an expression or a feel for the guy that you didn't get even when you were at the game.

You have to be a little bit of a nut to put in the time to do these things, but I believe they're necessary. This philosophy paid huge dividends when we drafted Robert Horry and Sam Cassell, two guys who were instrumental in helping us win world championships after being overlooked by many teams in the 1992 and 1993 drafts, respectively.

I knew a little bit about Robert Horry even before I looked at tapes on him because I had seen him play during the 1988 Olympic Trials. I saw the way he could go out on the floor for a 6-10 guy, and I made notes that he was a player to watch. When we got tapes on him his senior year at Alabama, he had moved to the center position.

He was playing in a guard-oriented offense with James

Robinson and Latrell Sprewell, so Robert didn't get many opportunities. But I watched his defensive ability and I noted that he would run back on defense. One of my pet peeves is what I call "stabbing." This is where a guy will give false hustle by running at the ball in the backcourt and allowing the opponent to go by him and create a numbers advantage.

Robert was getting low attitude marks from some scouts because he had a spat with his coach, Wimp Sanderson. But Robert talked to us openly about the situation. When we talked to the coach, we heard the same story from him. Robert made big sacrifices on that Alabama team, and from the fifteen or so tapes that I watched, I felt he did his job.

Then, you look at need. We were looking for a bigger, stronger guy at the small-forward position. Robert was a small forward who could block shots and had done a good job against Shaquille O'Neal in the Southeastern Conference. His interview with us was good. His workout was excellent.

Overall, we felt we had found a talent that some of the other people weren't even talking about. By getting Horry with the No. 11 pick in the draft, we had obtained a legitimate building block for a championship team.

One draft later, we had the No. 24 pick. As the season was winding down, Sam Cassell was a guy I didn't know. It just so happened that we were playing in Phoenix the day before the Phoenix postseason camp, and we got to watch a practice. I looked at Cassell because of his build and the way he carried himself. Right then, I didn't see anything special, so on my list I said he's probably a guy I'd watch a tape on and eliminate. There were other guards, guys like Greg Graham from Indiana and Rex Walters from Kansas, we expected to be available around our drafting slot. I'd watch tapes on all the players, but each day there was something about this Cassell guy that kept me coming back to him.

Finally, I just said, "Give me all the tapes we have on Cassell."

One play stood out. It happened in a Duke–Florida State game. Sam's man was at the free-throw line extended, and Sam played the passing lane and tipped the ball back toward his basket. His legs got tangled with his man and, as the ball was rolling toward the baseline at the other end, he was in a stumble.

Sam stumbled about fifteen yards and dove headfirst as the ball was going out of bounds. He managed to knock the ball toward a teammate, and the guy went for a layup and missed. But Sam had bounced off the floor and he was there to tip the ball in.

I just thought that was one of the greatest hustle plays I had ever seen.

We brought Cassell in and I had a long talk with him. He reminded me of someone from my era. He could have been a guy living down the street from me when I was growing up in Hamtramck; he could have been a Dequindre Jet, because his background was the playground.

I felt a bond to Sam Cassell. Here's a guy who wanted to be a great player. You could see it on the floor and hear it in his voice. To me, it was old-school stuff.

It was a fortunate coincidence that Sam had gone to nearby San Jacinto Junior College. Carroll Dawson had a good relationship with San Jacinto coach Scott Germander, and Germander had the same basic feelings about Sam that we had.

"Sam was such a strong personality and wanted to win so badly, I felt I had to be on my toes and do a good job or he'd get on me," Germander told us.

As we prepared for that 1993 draft, we kept asking the players we brought in where they had visited. To our surprise, Sam told us nobody else had invited him in. There were teams out there with multiple picks who could have gone big and small in the first round. We couldn't believe Sam wasn't drawing more interest.

I felt so strongly about this guy, and it was obvious nobody else shared that view. Both Graham and Walters were taken before Cassell, whom we grabbed with that No. 24 pick. I started wondering if I was crazy. But you have to believe in yourself and do what you think is right for your team. You can't just go with the pack mentality.

Back when I started scouting, a lot of the scouts had enjoyed long tenures in the league. There were a lot of cliques among the older guys, and they would get together and discuss players without giving away the family secrets. It was hard not to want to belong and be around these people, but I made up my mind that I would stay away from what they were saying and make my own evaluations. Maybe you miss a rumor here or there, but if you depend on getting your information from a league counterpart, you don't know if you're getting the straight scoop or if they're trying to throw you off the track. It's all part of the game.

I told myself to take everything cold. You might make a mistake, but at least your team is getting a fresh, personal opinion. My approach was to work at it and to keep things in perspective by respecting the human factor in scouting.

Nobody has all the right answers. When Michael Jordan was at North Carolina, I don't think there was one scout who would have said he'd be the leading scorer in the NBA. We all said he was a great player and would probably be an All-Star, but to say based on what you saw in college at North Carolina that this guy would be the best scorer ever? If anybody made that statement, I'd like to know who it was.

In reflecting on my time as an NBA scout, I think back to a story that seems humorous now, but wasn't so humorous when it happened several years ago. It's a glimpse of the not-so-glamorous life of someone in this line of work.

I once had a road trip in which I could relate to what Jack Lemmon went through in *The Out-of-Towners*. I still refer to it as The Trip from Hell.

It started early one morning as I prepared to depart Houston. I was headed off to scout a college game in Rhode Island, and then I was planning to drive to Boston and scout a Celtics game. When flying out of Houston, I was usually able to get a seat with extra leg room—the bulkhead seat in the front row of the coach section. I was sitting there this time and I was looking forward to some breakfast and a little nap. They started serving from the rear, and when they got to me a flight attendant informed me they were sorry but they had run out of meals. I was given a voucher for a meal when I made my connection in Atlanta.

When we landed in Atlanta, we were informed that our gate was being occupied by another plane. We would have to wait a short amount of time. I wasn't overly concerned because my lay-over time was one hour; I was really hungry and looking forward to my complimentary lunch.

But it wound up taking us forty-five minutes to deplane, and my thoughts shifted from eating to getting on my next flight. If I missed the flight, I wouldn't be able to make it to the game on time. I asked an attendant what gate my next flight was leaving from, and she told me it was two terminals away. I had to catch a train to get there.

I broke into a trot and made it to the gate with five minutes to spare. I asked if there were seats with extra leg room to ac-commodate my 6-8 frame, and the attendant explained that if I wanted a special seat assignment, I should get to the gate early.

I was sweating from the running and didn't feel like explaining. So I was assigned a seat in the last row of the airplane.

The plane was full except for the two seats next to me. Hey, maybe I'm about to finally catch a break, I thought. I had enough room to stretch out. I asked the flight attendant if they would be serving food, and she assured me this was a lunch flight. I assumed I'd be served first, since they started from the back of the plane on my last flight.

Things were really looking up.

Then I saw them. A mother and a child coming down the aisle. I got that sinking feeling because I knew their destination had to be the two seats next to me. As the plane departed, I tried to doze off in a sitting position. But I was jarred by a scream. The child wanted bubblegum.

The mother explained that the child had chewed all the gum and there was none left. This had no effect on the screaming child. I got the flight attendant's attention and explained the situation, asking if she could *please* find some gum. She promptly came back with a whole pack of spearmint.

The mother thanked her and unwrapped a piece for the child. This didn't help. The screams got louder. The little girl wanted Bubblicious.

By now, my nerves were really on edge. I tried to doze off

despite the screams, but I was awakened again, this time by the flight attendant. She had a meal in her hands. I smiled. She didn't smile back.

She informed me this was the only meal left. Was I dreaming all this? How could there only be one meal left?

"Sir, on this plane we serve from the front," she said. "We are sorry . . ."

"I know. I get a voucher," I glumly replied.

The mother and the child got the last meal. I asked the flight attendant if there was any more gum. She told me the child chewed the last piece. As I turned to the little girl, she said, "I like spearmint, too."

Think this is bad? Stay tuned. It gets worse.

The captain came on the speaker and announced that the Providence airport was fogged in. We would have to circle awhile and wait for the fog to lift. This delayed us another hour. I had thirty minutes to get a rental car and get to the game. I ran to the rental-car counter and was lucky to get there when nobody was in line.

I always rent a full-size car. But to my surprise, they were all taken. So were the midsize cars. All they had were compacts. "Are there any companies with bigger cars?" I asked.

They explained that there were none left because several conventions were in town. If I waited until the morning, I could get one—but then again, it would probably be difficult to get a room because of all the conventioneers.

I made it to the game on time, and they were introducing the starters when I got to my seat. Often, when scouting college games, they don't have a special section for NBA scouts. You have to sit in the stands with the college students.

On this particular night, I had a pretty good seat in the end zone where you didn't have to turn your head to follow the flow of the game. After a crazy day like I had, I was really looking forward to getting into the action. But as the game started, all the students got on their feet. And stayed on their feet. I couldn't see the game from a sitting position, so I stood. The yelling was wearing on my nerves to the point where I decided to scan the bleachers for an empty seat. I couldn't find one, and I spent most of the game standing in exits and moving along when ushers shooed me away. It was a nightmare.

And getting worse as the night wore on.

After the game, I squeezed into my compact car. I was not looking forward to the drive to Boston, because I felt like I was in a sardine can. The weather was still bad. The fog had come back and the visibility was terrible. I crept north at forty miles per hour, stopping a couple of times to get the cramps out of my legs.

I finally arrived in Boston well past midnight. I found my hotel, walked into the lobby, and, to my surprise, found the registration desk crowded with three lines about three people deep. These were fogged-in people. I got a terrible feeling they were going to run out of rooms.

I was exhausted, hungry, and about to lose it. "Do you have any rooms left?" I blurted.

The shocked hotel clerk said they had plenty of rooms and would I please bear with them. I didn't even get in line. I set my bag down, found a comfortable chair and sank into it. I let out a sigh of relief and tried to forget the terrible day I had experienced. It was comforting to know that nothing more could happen.

Just then, a man who had checked in turned to go to his room. His garment bag was on his back. It hit a standing ashtray, which toppled over and hit my bag at just the right angle to open the ashtray and spill sand into my bag.

I stared at it with my mouth open and started to laugh. It was the laugh you hear in the movies when they are dragging the guy away in a straitjacket.

I share this story to emphasize that life on the road for a scout can be brutal. But it's a vital job and, for me, it was certainly a rewarding job. Bottom line, I'm extremely grateful I had the opportunity to be a scout in this league. Those six years of scouting were like going to basketball school.

DEL HARRIS WAS the man in charge as the 1981–82 season opened, and I began making the transition from player to part-time scout. I remember first meeting Del in the Rockets offices, back when he came aboard as an assistant coach. He cast a striking presence, with all that white hair. He reminded me of the Marlboro Man. He had a soft manner, like Jimmy Stewart; as Del talked, you were waiting on pins and needles for that key point to come out.

As an assistant coach, Del did a great job of supporting the players. The head coach sort of separated himself from the team, which is natural because the head coach has to dole out the playing time and that means there are always going to be some players who are disappointed with him. Del was great at being the intermediary, a guy the players could talk to in confidence. Now he was the head coach and a good man for a young guy like me, trying to make a career change.

I wasn't a full-fledged member of the staff, but I did have a voice in some of the personnel decisions that were being made. Mainly, though, I watched that '81–82 season as a spectator and tried to learn as much as possible.

Coming off a trip to the finals, we didn't have a first-round draft choice. But we made a splash by trading two second-round picks to Washington for Elvin Hayes. Though he was in the autumn of his career, everybody was excited to get a player of Elvin's caliber. The Big E coming back to Houston—it made sense.

We had a decent regular season, finishing strong to close at 46-36. However, the playoff magic we had experienced the previous year just wasn't there. Seattle took us out in the opening round of the playoffs, and the organization had to make some major decisions with Moses Malone in the last year of his contract.

In '82, Moses had fully blossomed into one of the best big men ever. He averaged 31.1 points and 14.7 rebounds, and it was no surprise when the announcement came that he had won MVP honors for the second time. Meanwhile, in Philadelphia, the Sixers were still trying to get that elusive title for Julius Erving. They had a great Game Seven victory at Boston Garden to reach the NBA Finals, but the show-time Lakers stopped them in the championship series.

Philadelphia needed that extra push to get over the top. The Sixers had super players in Dr. J, Andrew Toney, Maurice Cheeks, and Bobby Jones. When the season ended, they set their sights on Moses and wound up giving him a six-year, $13.2-million offer sheet. It was an outrageous offer at the time and it created a real dilemma for our first-year owner, Charlie Thomas. Our attendance had been lukewarm, about 11,000 per game. So the question was whether Charlie would roll out the money bags for Moses, with no guarantee of a great gate or even a great team if Moses came back.

The Rockets had fifteen days to decide whether to match the blockbuster Philadelphia offer or to work out some sort of deal. On September 15, after Charlie met with Philadelphia owner Harold Katz, the announcement came that we had traded Moses to Philadelphia for Caldwell Jones and Cleveland's 1983 first-round pick, which Philadelphia had acquired for Terry Furlow several years earlier. The Cavs had played so poorly the year before that everyone assumed they would finish last in the East in '83. That meant we would have a fifty-fifty chance to get coveted senior Ralph Sampson in the draft.

Trading Moses was a gutsy move. I think Charlie and general manager Ray Patterson looked at the situation and decided it was better to take a step backward so that the franchise, for the long term, could take a big leap forward. Rather than being stuck in the middle of the pack with one superstar, we had committed to a rebuilding program.

THERE WAS SOMETHING of a building program going on around the Tomjanovich home at that time, too. I was already the father of two wonderful daughters when, on September 17, 1982, we had a baby boy. Since I'm an athlete, a lot of people might think I'd say, "I gotta have a boy. I gotta have a boy." But Sophie and I didn't feel that way at all. We were going to be happy with whatever our third child turned out to be. Trey came six years after our second child, Melissa, was born, and he added something different to the house; instead of Barbie dolls as he grew, there were the G.I. Joes and the camouflage helmets. Just a bundle of joy for all of us.

Prior to Trey's birth, Sophie and I would look at other families and say, "Well, when those families with girls finally have a boy, they sort of spoil him." We'd talk about it and say, "That would never happen to us."

But Sophie has such a strong attachment to Trey. I'll always remember coming home from a road trip one time when Trey was a baby. Sophie gathered the girls around the table and said, "Dad's home. We're going to eat as a family. This isn't 'grab a sandwich and go.'" As she sat there correcting the girls' posture, getting elbows off the table and showing the proper way to hold the fork, Trey crawled up on the table. The girls were thinking, Now the little prince is in trouble here. He's going to get reprimanded.

Trey just bounced around on the table, and all Sophie did was smile and say, "Doesn't he have good rhythm?" The girls said in unison: "I can't believe this."

WITH MOSES GONE, we came back with a team in '82–83 that just didn't have the talent to win. By then, I had signed on as a fulltime assistant coach, and the experience of going through a 14-68 season was certainly an enlightening introduction to coaching. We all knew going in that it was going to be a trying year. But even with that realization, it's still extremely depressing to go through loss after loss after loss.

We had some good players—Calvin Murphy, Joe Bryant, Allen Leavell, James Bailey, Wally Walker, Caldwell Jones. But overall, there just wasn't enough firepower to sustain us in the course of a 48-minute game.

We started 0-10, and then all the media wanted to talk about was "the Sampson Sweepstakes." For a while, it was shaping up as though we might have both sides of the coin in the Sampson flip: If Cleveland finished last in the East, we had that coin-flip pick, and we were certain to finish last in the West.

What we didn't count on was the stunning collapse of the Indiana Pacers. The Pacers managed to finish below Cleveland, meaning our chances of getting Sampson went from one hundred percent to fifty percent as the regular season ended.

Even though we lost with regularity, the '82–83 season taught me how to be a supporter. I had played with some of the guys who were enduring so much pain from the constant losses; trying to keep everyone positive was a big part of my job that first year in coaching.

One of the toughest lessons I learned in '82–83 came when, because we had so many guaranteed contracts, Del had to cut Larry Spriggs, a second-year small forward I had worked with on a personal basis. Larry was a hardworking player, and I developed a close relationship with him. He didn't have a good outside shot, and I spent a lot of time passing him the ball during drills and encouraging him to improve his individual skills.

When Del asked me to be present as he broke the bad news to Larry, it was an eye-opening experience. First of all, it wasn't fair; Larry was good enough to have made that team. But I began to see the other side of the pro-sports business. If you don't have a guaranteed contract, it can sometimes mean that a deserving player doesn't get his just reward.

With a better team, management might have been willing to pay off another player to keep Larry. But we weren't going anywhere, so management didn't take that route. For me, it was devastating. The pain of watching a deserving player not make the team really hit home. But the other side of it was that I saw how tough it is on a coach to make an unwanted cut. That's why Del had me present for the Spriggs meeting; he wanted me to see firsthand that this ugly chore is a part of coaching.

Years later I was scouting in Los Angeles and went to my favorite Italian restaurant on a main boulevard one day. As I sat down, I saw Larry Spriggs at the entryway. He came over and we embraced. I told him I was happy he was back in the league, playing with a good Lakers team.

"Do you come to this restaurant often?" I asked.

"Oh, no, I'm not here to eat," Larry said.

Larry had seen me get out of my car. He drove past, made a U-turn, and found a parking spot just to say hello.

That meant so much to me. I always say that coaching is a giving profession. But to get something back like that—just once every couple of years—makes you feel it's all worthwhile. If Larry hadn't seen me, I would never have known how he felt. I thought I had been a positive influence on him, but there are a lot of times when you do that with players and never get much of a response. You just have to accept it and stay in that giving mode. When a player like Larry expresses his appreciation, it makes for a special moment.

During that '82–83 season, I developed a real friendship with Del Harris. We played tennis and golf and shared ideas about basketball. We were all looking forward to getting through such a difficult season and reaping the benefits in future years. But as the season came to an end, the winds of change were blowing. We met at the office one day shortly after the season mercifully came to an end. Del was scheduled for a season-in-review meeting with management, and he went into that session with a lot of organized notes. He told Carroll Dawson and me he would meet us later at the golf course.

Carroll and I went ahead, and when Del caught up with us later in the afternoon he had a strange look on his face.

"I need to talk to you guys," he said. "I've been released."

Before we could express our shock, Del said, "It's okay. I'm going to be taken care of. I've talked to them about you two and how loyal you are. I told them, 'If you've got a problem with me, don't take it out on the assistant coaches.' "

I was completely destroyed. We knew it was a year in which we weren't going to win. I thought it was unjust, because we were about to get some extremely talented players in the draft. That was supposed to be the payoff for going through such a tough year. You say to yourself, "It's hell right now, but things will get better."

I began to question the whole business. The losses had taken an emotional toll, the fans had been cruel, everybody was edgy. Del had to endure all of this, and still there was no carrot at the end of the stick. I didn't have a positive feeling about the coaching profession at that point. Just as players sometimes get the shaft, so do coaches.

In retrospect, what influenced me most from Del's tenure was his penchant for drilling the inside game. He believed it had to be an everyday thing for your big guys to get comfortable with shots close to the basket. We constantly taught the fundamentals: how to show a target for the ball, how to catch the ball, how to make that first countermove. Del preached the importance of establishing a strong inside foundation and working from there.

I knew it was a good theory because, as a player, I had developed my inside game with this regimen. I said that if I ever became a head coach, drilling the inside game would definitely be part of my program.

After Del was let go, there was speculation that Tommy Heinsohn would be the next Rockets coach. Tommy had coached a couple of championship teams in Boston before going into broadcasting. He came down to Houston and met with team officials and the media, but the deal never materialized.

About that time, Bill Fitch announced he would be leaving as the Boston coach. Bill had won the championship against us in '81, and he had done a great job of building a Cleveland team from the roots of expansion.

The Rockets' situation was similar, in that we were basically starting from square one. As soon as the Heinsohn talk died down,

Fitch and the Rockets came together. Carroll and I had a great deal of respect for what Fitch had done, but we had also heard that he was a tough guy.

Some of the outside comments to me from people around the league indicated that I had better find something else to do: Bill Fitch didn't particularly like ex-players becoming coaches.

Truthfully, I could see where somebody could look at my situation and say, "Okay, here's a guy who has played his whole career in Houston. He wants to be around basketball, but he's not committed. It's a convenient situation for a guy to stay with one franchise."

But that's not how I was at all. I had really started to enjoy the job and I wanted to be part of Fitch's staff. I was prepared to show Bill how much I cared and how much I wanted to roll up my sleeves and go to work.

Carroll and I picked up Fitch at the Houston airport. Right away, we noticed his dry sense of humor. He joked about how I used to climb people's backs for rebounds. "Climbing the ladder," he called it.

We didn't have much time for a lot of chuckles, though. We had to get down to serious business, because the '83 draft was upon us and we had the first and third selections in the first round. Charlie Thomas had won the celebrated coin flip to give us the Sampson pick, but who would be the man at No. 3?

Carroll and I had been out prepping for the draft while management was settling on a head coach. Some of the names available in a rich draft were Rodney McCray, Dale Ellis, Byron Scott, and Clyde Drexler. There was a lot of debating about which way we should go. We all had different ideas, but the team decision was McCray, a heady small forward from Louisville.

So it would be Sampson and McCray leading the way for a Rockets renaissance. Ralph was 7-4 and had a lot of great tools. His slender build was something we were concerned about, but we all felt he had the potential to develop into one of the all-time great players in the league.

McCray was a team guy through and through, one of the most unselfish players I've ever been around. He was the kind of guy—

if you had the right players around him—who could be a championship contributor.

Besides Sampson and McCray, we also added third-rounder Craig Ehlo in the '83 draft. We had the makings of a good, young team and were excited about putting the ashes of that 14-68 season behind us. It got even better for us in August when Bill went out and got Lewis Lloyd through free agency. And then Robert Reid came back to us in October after a one-year sabbatical for religious reasons.

Lloyd was a great one-on-one player and was absolutely spectacular on the open floor. Reid had already proven himself and figured to be a stabilizing influence on a young team.

A new head coach. New players. A fresh era in Rockets basketball was upon us.

But remember, we were starting from the bottom. When you're in that position, it's going to take a while to get where you want to go.

12

RALPH SAMPSON WAS all the rage as we started our 1983–84 training camp. Everybody wanted to see how one of the most celebrated college players of all time would respond in the NBA, and media from around the country flocked to our early practices.

Let me just say that Ralph was such a multitalented guy that it sort of confused the issue. At 7-4, he was so tall that he had to play inside. But he also had some skills that enabled him to do things out on the floor. Ralph was a good ballhandler for his size, a good passer, and he ran well.

When he came out of college, some observers had compared Ralph to a Kareem Abdul-Jabbar in terms of what he might mean to an NBA franchise. But Ralph wasn't like Abdul-Jabbar, who was exclusively a post-up player. Ralph was a little bit of this, a little bit of that. He had great, great talent, but what was the best way to extract that talent?

Bill Fitch wanted Ralph to establish what we called a "basic." A basic is your pet shot, your bread and butter. Kareem, for example, had the sky hook as his basic; when the game was on the line, this was the shot he would use to get his team over the hump.

Ralph developed a turnaround from the baseline that was sort of a Kevin McHale move. Sampson also had a hook, though it was not nearly as refined as that of some players in the league.

Bottom line, Ralph didn't want to limit himself to the inside game. Some of that thinking was positive, but some of it worked against him. If your mind-set is to establish something strong inside, then you can expand and work off that. For whatever reason, Ralph did not want to take that approach.

In retrospect, Ralph's Rockets career didn't turn out the way we had envisioned it the day we drafted him. But if anybody concludes that he was a bust, that's not even close to the truth. What really happened to Ralph is something that happens to a lot of players with great promise: He got hurt.

Just look at the records. Though he didn't have that "basic," Ralph had two exceptionally strong years for us. First, he was the Rookie of the Year, averaging 21.0 points and 11.1 rebounds. The next year, when we brought back John Lucas as the point guard and drafted Hakeem Olajuwon, Ralph made the move to power forward and wound up averaging 22.1 points and 10.4 rebounds.

Think about how hard it is to be a "20-10" man in the NBA. You just don't do that at this level unless your overall basketball skills are extraordinary. It was only later, after Ralph suffered a knee injury, that his performance level took a decidedly negative turn.

In Ralph's rookie season, I basically had to follow the team from afar, since I was out on the road doing a lot of advance scouting. I started out with the team in training camp, but as soon as the season started, I did about two months of straight scouting, hitting one city after another. I also did the video breakdowns, which meant that I was always one step ahead of the team.

What I knew from the reports back home was this: An exciting new era in Rockets basketball had begun. Ralph and Rodney McCray were two solid building blocks, but we were nowhere near ready to be a contender. We were a respectable 20-26 at midyear, but then we lost 27 out of our last 36 and again finished with the worst record in the Western Conference. This meant another trip to New York for a coin flip, with the Portland Trail Blazers as the competition. The Blazers called "heads" and the coin rolled tantalizingly around the floor next to Commissioner David Stern. What a precarious business.

When the coin finally came to a stop, it was tails. Now we had a choice that everybody in the world would have savored: We could choose between Hakeem Olajuwon of the University of Houston and Michael Jordan from North Carolina.

People can look back now and talk about it; it makes for great coffee-shop debate. But the reality is that we had completely committed ourselves to Hakeem. Had we lost the flip, I'm sure we would have taken Jordan at No. 2. Portland didn't, of course; the Blazers went for center Sam Bowie, which moved Jordan down to No. 3. For that, the Chicago Bulls can be eternally grateful.

The feeling in our organization was that Hakeem would give us a tremendous defensive center. Ralph was such a lean guy that we didn't know if he could handle the constant pounding in the middle game after game, year after year. He was giving away a lot of weight in there.

But with the Twin Towers concept, Hakeem could anchor the middle and we hoped Ralph could use his versatility to give us a big edge at the other inside position.

I remember breaking down the tapes on Hakeem. We thought we were getting a defensive player in the Bill Russell mold. We didn't see him as a giant offensive force coming out of school, but to everybody's delight, he turned out to be much more than a defensive guy.

You can never be sure when you're scouting college players. Because of the zone defense, you just don't get to see the total offensive package. In college ball, if you've got any kind of big man, the other teams just aren't going to let you have room to make moves like the Dreamshake.

On film, you might get a glimpse of Hakeem's touch. You'd see a trace here or there, but nothing that would indicate he could become one of the most prolific pivot scorers in the history of the league.

The 1984 draft was good to us in another way, too. We took Minnesota's 6-10 Jim Petersen in the third round. This was a guy I had scouted when he went up against Kevin Willis of Michigan State, a surefire first-rounder. Jim didn't quite have the skills to compete with Kevin, but he battled every inch of the way. We all felt that, with some training and development, Petersen had the desire to carve out a nice career for himself in the NBA.

Back in '84, we held our draft at midcourt of the Summit, in full view of the fans. We were talking about various players when Fitch suddenly turned to me and said, "Rudy, you make this pick."

I was shocked. Bill always made the final decisions. He'd ask Carroll and me to give input, but Bill called the shots. Since we were in front of the fans, I didn't have the chance to get up and pace, like I usually do when I'm making a tough decision. I looked at the candidates left on our draft list and said, "Coach, I'd take Petersen."

"That's a good pick," Bill replied. Carroll liked it, too.

For me, it was an important learning experience. It was then that I learned the difference between making suggestions and making a final decision. The pressure is substantially greater when you're a decision maker. I really felt it that day.

Over the next couple of years, Pete became an important Third Tower for us and developed tremendously because of his weight training with strength coach Robert Barr. As the No. 51 pick overall, he had to be one of the best sleepers we ever came across.

Truth is, I was a driven person during those times, because I never wanted Bill to think he was getting a guy who was just using the Rockets to be in the public eye. I was a worker as a player and I was a worker as an assistant coach.

And I must say, Bill gave me plenty to do. It was a developing stage for a young coach because Fitch believed in putting in the time; whether we won by thirty or lost by thirty, we'd review the tape no matter how long it took. Whether it was 3 A.M., 4 A.M., or 5 A.M., we'd be there until the job was done and we were satisfied that we had the material assimilated to provide an adequate teaching aid.

I must say, though, that I didn't get off to a good start in winning Bill's favor. On my very first scouting trip, I was going to Notre Dame to scout an exhibition game. As we were flying over the city, I saw a lot of cars leaving the arena. I figured, Well, there must have been an event in the afternoon. I didn't realize it was a Saturday.

Saturday? Don't they often play college basketball games on Saturday afternoon? Uh-oh. I had missed my first scouting assignment under Fitch.

Making that call back to the coach wasn't something I was really looking forward to doing. He gave it to me pretty good about never letting anyone else do your schedule. Another valuable lesson along the trail of coaching: Check the details yourself.

Just so it wouldn't be a wasted day, I wound up driving about a hundred miles to Rockford, Illinois, to see a CBA game that night. It was a rather humbling experience, and I was on my toes from that point forward to make sure I never made another mistake like that.

As we headed into the 1984–85 season, we had the front line of the future in Sampson, Olajuwon, and McCray, but we needed some veteran leadership in the backcourt. Bill asked me if I would go out on the road and take a look at John Lucas, who had encountered drug problems earlier but had found his way back to the San Antonio Spurs.

"Can Lucas help us?" Fitch asked me directly.

I had loved playing with Lucas so much: the energy, the upbeat approach. Yes, we knew there had been drug problems, but he was playing as though he had himself together.

"Yes, I think Lucas would help our team," I told Fitch.

We wound up trading for Luke in the preseason of '84–85, and now we had that distributor to bring out the offensive potential in our big people. From the very first day, Lucas was a catalyst, and what a one-two combination Ralph and Hakeem turned out to be. Not only could they score, but both were adept at blocking shots. If you took the ball strong at Hakeem, where was Ralph? And vice versa.

Offensively and defensively, we were the talk of the league. We started 8-0, but then our youth began to show during the wear and tear of a long season. Keep in mind that these were just kids who were used to playing a twenty-five- or thirty-game college season. As talented as we were, we still lacked the maturity of a championship team like the Celtics or the Lakers.

Mitchell Wiggins was a 6-4 guard who joined us that year and would eventually become a key figure on a Western Conference championship team. Wiggins was a talented but moody player, and his situation was another that helped me learn what the coaching profession is all about.

Early that year, Fitch conducted some toughness drills in practice in which guys really had to gut it out. It was a barometer; Bill wanted to see who was willing to pay the price and who wasn't. Wiggins wasn't putting out the effort that Bill wanted, and the coach sent the player a message by keeping Wiggins home on the first preseason trip.

Bill asked me to talk with Wiggins while the team was gone. My assignment was to talk to him and basically say, "You have to do what the head man wants."

Wiggins and I had a good talk, and I think that not traveling on that first trip really got his attention. He became a tough player for us, largely because he loved to be an offensive rebounder from the big-guard position. Many, many times he would soar in for a tip-in that would serve as a dagger to the opponent's heart.

We wound up winning 48 games and had the No. 3 seed in the opening round of the playoffs. Our opponent was a veteran group of Utah Jazz. It was their experience against our youthful talent.

Adrian Dantley, the small forward, was Utah's top scorer. He was an amazing player at only 6-5. He was one of the best post-up guys in the league. He used his solid body to get position close to the basket, and he could also move out on the floor and face up. Adrian had excellent footwork; if he got by you on the first step, it was over. He was going to score on a layup or you were going to have to foul him. Dantley was always on the free-throw line because he constantly challenged the defense.

Darrell Griffith was their high-scoring big guard. He had three-point range and was a nice complement to Dantley's inside game. Griffith was a great leaper, which earned him the nickname "Dr. Dunkenstein" back in his college days at Louisville. His running mate at point guard was Rickey Green, one of the fastest players in the NBA. They had Thurl Bailey, a promising young forward, and in the middle Utah had a mountain of a man: At 7-4, Mark Eaton was one of the best shot blockers in the league. The Jazz also had experienced reserve centers in Billy Paultz and Rich Kelley, as well as a dynamic rookie point guard named John Stockton.

It came down to a decisive Game Five in Houston, and we had a double-figure lead in the second half. But Paultz, our wily old friend from the Cinderella days of 1981, used every trick in the book to try to get Hakeem off his game. Billy kept sticking his fingers into Hakeem's midsection, and eventually Hakeem reacted and lost his temper. Hakeem took a swat at Paultz; the fired-up Jazz began a determined comeback, and we wound up losing the game. It really hurt to go out that way after such a promising season.

Still, we weren't about to overreact. We knew the future was bright and that there weren't going to be a lot of changes in the off-season. In our postseason meetings, the overriding message was that we wanted to continue what was already in place. Maybe add a nice draft pick and work from there.

As draft day neared, we zeroed in on four guards: Joe Dumars of McNeese State, Sam Vincent of Michigan State, Terry Porter of Wisconsin–Stevens Point, and Steve Harris of Tulsa. McNeese State is in Lake Charles, Louisiana, just a couple of hours' drive from Houston. I had been over to scout Joe a couple of times and really felt he was the best of the group.

Our organization felt we had a great shot at getting Dumars. But as it turned out, the Dallas Mavericks hindered our plans. Dallas had three first-round picks that year, and we figured maybe they would take two big men and one little guy. Detroit had the No. 18 pick, just one notch above us. If a quality big guy had been on the board, the word was that the Pistons would take him. But the Mavericks used all three of their picks on bigger guys, and that left Detroit in the position of having to take a guard.

The rest, as they say, is history: Dumars went one pick ahead of us and wound up having a sensational career. We'll never know what an Hakeem–Dumars combination might have accomplished. Our pick turned out to be Harris, who stuck around a couple of years but never found his niche in the league.

You win some, you lose some. But even though we barely

missed out on Dumars, we were still darn good. We started 1985–86 with a 20-0 home record and lost only five home games all year.

We weren't nearly as proficient on the road, but our 51-31 record was the best in franchise history. Purely in terms of offense, it would be tough to match our '85–86 team. We averaged 114.4 points and shot 49 percent from the floor. Our team speed was amazing. We had the inside game and timely outside shooting from the likes of Lucas and Robert Reid. McCray was solid all around, and Wiggins and Petersen helped us off the bench. And when we needed that one-on-one surge, it was "Sweet Lew" Lloyd to the rescue.

We gained the No. 2 playoff seed in the West behind the Lakers, and that meant we were paired against Sacramento in the opening round. There was never any doubt about that series; we were outstanding in a 3–0 sweep.

The next opponent for us was Denver, and a television reporter asked Joe Kleine after the last Kings game if the Rockets could whip the Nuggets.

"If Houston plays like they played against us," Kleine said, "they'll win the whole thing."

We had a much tougher time with the Nuggets, but we prevailed in six games. The finale at McNichols Arena was a double-overtime classic in which our twelfth man, Granville Waiters, became a hero. With Hakeem and Ralph both out of the game, Granville had a key basket in the second overtime to help pull us through.

When you talk about twelve men pulling together, that was the essence of it right there.

It had been a great ride to the Western Conference Finals, but most people figured the vaunted Lakers would put our young upstarts in their place. That theory was reinforced when Magic Johnson and company nailed us, 119–107, in the opener at the Forum.

But we learned an extremely important lesson in that series. At the time, the Lakers had the best rotating defense in basketball. They were big and athletic and extremely proficient at double-teaming a post-up player. Then they would recover quickly to guard the outside players.

Their doubling man was getting to Hakeem and Ralph quick enough to take away high-percentage shots inside. But Bill came up with an adjustment that I believe changed the series. On one of our basic plays that the Lakers had been shutting down, Bill changed the route of the player cutting up to the top of the key. Instead of coming up on the strong side, Bill had him cross the midpoint just on the weak side of the basket. A difference of about five feet.

Now, because of the illegal-defense rules, the double-teaming man guarding this player couldn't cheat and sag in front of our big men since his man was on the weak side of the midline. He had to wait until the ball was passed inside, then try to double quickly. This little wrinkle paid enormous dividends. It gave our big guys just enough time to get off their best shots.

As a young coach, it really taught me something: You don't always have to do something drastic. You don't have to change your whole system. A very subtle adjustment can make a big difference.

We still use this play today. We call it "L.A."

The stunner was that we came back and handled the Lakers, 112–102, in Game Two. When you get your momentum going, it's hard to beat a team with a lot of energy. The key in that game was that Lewis Lloyd—who wasn't known as a good defensive player— did a wonderful job of keeping a body in front of Magic all over the floor. Suddenly, we were coming home with an enormous wave of confidence, and that confidence manifested itself with solid victories in Games Three and Four. Hakeem was a sight to behold, getting 40 in Game Three and 35 more in Game Four. No matter what the Lakers tried, they couldn't hold him down.

The really amazing part about all this was that we were doing it with a makeshift lineup operating without a true point guard. Back in March, we had a practice scheduled at the Summit one day, and John Lucas failed to show up. A couple of days later he took a drug test that proved positive. He was gone for the year.

Robert Reid had been our sixth man, but he moved into the

starting point-guard slot after Lucas departed. Reid's contributions were especially significant since our backup point guard, Allen Leavell, suffered a fractured left hand late in the regular season and was basically trying to get by with one hand and a lot of guts.

Back to L.A. for one day. We knew the Lakers were great champions, and we didn't want to let them get in a position where they could smell blood. We figured they would have great energy early, and they burst to a big lead. But our guys hung in, and we were in position to win down the stretch when Reid drilled a key three-pointer to tie it. Byron Scott went for the win and missed, and we called timeout with the score tied and one tick left on the clock.

What happened next will forever live in the minds of Rockets fans. McCray lobbed the ball to Ralph, who turned and flung the ball toward the basket. The ball bounced around and it was as though some magnetic force caused it to settle and drop through as the buzzer sounded.

Our bench went wild and, to this day, the television cameras still show the poignant pictures of Michael Cooper lying on his back, eyes closed, under the basket. The Lakers had given their all to keep the series going, but it wasn't enough against a Rockets team that had blossomed from the seeds that had been planted in successive coin flips for Sampson and Olajuwon.

In another year, that '86 Rockets team might have been an NBA champion. We just had the misfortune of running into an '86 Boston team that has to rank as one of the best of all time. The Celtics went 40-1 at home during the regular season and whipped us convincingly in their three home games during the title series. We won Games Three and Five at home, but a key offensive rebound by Bill Walton broke our backs in a 106–103 Game Four loss.

Boston was simply outstanding. Larry Bird, Kevin McHale, and Robert Parish formed one of the greatest frontcourts ever. Dennis Johnson and Danny Ainge got it done in the backcourt, and having a player like Walton—a Hall of Famer who was willing to serve in a reserve role—coming off the bench rounded out a superb ballclub.

We were blown out in the finale, 114–97, but the future seemed bright indeed—until, that is, the impact of drugs tore a hole in the franchise that we wouldn't recover from for several years.

We had survived the Lucas episode, but early in the 1986–87 season, the jarring announcement came that both Lloyd and Wiggins would be leaving us because of drug violations.

Think about the impact: We had our three top guards leave in an eight-month span. And we got nothing in return. No draft picks. No players via trade. Nothing. How do you recover from that?

Despite it all, we came back in '86–87 and did a good job of battling to reach the conference semifinals. We were 42-40, but what really hurt was that Ralph injured his knee and played in only 43 games, which cast a shadow over the rest of his career. We made a short-term bid to fortify the roster by giving up a first-round pick for Cedric Maxwell. He helped us beat Portland in the opening round of the playoffs, but then Seattle took us out in double-overtime of Game Six.

With a patchwork guard rotation, an injured Sampson, and limited options in the draft, the ship was on rocky waters. Hakeem was a stalwart through all this, but now his frustrations were beginning to show.

When we got off to a lukewarm start in '87–88, management figured it was time for a major move. Watching Ralph on film, it had become apparent that the knee injury was taking a toll. When he tried to get his body to do what once came naturally, it was just too much.

It hurt him most at the defensive end; he couldn't change directions quickly or stop on a dime. He could still play, but not with balance. Ralph needed a strong base, and it just wasn't there.

Ray Patterson had been talking with Warriors boss Don Nelson, who really coveted Ralph. Don was willing to give up two All-Stars—Sleepy Floyd and J.B. Carroll—for Ralph. On December 10, Ralph went through a game against Utah in which he didn't score a point. Ray got on the phone with Nelson, and the trade came down a couple of days later.

This was a huge gamble, because we didn't know if Ralph

would come back physically. But that's basically what it was all about: Ralph didn't lose his talent, he lost his body.

Very unfortunate. I thought he was on schedule to be a perennial All-Star, but his body simply wouldn't allow it.

With Floyd and Carroll trying to fit into the system, we won 46 games, but Dallas took us out in four games in the first round of the playoffs. Carroll and I were called into meetings with management concerning Bill Fitch. I felt we should continue with the status quo. My philosophy always has been and always will be that you support the head coach. I know Carroll felt the same way.

It wasn't to be. Management decided to make a change, and there was immediate speculation about two assistants in the league: Don Chaney and Jerry Sloan. Chaney was the choice.

I learned a great deal of basketball from Bill Fitch. He was a great teacher and a master at taking a team with no direction and establishing a foundation. He does this by constant drilling and repetition of the fundamentals of basketball. It's an everyday thing. It becomes a way of life. The players learn to expect the routine. They become comfortable with it and start to rely on it because they begin to see that it works, and their confidence grows.

Bill would start with very simple things, like the proper way to take the ball out of bounds. It's amazing how many mistakes are made if the fundamentals are not explained. He'd graduate to more complex things like running an effective fast break. So many little things go into it: how to pivot after the rebound; where the outlet men should position themselves; the communication the players must have to create the proper spacing; what passes were the best to use.

As more and more things were taught, Bill was putting in his system. It was a gradual process, but it was solid as a rock because it was based on fundamental basketball. It took commitment, persistence, and a lot of patience on his part.

I witnessed and was a part of this process, and I have a great deal of respect for Bill as a coach. Working with him, I also learned what work ethic really means. Hours mean nothing. A nine-to-five workday doesn't apply. You do what you have to do to get the job done, no matter how long it takes.

Bill had a routine of watching the videotape of every game we played. Videotape is a great coaching tool. It helps a coach know his team better. You can't see everything while the game is being played; studying videotapes has become a consistent, everyday part of my job, whether I'm preparing for an upcoming opponent, analyzing our team, or evaluating personnel.

My five years with Bill Fitch were a great learning experience. He had a tremendous impact on me, showing me just how important preparation is at the NBA level.

13

WHEN DON CHANEY was named the Rockets' new head coach for the 1988–89 season, I thought back to when I first came to Houston with the Rockets, and Don was playing with the Boston Celtics and living in Houston in the off-season. A group of us would get together at Fonde Recreation Center and play pickup games. I found Don to be one of the most genuine people I've ever been around. I later had the opportunity to play with him on an All-Star team that went to Japan, and it was a pleasure to play with him because he was a team player through and through. He'd do whatever it took to win and he was an outstanding defensive player. I respected Don not only for the way he played, but also for the way in which he handled himself. He was a tough competitor on the floor and a gentleman off it.

As when Bill Fitch came in, we had a situation that was pretty rare in the NBA: Management was bringing in a new head coach and retaining the assistants, Carroll and me. We were very fortunate, because a new head coach often insists on bringing in a whole new staff.

There's no way anybody could say we had all the pieces at this time. But considering what Don had been through in his first head-coaching job with the Clippers, this was a tremendous opportunity. With the Clippers, Don just didn't have much to work with, and the organization always seemed to be in some sort of turmoil. I remember scouting a 12-70 Clippers team and feeling it was almost a no-win situation for the coach. Coming from that environment, Don was really excited to have a great player like Hakeem Olajuwon to start with as a foundation.

One of Don's first moves was to go after a power forward who could augment Hakeem. Otis Thorpe hadn't been able to work out a contract with Sacramento, and the Kings started shopping Otis around rather than giving him the type of financial package his agent felt he was worth. We got involved because we felt having Otis next to Hakeem would be a major step in getting our team back on track. The asking price? It was tough: Rodney McCray and Jim Petersen, two players who had been major contributors on our '86 Western Conference championship club. Though it was extremely difficult to lose two players of that quality, the organization felt the chance to get a consistent double-double guy like Otis was simply too good to pass up.

With Hakeem and Otis, we were ready to take a giant step forward. We had the center and we had a true power forward. Then we went to work to try to build around that strong inside combo.

In '88–89, Hakeem and Otis weren't enough to sustain us through a topsy-turvy season. We got off to an 18-9 start, but all that did was create a false sense of security within our ballclub. We started to think we were better than we really were. We had what Don called "happy feet." We were getting complacent, fattening up on the two new expansion teams and winning games at home, but we began to struggle when we went out on the road against better competition.

My role as an assistant changed under Chaney. I had always been a step ahead of the team, scouting the pro competition or college prospects, but when Don took over I went to the bench on a full-time basis. It felt great to be around the team and to experience again the ups and downs that NBA teams have during the course of a long year. As a scout, you sometimes feel you aren't in touch with what's going on; you're out on the road, isolated. You just hope to catch highlights of your team on ESPN, or catch a score on the sports-ticker update.

From the time of my retirement as a player, I had traveled so much; I can't emphasize enough what a great foundation it was for me as a coach to go out and learn everybody else's system, but now I was ready to be there to help with the everyday problems and to work on drilling players on the basics of their individual games.

While we had some talent, we didn't quite have a championship mix. Sleepy Floyd, a former All-Star, was our starting point guard. Purvis Short was an excellent spot-up shooter and was still capable of having big scoring nights. We acquired Mike Woodson as our big guard, which made a lot of sense for our team because he had been one of the purest shooters in the league. Buck Johnson was our starting small forward. We also picked up a great one-on-one player in Walter Berry, but he was a guy who struggled when he had to run a five-man play. Derrick Chievous, our first-round draft pick, showed some promise but lacked consistency, which is common for a rookie.

In short, there were good moments, but not enough of them.

A highlight that year was having All-Star Weekend in Houston. Our city really put on a show that made everybody proud. There was a big Friday-night party at the George R. Brown Convention Center, and Saturday's activities at the Summit featured an old-timers game in which several former Rockets players were featured.

I had worked out a little in preparation for the event, but it quickly became apparent my body wasn't what it used to be. I injured my hamstring in practice and wasn't able to do much in the game, but Calvin Murphy—who always stayed in great shape— put on a show and wound up sinking the winning shot for the home fans. The next day, it was tremendous to see 44,735 fans pack the Astrodome. It's an All-Star attendance record that stands today, and it meant a lot to some of us pioneers, who remembered what it had been like playing in the tomblike Astrodome back in the early Seventies.

We wound up winning 45 games, and that matched us against Seattle in the first round of the playoffs. Leading the series 2–1, the Sonics inbounded from midcourt in the final seconds of Game Four with the score tied. They set a backpick looking for a lob near the basket and really executed well. Allen Leavell wound up beside Derrick McKey, who grabbed the ball, came down, and shot over Al. McKey was 6-9; Leavell was 6-3. McKey's short basket at the buzzer sent us packing for the summer.

It looked to the fans as though those two were matched up, but that wasn't the case at all; Leavell was guarding the man who set the pick, and when he saw that Buck Johnson was blocked from behind, Leavell switched to McKey and tried his best to hold McKey off until help arrived, but the help got there too late.

That play turned out to be Al's last in a ten-year Rockets career. What a career he had for a guy who had been the 104th pick in the 1979 draft. He really made the most of what he had. He was basically a right-handed player, and his penchant was to drive right or straight up for a set shot. But through determination and willpower, he played in two championship series and was a solid, productive player for the Rockets. For young players who aren't drafted high or even drafted at all, there's a lesson to be learned. If you have the heart and the belief that you can do it, there's a chance for sleeper guys to have fine careers in the NBA. It isn't just the first-round picks who go on to fame and fortune.

We didn't even have a draft pick in 1989, as the league cut the draft to two rounds. All we could do was sit by and hear commentator Steve Jones say, "In Houston, the lights are out and nobody's home."

For us, with no draft assets to rely on, it was back to the future. The three guys who had been instrumental for our '86 team before experiencing drug problems—Lucas, Wiggins, and Lloyd—were all with us as the '89–90 season commenced.

Unfortunately, they didn't have nearly the same impact as a backcourt group that we had seen three years earlier. Wiggins was the best of the trio now; he had become a real fitness guy and averaged 15.5 points for us. But Lloyd had developed a weight problem, causing him to lose the explosiveness that once made him so feared in the open court. In training camp, Don said of Sweet Lew, "I can't have a guard who weighs more than my centers."

Lucas? John had some shining moments early; he replaced Sleepy Floyd as the starting point guard for a stretch, but it's hard for a thirty-six-year-old point guard to keep up the pace against guys who are ten years younger. Luke spent the latter portion of the season on the injured list, and that was the end of his dynamic Rockets playing career.

We bottomed out with an overtime loss to Detroit on February 27 to fall to 24-31. Something had to be done to pump some enthusiasm into the program—so here came Vernon Maxwell. Spurs coach Larry Brown had been leery about Maxwell's off-the-court problems in San Antonio and was looking to unload him. Chaney was intrigued by Vernon, especially his quickness. We had scouted Vernon and definitely felt he had NBA talent; Carroll had seen the Spurs versus the Lakers in Maxwell's rookie year and came back raving about the defensive job that Vernon did on Magic Johnson.

"This kid has the quickness and the toughness to be one of the few guys in the league who can play Magic," Carroll said.

We were willing to give Vernon a clean slate, and his energy pumped new life into our team. We were looking like a surefire lottery team, but we went seven games over .500 the rest of the year and snuck into the playoffs on the last day. Golden State opened the door for us by beating Seattle, which meant we had to win a 5-P.M. home game against Utah to get in the playoff field. We took care of business, 100–88, and were off to face the Los Angeles Lakers in the first round. By then, Floyd and Maxwell were developing some backcourt chemistry to the point where the L.A. media was calling them "Sleepy and Speedy."

After the Lakers won the playoff opener handily, we shocked them by jumping out to a 19-point lead in Game Two. Los Angeles was still an excellent, resourceful team, though not quite what it had been in the 1980s. The Lakers came back to nip us by four, but I think we had earned their respect; that respect was reinforced when we came home and beat them, 114–108, in Game Three. It's called progress: In those dark days back in February, it didn't seem possible we could win a playoff game against a club the caliber of the Lakers.

Los Angeles was able to finish us off in Game Four, but we were at least seeing hope. Now we had Olajuwon, Thorpe, and Maxwell. Piece by piece, we were getting somewhere.

It was at this juncture that Ray Patterson announced he was stepping down as president of the Rockets after an eighteen-year run. Ray was a crafty guy who knew the league; his son, Steve, would be moving up as the number-one man in the front office and had the training to do a great job. Steve had a law degree and was an expert on the league's salary-cap system. Knowing the nuances of the cap was an integral part of running a team in the early 1990s. If you could find a way to fit an asset into the many intricacies of the cap, you could really help your ballclub.

In pinning down what Ray Patterson meant to the Rockets over his eighteen-year reign, I would say the key word was *determination*. Starting a pioneer NBA franchise in football country, he was fiercely determined to make it work. If Ray hadn't hung in there and kept the ship afloat through the turbulent Seventies, there might not have been Rockets teams for the public to enjoy today. It's a legacy I know Ray is proud of, and rightfully so. I'll always remember the way Ray treated me and how, after my playing career, he gave me the open invitation to help the Rockets any way I wanted. And I'll remember how loyal he was to Carroll; Ray made it possible for us to serve under three different head coaches in the same organization.

We made a significant deal that summer, getting Kenny Smith from Atlanta for Tim McCormick. On the surface, it seemed like a no-brainer trade for us, but there were some stipulations: If McCormick, who had questionable knees, failed to play 100 games over the next four years, we would have to surrender our 1994 first-round draft pick.

Turns out, we did have to surrender that pick. But even with that arrangement, getting another backcourt weapon in Smith was a great move for us. Kenny quickly won the starting point-guard slot and went on to finish third in the league's Most Improved Player balloting, with marks of 17.7 points, 7.1 assists, and .520 shooting.

Indeed, "Smith" was the name of our game in 1990–91. On January 3 against Chicago, disaster had loomed: Hakeem had the orbital of his right eye shattered by an inadvertent Bill Cartwright elbow. But Larry Smith came to the rescue in phenomenal fashion.

We had picked up Larry as a free agent after his long tenure with Golden State. He wasn't known for his shooting, but he put bread on the table by being one of the game's most tenacious rebounders. Larry gave us toughness and a no-nonsense approach. You talk about a guy changing personalities between the lines—that was Larry Smith. Off the court he was soft-spoken and a true gentleman, but when he crossed that line, he'd do anything to help his team: hit the floor, set a bone-crushing pick, play blue-collar defense. Whatever it took.

Somehow, some way, we began to thrive without Hakeem, who was out for two months. We had a three-guard rotation in Smith, Maxwell, and Floyd that hit a groove. Inside, Larry began dominating the boards with a siege of 20-rebound games. Suddenly, everybody was pitching in at the defensive end, and our team went on a nice roll. We were 17-13 when Hakeem was injured and 32-23 when he came back.

In a game against Denver, with Hakeem still out and Larry starting at center, Smith put on an unbelievable display of sheer hustle. On one possession, Larry grabbed an offensive rebound. He was in traffic, so he passed the ball out to an open Kenny Smith. Kenny shot and missed, with the ball hitting the rim and bouncing toward the corner. Larry was again battling inside for position. When he saw the direction of the rebound, he busted through two defenders who were trying to keep bodies on him. Larry dove and hit the floor hard. He grabbed the ball and quickly passed to Vernon Maxwell. Max drove and shot a layup. It rolled off the rim, but somehow Larry was there to tip it in. He was everywhere!

It was the only time since my retirement that I felt like putting on a jersey and being on the floor. Larry's performance was so inspiring that I wanted to be out there battling beside him. It sent chills through my body. And Larry had that effect on the whole team.

People wonder how we could possibly hold up defensively without a great shot-blocker like Hakeem, but again Larry was a big part of the answer. He was a great fighter for position in the post and had quick hands for a guy so big. He would often strip the ball from the offensive player, a lot like Karl Malone does these days.

Offensively, we still had a post-up game with Otis inside. But the pick-and-roll play became a bigger part of our attack. Kenny, Sleepy, and Max got a lot of mileage out of it, especially with Otis setting the picks. Thorpe was one of our best screeners and had great hands; when he'd catch the ball on the roll, he could palm it and dunk it quickly before the defense could rotate over.

Hakeem expressed great pride in the team's performance without him. When he came back, you could see he was fired up about taking us to an even higher level. The team found great chemistry, and a staggering 29-5 spurt propelled us to a 52-win season, the best in franchise history. Don displayed a masterful touch in directing the various attacks he had available: When Hakeem was with us, we exploited the inside game; when Hakeem was out, Don utilized the quickness of his guards.

For a young assistant coach like me, that '90–91 season was a lesson in the importance of chemistry. You might not have your powerhouse player out there, but if you have chemistry, play together, and play tough and hard, you have a chance to win in this league.

The rough part about that 52-win season was that we again had to face the Lakers in the playoffs. The key was Game One at the Forum when, with the game tied, Byron Scott was credited with making a shot at the buzzer for a 94–92 Lakers victory. This was a case where we sure could have used instant replay; we felt that Scott had released the ball after the buzzer, but there was nothing we could do except walk away when the goal was ruled good.

That play seemed to deflate us, and the Lakers wound up winning the next two games for a 3–0 sweep. In the clincher, Magic Johnson was magnificent, scoring 38 points. Who would have believed that would be the last time we'd face Magic until his brief return in 1995–96? The Lakers lost to Chicago in the 1991 finals, and Magic revealed in the preseason the next fall that he was leaving the game because of HIV.

Despite the playoff sweep, Don's ability to win 52 games in a season in which Hakeem played only 56 games was duly noted by the media. Don was named 1990–91 Coach of the Year. So there we

1

With some pals from the neighborhood. My sister, Frances, is second from left; I'm at center; and my cousin Mark, the Little League star, is next to me in front.

2

3

Skying for a rebound while at Michigan, despite some unorthodox defense by Michigan State.

A very special way to start a new life: with Sophie, on our wedding day.

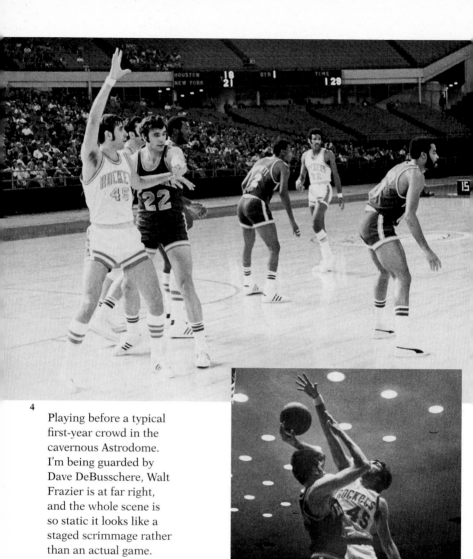

4

Playing before a typical
first-year crowd in the
cavernous Astrodome.
I'm being guarded by
Dave DeBusschere, Walt
Frazier is at far right,
and the whole scene is
so static it looks like a
staged scrimmage rather
than an actual game.

Soaring to reject a shot
by Phil Jackson as we
clinched our first-round
playoff series against
the Knicks in 1975.
Beating New York in a
playoff series was a
breakthrough for our
franchise.

5

These pictures show the event I could not remember: the devastating punch thrown by Kermit Washington.

6

7

8

Four proud Tomjanoviches on the night the Rockets retired my number: (clockwise) me, Sophie, Melissa, and Nichole.

I've enjoyed Calvin Murphy from the first time I saw him play in college. In the pros, I was very lucky to call him my teammate, my roommate, and my friend.

The Rockets coaches gather to watch the announcement that we were drafting Ralph Sampson. From left, head coach Bill Fitch, me, and Carroll Dawson.

9

At the press conference where I was named to the job I never expected and wasn't sure I wanted, head coach of the Houston Rockets. I felt every bit as tired and pressured as I look.

10

Making a point to Hakeem Olajuwon during the 1993 game in New York where we tied the NBA mark for best start ever at 15-0.

11

12

In a gesture as unselfish as his play, Hakeem shares his 1993–94 Most Valuable Player trophy with his teammates.

Vernon Maxwell drives against the Knicks' John Starks during the 1994 finals.

A sweet moment of triumph in the closing seconds of our first NBA championship.

It was a privilege to give a jersey to President Clinton at the White House in February 1995. Sam Cassell, Hakeem, and Kenny Smith were three of only five players from the '94 champions who were still with the team when we made our visit.

16

Good friends, college teammates, and now NBA champs: Hakeem and Clyde Drexler celebrate the four-game sweep of Orlando as Hannah Storm looks on.

The Tomjanoviches today (from left to right): Sophie, me, Nichole, Trey, and Melissa.

17

were, ready to build on the '91 success with Don's trophy still shiny and new.

But in this league, you can never *ever* know what to expect from year to year. I always say, "Expect the unexpected." We just never got it going in '91–92. It was as though we were chained to the .500 mark.

After we lost that infamous 24-point lead to Minnesota on February 17, management decided to make a head-coaching change. Chaney was relieved of his duties the next day and suddenly, shockingly, my life was about to take on an entirely new dimension.

We've come full circle here, right back to where this book began. As I said right from the start, I didn't want to be a head coach and I didn't think it was right that Don was let go.

Don Chaney was an outstanding defensive coach. He had played on Celtics teams that always played tough defense, and he worked under Mike Fratello, honing the philosophy that would enable him to devise an excellent double-teaming scheme. The Rockets hadn't used it prior to Don's arrival, and that rotating, double-teaming defense that Don brought in was an influence that has always stayed with me.

On February 19, 1992, I woke up as the man entrusted with guiding the Houston Rockets through the rest of the season. There was so much to be done and so little time to do it.

We were 26-26. All I really wanted to do was attack the last 30 games of the '91–92 season with as much energy and class as I could muster. Above all, I had always been loyal to the organization. Now the organization was reaching out and asking me to perform a new role, and I was going to do it the best way I knew how.

When it was over, when the dust had settled and all the emotion of a disappointing finish had run its course, I felt something in my heart.

Yes, I felt I could make a contribution as the head coach of the Houston Rockets. And I was thrilled and honored that Charlie Thomas was giving me the chance.

14

IN THE SUMMER of 1992, after Charlie Thomas uttered the words, "You're the guy," and gave me a three-year contract, Carroll Dawson and I spent many hours talking about what coaching is really all about.

As the interim coach the year before, I was doing things on the fly. There wasn't much time to sit around and discuss the nuts and bolts of coaching. I was extremely fortunate to have someone like Carroll for these discussions; he was an experienced coaching teacher. Carroll was in his early thirties when he took over the head coaching job at Baylor University, and he had been an NBA assistant for more than a decade and had experienced the transition process that takes place when a new coach takes over.

Carroll told me that going from being an assistant, whose job is to help execute the head coach's program and make suggestions, to the guy who creates the system and makes final decisions is a giant step. I had gotten a taste of this transition when I took over during the season, but he let me know that things were completely different now that the *interim* had been dropped from my title.

"It's your team now," Carroll said. "You're the man standing in front of the troops, leading them into battle. They need to know what you believe in, what you stand for."

This was a crucial time for me. I had to establish my own philosophy.

Then Carroll said, "Rudy, coaching can be the loneliest job in the world when things aren't going well. There will be times when you'll feel you stand alone. It's comforting to know you have loyal assistants, but we can't help you in a lot of situations. You have to be the one who faces the media and answers the tough questions when we lose. The fans live and die with their teams. When we lose, they'll hold you responsible. They'll want your head.

"You're the one who has to meet with the owner and explain why things aren't going the way he expected. You have to talk to the players we decide to cut and you have to break the news to the players we trade. Most of all, you have to stand in front of the team when losing has made them lose confidence and faith. You have - to ease those doubts by being strong and positive. It takes a lot of courage."

I stared at Carroll for a long time and said, "Aren't you the guy, when we were sitting in Steve Patterson's office, who said, 'You've got to take this job'? What the hell are you getting me into?"

We both laughed.

"C.D., I know it's a tough job. I'm going to do what I always do—give it my best shot."

I did feel some apprehension, but mostly I was excited. Basketball was on my mind every waking moment. I even dreamed about it.

I was constantly jotting down notes of things that came to mind. I got a lot of ideas while driving. It was difficult to write while motoring down the freeway, so I bought a tape recorder. I taped conversations I had with Carroll when we would go up to Lake Conroe and talk basketball until two or three in the morning. Then I'd play them back on the ride to Houston the next day.

I considered this summer's time away from the team precious, and I wanted to use it wisely. I began mentally sifting through all the influences I had experienced, starting with my playing days all the way through my years as a scout and an assistant under three fine coaches.

I had been exposed to so many different approaches. All coaches want the same thing, to win, but there are a lot of ways to get there. I had to find the best way for me to help the Houston Rockets become a successful team.

I knew I had to coach my players in a manner consistent with my personality. I couldn't put on a different face now, just because I was named head coach. It wouldn't have worked anyway; the players knew who I was and, they would have seen right through it.

Some people felt I didn't have the right personality to be a head coach in the NBA. I was too nice a guy, not assertive enough. I wasn't confrontational. These were some of the things I heard, and those observations were not far off the mark.

"How are you going to deal with the egos of the players?" That was a question I was often asked. I didn't have a definite answer yet because I hadn't had any major problems in my first year. The players had been very cooperative with me.

It made sense to me that I should treat the players the way I wanted to be treated when I played—with respect, understanding, and honesty. These guys were not kids anymore. I would treat them as adults. Some of them were married and had children of their own. I knew what they were going through in this highly competitive business: fighting to win a job on the team, fighting to beat the opposition. There is tremendous pressure to perform. When I played, I felt I performed better when the coach was positive and supportive. When I knew he was pulling for me to do well, I felt that I had an ally on the sidelines. I also wanted him to be honest with me and tell me when I wasn't doing my job. I didn't want to be penalized for something I didn't realize I was doing wrong.

I was like all players: I wanted to play. Just let me know what I needed to change and I would do my best to correct it.

Players want to do the right thing when they're in the game. No one wants to make mistakes. But the fact of the matter is, mistakes are part of the game. Because of the fast pace of the game and the competitiveness of the other team, they're going to happen.

Correcting mistakes is one of the most important parts of coaching. If you can get your team to eliminate errors, you have a chance to improve and grow. The majority of the things a coach says to a player involves correcting him, and the manner in which you do so is vitally important. No one wants to be embarrassed in practice in front of his peers or especially in a game, in front of the crowd with family and friends in the stands.

I learned a valuable lesson when I was an assistant coach under Don Chaney. We were going through a tough period, and Don called a team meeting to air out our problems.

We talked about several issues, and then Sleepy Floyd asked to speak. He said it was hard to play with confidence when he would make a mistake, look toward our bench, and see me making a gesture of displeasure with the play.

I was shocked. I knew I could get totally wound up in the game, but I didn't realize my body language was sending negative signals to the players.

I did two things: I apologized to Sleepy and then I apologized to Don. That was not proper behavior for an assistant coach.

The incident made a tremendous impact on me. I really felt terrible, and I made a vow never to show any outward signs of negativity toward a player.

The respect factor is very big with players. They realize the coach has to do his job and that there are times when he'll get emotional and even angry, but they want to be treated like adults, not like children being reprimanded. I planned on doing my correcting in a civil manner. I wasn't going to attack the player, demeaning him. It was a basketball technique I was addressing, not something personal.

I feel a good way to change a negative is to add a positive to the formula. For instance, if Vernon Maxwell wasn't using the pick properly on the pick-and-roll, I'd say, "Max, you've got great quickness. You're hard to stop when you drive to the basket. Just think how much more pressure you'll put on the defense if you do it this way."

Then I'd explain the proper technique; I'd let him know I think he's good at a skill, but I'd also shown him a way to be more effective. It's much better than going "No, no, no. You're doing it wrong. Do it this way."

The key is, the positive you use has to be true. Otherwise, the player will think you're conning him and it will cause a breakdown in trust.

I knew I couldn't deal with every player the same way. I expected them all to follow the team rules and give a hundred percent when they were in the games; those things applied to everyone equally. But when I had to address a player one-on-one, I had to use some sensitivity. They are not rocks; they are human and they have feelings.

Some players are more sensitive than others. Some need an arm around the shoulder when you're correcting them, and some don't like to be touched—just let them know what needs to be done. Some need a soft approach. Some need a firmer one.

I also knew there would be occasions when a player would fail to act like an adult or would put himself above the team. Then he would lose my respect. I would call him aside for a private meeting and let him know he had let the team down. Still, I wouldn't address him in a disrespectful way; I'd be direct in letting him know I expected a change in his behavior.

All the things it takes to be a good coach were not going to come overnight. I was going to have to learn a lot of things by trial and error.

In the NBA, you can't use fear as a weapon to gain respect from the players. Maybe some coaches use it on the high school or college level, where the players are younger and the coach is more of a father figure, but on this level the player-coach relationship has to be one of cooperation, with respect flowing both ways.

I wanted to gain their respect through how I conducted myself. If I was going to expect them to be a hardworking and unselfish team, I would have to set the example. I would show them I was totally committed and dedicated to my job. I would always be well-prepared. I would let them know I believed in them and cared about them, not only as players but as people.

I wanted to create an environment where every player felt appreciated, whether he was a star or a reserve. They would know the coach and his staff were there to support them and willing to give of themselves to help the players improve.

There would be little insecurity. They would have confidence because of this overpowering feeling of support. It would be like a family: We would take care of each other, we would draw energy from each other and always defend each other. I would never single out a player to the media for playing poorly. After losses, it would be "we played poorly." After wins, I would single out basic contributors.

The players would do the same for their teammates. It would be a team that knew its strengths and weaknesses and worked to improve on the weaknesses.

There would be a strong team pride that our system—the way we do things—is right for us. It's our identity. It's how we get it done. It's how we win.

I not only spent time thinking about how to coach, I had to make decisions on *what* to coach. What plays would we use on offense? Which defensive tactics would we employ?

I had to choose things I firmly believed in. They had to be things that would help us become a successful team. And my choices had to fit the talents of the players I had.

If I believed the passing-game offense was a great offense but I didn't have the kind of players who could execute it, I would be making an unrealistic choice, one that wouldn't win many games and would cause frustration for the players. Just because I liked it didn't make it the right choice.

A month before training camp began, I called my staff together for meetings to kick around different basketball ideas. Assistants Carroll Dawson and Bill Berry, veteran head scout John Killilea, advance scout Joe Ash, and new video coordinator Jim Boylen participated in these skull sessions.

I believe in involving everyone. If the guys on my staff knew I had respect for their opinions, I believed, their commitment to the team would become just as strong as mine.

I had some definite ideas on what I wanted to do in putting in our system. But it would have been foolish not to use these guys' knowledge.

Everyone got a chance to express his views. Carroll and Bill, who had coached college teams, where you do a lot of teaching, suggested drills we could use. John had some great drills for teaching defense. Joe had some ideas on new plays.

Jim, a novice to the NBA, came up with some good ideas regarding terminology. I felt fortunate to have such dedicated guys to help me get started.

In the past, we had always held training camp in Houston. We didn't have a hockey team, so the Summit was always available. It was convenient, but I wanted to make it clear to the team that we were putting in a new system. I wanted it to register.

I decided to take the team out of town to change the setting. I wanted to get away from the hustle and bustle of the big city and go someplace with a more relaxed atmosphere so the players could better concentrate on basketball.

Galveston was my choice. It was only fifty miles from Houston and they had built an impressive hotel there, the San Luis. There were plenty of good restaurants on the seawall, and I found a gym at Galveston Ball High School that had a good floor that wouldn't put a lot of stress on the players' legs.

It was an old gym, built in the 1950s. It reminded me of my high school gym back in Hamtramck. I did have some concerns because it was not quite up to the standard of places that NBA players were accustomed to playing; the gym wasn't shiny and new, but it felt like the kind of setting where work and sweat should take place. It had a blue-collar feel. I hoped it would make the same kind of impression on the players.

This is where the foundation of Rockets basketball would be established. My summer was filled with excitement about my new basketball challenge, but I also had an underlying feeling of worry and concern.

At the end of the previous season, Hakeem Olajuwon and owner Charlie Thomas had had a contract dispute, and things didn't look good. Charlie felt it couldn't be resolved and that the only solution was to trade Hakeem. I was caught in the middle. I wanted to keep Hakeem; there was no doubt in my mind that I had a better chance to succeed with him on the team.

I had a great deal of respect for Hakeem, but I worked for Charlie. When trade possibilities came up, I had to give my opinion of whether it was a good basketball deal or not.

I felt there was no way we could get equal value for a player of

Hakeem's caliber. He was an A-plus player, and the offers that came in were, at best, a couple of Bs and a C. You don't win big in this league unless you have at least one A player. Most good teams had two and some had three, like the Lakers with Magic Johnson, Kareem Abdul-Jabbar, and James Worthy. I was a new coach raring to go and I didn't even know who was going to be playing for me in the upcoming season. I was in limbo as far as preparing the system to fit the talents of the players.

Who were the players going to be?

I had uneasy feelings about the situation. I could see into the future: "Yeah, Tomjanovich. Wasn't he the guy that coached the Rockets after they traded Olajuwon? He wasn't around long. They never made the playoffs."

I believe that history will smile kindly on Hakeem Olajuwon. When you talk about the all-time great centers, he belongs in the same category as Wilt Chamberlain, Bill Russell, Kareem Abdul-Jabbar, Bill Walton—all guys who have won championships.

You could make a strong argument for Hakeem being *the* best. When you look at him and really watch the things he does, it becomes apparent that he's a combination of the great ones. He's got the strength of a Chamberlain, the quickness of a Russell, and the shot-making ability of an Abdul-Jabbar. When you talk about Hakeem and Kareem, the connection is that the defense can do almost nothing about each guy's pet shot. Kareem had the nearly unstoppable sky hook; Hakeem has the shake-and-bake fadeaway jumper. I won't say Hakeem is as good a passer as Walton, but he has worked on that part of his game to the point that it eventually helped make Hakeem a champion.

I first saw Hakeem play basketball at the University of Houston, even before he became a starter for the Cougars. I had heard about his background—that he hadn't played much basketball before coming to Houston. My first impression was based on his quickness to the ball. As a shot-blocker and rebounder, he was eye-catching.

In the early 1980s, I basically projected Hakeem as a defensive player who could use those catlike assets to help his team. I didn't know how far he would go in basketball, but when you saw him out there as a young collegian, he was a presence that you noticed right away.

As his college career continued, we kept an eye on his constant improvement. He would play against Moses Malone in those famous Fonde pickup games, and his progress was amazing. When it came time for the 1984 draft, Hakeem was the guy at the top of our list as we held the No. 1 pick. Yes, Michael Jordan was in that draft, but nobody then could have dreamed Michael would become what he is today. We all agreed Jordan was by far the best two-guard in the draft and the best two-guard to come along in a long time, but he has done things no one could even imagine back then.

The general consensus among the Rockets staff was that if you have a choice between a great big man and a great guard, you go with the size. Big people just don't come around that often. Hakeem's connection with the University of Houston was a factor as well. Ralph Sampson had had a good first year, and his presence, plus Hakeem, would give us two dynamic athletes with size.

In the first few days of Hakeem's rookie training camp, we were delighted to watch him shoot the ball. The spin on it, the feathery touch—it was something we really got excited about and something we hadn't seen that much of when he was in college. My initial thought that he would be more of a Bill Russell–type player was wiped away. This young man had another dimension!

The other thing we saw from the young Hakeem was the emotion and the fire. Once he got things going, his energy level was just amazing. Right from the beginning, he had people on the bench turning to each other to say, "Wow, did you see that?"

Some of his athletic feats as a rookie were just awesome. By his second year, Hakeem had jumped from a 20.6 scoring average to 23.5. He was like a kid in a candy store, because he no longer had to deal with the zone rules that shackle a big man's offensive maneuverability in college. There, you've got a man behind you and a man in front of you at all times, and there's no place to go. But in the pros, Hakeem had enough room on the court to develop new moves and new shots that seemed to come naturally to him.

The national reputation really set in when Hakeem went up

against Kareem and the Lakers in the 1986 Western Conference Finals. Olajuwon had 40 and 35 points, respectively, in Games Three and Four as we stunned the defending champs in five games. *Sports Illustrated* put Hakeem on the cover with THE NEW FORCE as the headline. With Hakeem and Ralph, there was a feeling that this was just the beginning of a team that could be title contenders for many years to come.

But as the cast around Olajuwon changed, largely because of the drug problems that ravaged our backcourt, Hakeem became frustrated because he was such a great competitor and wanted to win so badly. Because he was so young and explosive, Hakeem was quick enough to beat most double-teams. With our supporting cast in flux, I'm sure there were times when he felt he had a better chance of scoring against a double-team than we had of making an open shot. But the percentages say that you can't succeed that way over a sustained period of time. As the Rockets stabilized in the early 1990s, Hakeem matured as a team player. We would get the ball in to Olajuwon, and the offense could start from there, based on the defensive reaction.

With the three-point shot becoming more of a factor in the NBA, we came up with a spacing scheme intended to stretch the floor. We wanted to keep people spaced so that one man couldn't cover two. For the center with the ball, there's an option right in front of him, an option out on top, and an option diagonally on the outside. The other big man attacks the front of the rim, and if the defense doesn't pick him up quick enough, there's a pass available for a layup.

We ran variations off this concept, but basically that was the system we believed in. I'm not going to say I devised it; it's pieced together from different little things that other coaches did. But this was our bread-and-butter offense, the way we made our living.

Hakeem took to the system very well in reading the defenses and making people pay for the double-teams. And when teams stayed with our outside people, Hakeem had the freedom to use his one-on-one skills—and nobody could stop him.

In trying to put a championship cast around Hakeem, we went out looking for people who could make the spot-up shot—the open, standing shot—that is essential in our system. In our scouting, one of the first questions was, "Can he spot up with three-point range?" Of course, we didn't want just that one dimension; we wanted drivers, passers, defenders. But if we could find guys who could do those things *and* make the spot-up shots, we felt we could put together a dangerous offensive team with Hakeem serving as the hub of the wheel.

There's no single moment when the light bulb comes on in a player's mind as far as making the right pass at the right instant goes. It requires a lot of practice, togetherness, and dedication to get all five guys instinctively moving the ball to the right place within the system.

As our team was evolving, the double-teaming defenses around the league were getting better and better. The Lakers of the late Eighties started the trend with their big, rangy athletes. When other clubs began to get more adept at the rotations, it put great pressure on a center looking to make the play. But once we got the right system and the right personnel around him, Hakeem was very comfortable with how you defeat the double-team.

From a defensive standpoint, Hakeem's problem early in his career was foul trouble. This happens with most young, athletic big men. Again, it takes maturity to learn how *not* to get into foul trouble. Hakeem was so active and competitive that he'd go after balls in the backcourt, trying for a quick steal. I call this "stabbing," and we try to stay away from that because it causes fouls and you will take yourself out of the play on the fast break if you don't come up with the ball. Hakeem had some success with steals in the backcourt because of his great athleticism, but the percentages didn't work out and it took time for him to understand that. Bill Fitch, Hakeem's first pro head coach, really worked and drilled Hakeem on that aspect of the game.

When I think of Hakeem Olajuwon's greatness, the word I keep coming back to is "competitiveness." In our practices, whenever a score was being kept, he would be out there giving it his all. When we've acquired guys in trades or brought in rookies, Hakeem has been a great leader by example. When guys see the intensity of a superstar—even in practice—it just lifts the whole program. He has never been what you would call a rah-rah guy, but he is very comfortable leading by example.

I remember Don Chaney saying to Hakeem, "I want you to be our cocaptain and take on a leadership role." Hakeem said he would do everything for the team, but didn't feel comfortable vocally addressing other players in a public way. But as time went by, he would often have something to say when we got into a crucial situation, and everybody would take notice. When the team could go one way or the other, his input was what got us going in the right direction.

Hakeem would get right to the point of where we needed to be as a team. Everything was about *we*. What are *we* going to do? Are *we* all committed?

Without Hakeem Olajuwon doing the right thing in the locker room, I wouldn't be writing this book, we wouldn't have become two-time champions, and I probably wouldn't have lasted very long as a basketball coach.

My relationship with Hakeem is based on respect. I don't pal around with him or any of my players, but we've had some very good talks about the direction of the team and about different ideas I have for the success of the team. The number-one connector between Hakeem and me is that we both want to win. We've both been around Houston a long time, and we both feel working for the Rockets is more than just a job.

What really strikes me about Hakeem Olajuwon is how he came up with very little basketball in his life during his teenage years. The whole story of this Nigerian kid coming to America mainly for the purpose of getting a college degree and then going on to win MVPs and championships just shows that truth can be stranger than fiction. A scriptwriter in Hollywood couldn't sit down and come up with a better story.

I feel privileged to have been involved in Hakeem's remarkable odyssey. Most of us who went on to play pro basketball started out in youth leagues or on playgrounds when we were kids. Here's a guy who didn't even know the sport existed during his early years—and now people are calling him one of the greatest of all time.

What Jordan means to Chicago, what Larry Bird means to

Boston, what Magic Johnson and Kareem mean to Los Angeles—
that's what Hakeem Olajuwon has meant to Houston.

IN THAT TENUOUS SUMMER of '92, no trade offers for Olajuwon were presented that made any sense. Fortunately. So I made
my preparations assuming Hakeem would be a Rocket.

In early October we started training camp. The night before our
first practice we had a dinner, and afterward I addressed the team.

I told them I thought we had a chance to become a successful
team. We had a good mix of talent, and I said there was only one
way I knew to reach a goal: through hard work. Not now and then,
but every time we stepped on the floor. We couldn't loaf in practice
and then turn it on in the game. It doesn't work that way.

Hard work would have to be part of our everyday life. We
would have no fat cats on our team. To be a successful team, every
one of us, including me, had to put the team first, above our personal needs and wants.

We would support each other, pick each other up when someone was down. On offense, we would obey the golden rule: The
open man gets the ball. And the most important thing to understand was that we had to become a good defensive team. We had
to believe that defense was the key.

We ended the evening with a highlight tape that Jim Boylen put
together. The tape consisted of a series of great plays that each
player made the previous year, even the rookies. It really got the
guys fired up. They seemed anxious to get started.

The 1992–93 Rockets had Olajuwon at center and Otis Thorpe
at power forward. Rookie Robert Horry—our No. 1 draft choice—
was a strong candidate at the small-forward position; Robert had
signed early and attended our summer program, which was rare
for a lottery pick. He showed a good attitude and was picking
things up quickly. At 6-10, he had the ability to block shots from
the forward position.

Vernon Maxwell returned at big guard and Kenny Smith was at
the point. Carl Herrera, a 6-9 forward from Venezuela who had
played at the University of Houston, would back up Thorpe at forward. Our players called Herrera "Amigo."

The veteran Tree Rollins spelled Hakeem. We had Matt Bullard, a 6-10 sharpshooter who could play both forward positions, as a reserve. Another newcomer was 5-11 point guard Scott Brooks.

The previous summer, we had gotten a call from Minnesota general manager Jack McCloskey. He needed to clear some cap room to sign their No. 1 draft pick, Christian Laettner. McCloskey asked if we had any interest in Brooks.

Scott had broken into the league with the Philadelphia 76ers. I remember the exhibition game he had against us at Vanderbilt: He made four straight shots on the pick-and-roll to beat us. On first impression, you'd say he didn't have the height or the weight even to be in the NBA, but he had a great heart and he played so damn hard.

The Wolves only wanted a second-round draft choice in return for Scott. My immediate reaction was that a pesky, gutsy guy like Brooks was just what our team needed. He was an inspirational player.

Sleepy Floyd was a backup at both guard positions. Kennard Winchester was a reserve swingman, and we would later bolster our backcourt depth with the signing of Winston Garland.

Our first practice was critical. I wanted to make a point about the importance of defense. It would be the first thing we covered. Every coach in the history of basketball has advocated that his team play defense, but preaching it and really getting it done are two different things. Defense is the hardest part of the game. It takes both physical and mental toughness to play it well.

There are a few stats, like steals and blocked shots, that give players credit for playing good defense, but basic, solid defense has no individual stat. Many times, it goes unnoticed by the casual fan. As a coach, you can't just tell your player to play good defense and expect him to stop the man he is guarding. The offensive players in this league are so good it is almost impossible to stop them with one man. Even if a defender has great quickness, he's still at a disadvantage against a versatile offensive player—one who can either shoot outside or drive left or right. The offensive man is facing the basket and knows what he wants to do; the defense has to guess which way he's going and has to move backward. Everyone moves faster going forward than backward.

175

The solution to this problem is team defense. The defender guarding the player with the ball must get help from a teammate to stop a tough offensive player. As the helping teammate leaves his man, a third teammate must cover the man left open. This helping and covering takes all five players working in harmony. If one man is left open, you want him to be the man farthest away from the ball. The term *teamwork* is usually applied to passing the ball on offense, but it's also the basis for good team defense. This concept of working together and helping together builds confidence that you can play your man aggressively and feel secure there will always be a teammate there to support you if you happen to get beat. It takes time to perfect this defensive system; it must be taught step by step, starting with the stance and footwork of the individual defender. You progressively move to two-man situations . . . all the way to five men helping each other.

We had drills to cover every offensive situation we were likely to face. We stationed coaches at four baskets. Carroll had the big man working on post defense. Bill was working on various ways to defend the pick-and-roll. John showed different stances for strong-side and weak-side defense. Jim and Joe worked on defending pin-downs and backpicks.

I'd move from basket to basket, reinforcing the techniques the coaches were teaching. We were gradually making progress.

Offense was a lot easier to put in. It's the fun part of the game. Players will always be attentive when you're showing them ways to score.

I wanted us to become a better running team, utilizing the fast break. We were athletic at all positions, and I wanted to get as many easy baskets as we could. Hopefully, our new defensive system would cause some turnovers leading to breaks. On every team I've been involved with, the players want to fast break—even the slower-tempo team that Del Harris coached to the finals. Everyone likes to get easy baskets.

Just wanting to be a running team is wishful thinking. To really become one, a team that scores on a high percentage of its attempts, takes a tremendous amount of hard work. The team has to be in great physical condition. You must run hard on every opportunity, even when you know you probably won't get the ball. Sometimes you have to sacrifice yourself by making a defender guard you to open up opportunities for your teammates. The toughest thing about running the break is that you have to make quick decisions at top speed. Bill Berry came up with an excellent fast-break drill that calls for the offense to make the play quickly before trailing defenders catch up to the play.

When we do have to set up in the halfcourt offense, most of the plays we run stress getting the ball to our inside players, Olajuwon and Thorpe. Whenever we pass the ball inside to one of them, the other big man positions himself close to the basket for a pass or an offensive rebound. The other three players space themselves around the three-point line to keep their defenders honest and give us good spacing. They should be ready to shoot three-pointers if the defense decides to double-team. We run a lot of pick-and-rolls from various positions on the floor and from all kinds of angles, creating different problems for the defense. No matter what play we run, the open man should always get the ball. I don't care who scores as long as it's a Rocket.

The foundation of the new Rockets system was in as we closed preseason with a 5-3 record. We had a terrible schedule: We played our last preseason game in Mexico City, and then had to travel halfway around the world to Yokohama, Japan, to face Seattle in the opening two games of the regular season. This torturous trip had a silver lining; Hakeem and Charlie Thomas wound up sitting next to each other on the fourteen-hour stretch from Dallas to Tokyo. They had a chance to talk through their differences, and a compromise was reached. All the talk about Hakeem being traded came to an end.

We went into our first game shorthanded: Otis Thorpe had sustained a bruised kidney in an exhibition game and would be out at least two weeks. It was a rare injury for Otis, who had been an iron man, playing in 542 consecutive games.

We started Matt Bullard in Thorpe's place at forward. Matt would have to go against Shawn Kemp. It was a tough matchup. Kemp got off to a strong start, getting three dunks in the first quarter. Seattle's superior size and strength wore us down, and they began dominating us on the boards. The Sonics won easily, 111–94. In the second game, we played much better. We outrebounded *them*. We had a six-point lead at the half and led by one going into the fourth quarter. But Nate McMillan wound up being the hero of the game. After Kenny Smith put us up by two with a three-pointer at the 2:40 mark, McMillan chased a loose ball into the corner and shot it as the 24-second clock was winding down. It was a clutch three-pointer that put them up by one. Then, a minute later, McMillan made a spot-up shot to put them up by three. He wound up with 24 points.

It was a tough 89–85 defeat. I was down about our 0-2 start, but our problems were not over. Teams who had played their opening games in Japan said that it took them about a week to recover from the jet lag.

How would our guys react to such a tiresome journey?

I was a little apprehensive, but we went home and had a strong win over Atlanta. Usually, I don't go overboard about a victory, but this one was crucial. It was my first as the official coach of the Rockets. I didn't want to get off to a poor start and have the players lose confidence in our system.

"I love you guys," I said as we gathered after the game.

I knew they were still feeling some effects from the Japan trip, and I wanted to let them know how much I appreciated their effort. The players were in great spirits, but they looked at me as if to say, "I hope this guy isn't this emotional after *every* game we win."

We were a respectable 14-9 when the real trouble began to set in. First, we gave up 132 points to Golden State on our home floor. The next night, we surrendered 133 points at Phoenix. Then came another loss to the Warriors in Oakland.

Our next game, in Portland, took place on a day Houston sports fans will not soon forget. Early in the day, the Oilers let a 35-3 lead in the third quarter slip away in their playoff game at Buffalo. On cue, it seemed, we followed up by losing a seven-point lead in the final minute of our game in Portland. Up by two in the final seconds, we inbounded from midcourt. We had always managed to get the ball in safely, using what we simply call the "get-in" play, but one of our players failed to move to the proper position and Rod Strickland wound up making a big steal on the dead run. His layup tied the game, which we eventually lost in overtime. Four consecutive losses. We were finding ways to lose. We couldn't execute a basic inbounds play to secure a game. We were not doing the little things that it takes to win.

But the major problem during this period was defense. It was nonexistent.

I called three team meetings during the skid, hoping to stop the bleeding. I tried to impress upon the team that we couldn't beat anyone in the league if we didn't work harder on the defensive end. The main problem was that we weren't running back hard when the other team ran their fast break. We were giving up layup after layup. If our opponents happened to miss, they were there to rebound and put it back in.

During our games, Bill Berry keeps a record of how many points we give up on the fast break. We consider giving up less than ten points excellent. Ten to 15 points is good, 15 to 20 is fair. Any more points indicates that we're not doing a good job of getting back.

Bill's statistics were staggering: During this losing streak, we were allowing teams to score 30 and sometimes 40 points on the break.

We couldn't have beaten a good college team giving up that many cheap baskets. After these losses, C.D., Bill, and I worked well into the morning hours reviewing and editing tapes of the games. It was painful to watch them a second time. In fact, it was even worse on tape. The good players on these teams had field days on us, scoring at will, but what really was gut-wrenching was how players who had reputations for being lazy were running by us, outhustling us to the other end of the court. It was humiliating.

Losing causes more than a number in the loss column. It tests your constitution. It tests your faith. It clouds the true issues. Everyone starts searching for reasons why this could be happening to us. What usually occurs is that some players feel they could help the team win if they got better opportunities to score. They think offense.

This is natural, because putting the ball in the basket is what they feel got them to be pro players in the first place. It's what they do best.

I knew we had some grumblings about the number and the quality of shots some guys were getting. When you lose, that's as predictable as the sun coming up. It happens to every team that goes through a losing streak.

I had to get the team focused on the real problem: defense. I knew players hated to watch tapes showing them making mistakes and playing poorly. When I played, I dreaded those tape sessions. But we were at the point where player feelings were not the main issue. The main issue was the survival of the team.

We were at a crossroads. Would we waste energy trying to place the blame where it didn't belong and continue to struggle? Or would we face the reality of our problems and start working to improve them?

As we viewed the tape of our horrendous play, there was complete silence in the room, except for my comments. I didn't have to make many; the pictures on the monitor were spelling it out loud and clear.

Layup. Layup. Layup. When the tape ended, the players' heads were dropped, eyes looking toward the floor.

"What we just saw was embarrassing," I said. "I wish I could say that us coaches invented this tape just to make a coaching point. But the truth is, what you saw was really us. That's the way we've been playing."

I then read off the terrible fast-break statistics.

"It has to hurt when you see yourself getting beat so easily," I said. "It hurts me to think I haven't gotten the point across to you about defense. We started from day one working on it. We work on it every practice. It's just not sinking in. If you don't believe in your heart that defense is the key, we don't have a chance."

Their heads remained down while I was talking. I then said, "I want you to look up here and watch the same Rockets team play the same opponent. But this time with a different result."

I pushed the tape of our positive defensive plays into the VCR. It showed plays where all five men were sprinting back on defense to slow down the running game. There was a play where Vernon Maxwell was caught behind the fast break and gave extra effort to catch up and break up the play from behind.

On another play, Otis made a steal. Then Hakeem blocked a shot. Then Horry blocked a shot.

"This proves we can do it. We have the ability to play good defense. We just have to do it more consistently. It would be different if I was asking you to do something you're incapable of doing. You're cheating yourselves. You're not getting the most out of your ability."

This was our third meeting in a week. I hadn't received much feedback from the players in the earlier meetings. The feedback I got from the games showed my words were not making any impact.

"I'm not going to lecture anymore," I said. "It's our team. It isn't me against you. I'm with you. We're in this together. I'm just telling you I believe the reason we're losing is we give up too many easy baskets. If any of you guys have different ideas, bring them up now. We can't get this problem solved talking about it in small groups or keeping our ideas to ourselves. We have to do it as a team."

I waited. Max was the first to speak up.

"I've got to be honest," he said. "I've been playing terrible. I'm letting guys score on me too easily. From now on, I'm going to come out more aggressive. I'm tired of losing."

Then Otis.

"We all have to work harder," he said. "It's not one or two players, it's all of us. We all have to do our part to get this thing turned around."

Finally, Hakeem.

"After watching the tape, it's obvious what must be done," he said. "We must all make a commitment to play harder. We cannot just talk about it. We must stick to that commitment."

The leaders on the team had stepped forward. After the meeting, I had a feeling it was a step in the right direction.

We played the Nuggets on the road that night. I could see we were trying harder, but we wound up with the same result—a 25-

point blowout loss. It was the second leg of a back-to-back, and we were a tired team both physically and mentally. The thin air in Denver didn't help matters.

Seven losses in a row. Here was one of those instances that Carroll had told me about. The feeling of isolation was overpowering.

What was I doing wrong? Why couldn't I make them see the obvious solution?

In my gut, I felt our ills were not incurable. What made the situation more difficult was that with back-to-back games and the travel, there wasn't time to have live practices, where we go full tilt and work to iron out problems. We had to save some energy for the games. I had to try to get us on course through nonphysical practices where we walked through situations and had chalk talks and video sessions.

I knew the players on the team were good guys. We didn't have one prima donna. They all practiced hard. They all had good attitudes. They were willing to listen and they all wanted to win.

Why were we losing concentration on defense?

I had the feeling that the early success we had—going 14-7 after those first two losses in Japan—had given us a false sense of security.

I could see we were gaining confidence. We believed we were going to be a good team, but we somehow forgot how we had been winning. We began to think we could just take the floor and outscore our opponents. For some teams, that might be possible, but we were being totally unrealistic if we thought we had the firepower to win that way. If there wasn't a change in our approach to the game, we were going to have a terrible season and I wasn't going to be coaching long.

Our next game was at home against the Utah Jazz. They were a consistently solid team. They had a strong halfcourt game, posting Karl Malone, and a dangerous fast break with John Stockton handling the ball.

It was a physical game, and I began to see signs that our players were serious about changing our ways. The transition defense was excellent. We didn't give Stockton many opportunities to do what he does best—find open teammates. We had a great team effort, holding them to 90 points as we won by seven. It was a relief finally to be off the schneid and put one in the win column.

After the game, I said, "There was a noticeable difference out there tonight. This should be a great lesson for us. We beat a good team. Defense was the key. Let's not stop here. We have to build on this."

We *did* build on it. The Utah win was the start of an eight-game winning streak. We then leveled off a bit before enjoying a remarkable 15-game winning streak that lasted from mid-February to mid-March. In 11 of those 15 wins, we held the opponents under 100 points; twice we gave up 102 points, and another team scored 104 on us. The most we gave up was 111, but that was in a 38-point blowout victory where there was a lot of garbage time.

There was a remarkable transformation occurring on our team. In huddles, instead of the topic of conversation always being offense, players began to communicate with each other about defensive situations.

The coaching staff kept reinforcing strong defense, keeping the team informed of the impressive defensive stats we were compiling. The players began to take more and more pride in our defense. We were winning games on the road when our offense wasn't hitting on all cylinders, because we made it tough to score against us. Our defense always seemed to give us a chance to win, even when other parts of our game weren't up to par.

Before this transformation, we were a team that all wore the same uniforms, but in reality we were all individuals moving in our own directions. I have no doubt every player wanted to win, but there were different ideas of how to get it accomplished. We didn't have a common theme. We had nothing to hold on to when things got shaky. We needed a foundation. But, finally, we had a team identity, one that worked for us, one we could take pride in. We now believed we were a defensive team.

We'd fight on every possession, and we believed we had to be unselfish on offense. We would exploit our strong inside game, then read the defense. When the double-team came, we would find the open man.

It sounds simple when stated in general terms, but it took a lot of sweat, sacrifice, and commitment to execute it. I felt fortunate that I had players who were willing to pay the price to make it work.

Looking back on it, as painful as it was to go through the seven-game losing streak, I'm not certain things would have turned around so drastically if we had lost two or three games, won one, then lost a couple more and won another. The magnitude of the losing streak brought things to a head.

It tested us to the core. When we were standing at the cross-roads, I'm proud to say the Rockets players had the character to be honest with themselves and consciously make changes in the way they approached the game.

After a 14-16 start, we won a phenomenal 41 of 50 games to clinch the Midwest Division crown going away. Could I have predicted anything like that? Of course not. But the philosophy wasn't that hard to grasp. We had seen what would happen if we didn't run back. We were always hustling to get five men in defensive position, and then we always played percentage basketball at the offensive end.

The only problem was that we didn't quite finish the way we wanted, losing our last two regular-season games to Dallas and San Antonio for a 55-27 record. As it turned out, we needed one of those two games for a second-round homecourt advantage.

Garfield Heard was coaching the 10-71 Mavericks in our 81st game, and it was all over for those guys. He just told his team, "Go out and have fun." No pressure. One of their big guys, Terry Davis, was even taking three-pointers and making them. This is what's known in the NBA as "free-stroking." Guys you never thought would take a shot were firing them up and they were going in.

The Mavs beat us, 128–123, meaning we had to win at San Antonio to get second-round home court. We were up by two when David Robinson put in a shot that replays showed was after the buzzer. Hugh Evans was the lead official and ruled it good. There's no way in the world you could fault Hugh for a call that close, because after the game we had to run the video back a couple of times to make sure ourselves. But in a situation that important, I think the powers that be in the NBA should do anything and everything to ensure that the proper call is eventually made. If that means looking at a television replay, so be it.

Think about this: If the right call is made, we have homecourt advantage in the second round. It could be the deciding factor in that series. And think about the business aspect, the additional revenues that clubs reap for an extra homecourt playoff game. For the fairness of the sport, I believe there are times when the replay can be a tremendously useful tool, especially when the clock has run out.

We had to get over that sting and play the Los Angeles Clippers in a best-of-five, first-round series. We had beaten them 4–0 in the regular season, but I've always believed that too much is made of head-to-head results in the regular season. The slate is wiped clean once the playoffs begin.

The Rockets hadn't won a playoff round since 1987, but we were extremely sharp in a 117–94 opening-game win. However, Larry Brown—a coach I really admire for getting his teams to play tough defense and display high intensity—had them ready in Game Two, and they evened the series with a 95–83 win.

The big factor was that we didn't have Vernon Maxwell, who had suffered a left wrist injury and was wearing a cast on it. We had to go with 6-2 Winston Garland against a 6-6 Ron Harper at the two-guard position. Winny really hung in there and battled, but we could only gain a split in the two games in Los Angeles. So it came down to Game Five on a Saturday afternoon at the Summit.

That fifth game really forged a bond for me with Vernon Maxwell, who could have been a hero just by missing the whole series, which would have demonstrated his value to the team. But Max was determined to play in Game Five, wrist injury or no injury. The doctors were recommending that he not play, but Max took off that cast and went to work. In a tense, roller-coaster game, we were down by one with less than a minute to play when Maxwell reared up in front of the Clippers' bench to hit a three-pointer that proved to be the difference.

It's hard to put into words the vast ramifications that Maxwell's

shot had on our franchise. Had we lost that series, the whole public perception of Rockets basketball would have changed. People
would have forgotten our 41-11 finish. People would have forgotten about Maxwell missing most of the series. To be honest,
I didn't feel that viselike pressure at the time, but in retrospect I
can see how we might have been viewed by the public as just
another first-round Rockets flop if Max didn't sink that three-
pointer.

It was almost like a movie. Maxwell had always been a thorn in
Larry Brown's side after the Spurs traded him while Larry was the
coach. It was as though Max just had that special wand against his
ex-coach, and Vernon came back from that wrist injury just in the
nick of time.

Bottom line? We had survived. We had finally made that definitive first step in the direction that an aspiring champion must
inevitably take.

Against Seattle in Round II, it was strictly a homecourt series
through six games, with each club responding in its own building.
During that series, the Coach of the Year Award was announced:
Pat Riley won it, and I was just one vote behind. I considered it a
great honor to be up there so high in the media voting. Meanwhile,
The Sporting News named me as its Coach of the Year. That meant
even more to me, because the voting was done by the coaches. I
can't express how flattered I was to be recognized by my peers. It
melted me.

In Game Seven at Seattle Center Coliseum, we came out and
played a first half that indicated we were ready to break the homecourt trend. We were up by ten at the break, but Seattle came
out strong in the second half, chipping away at our lead and eventually going up by as much as six in the fourth quarter. We fought
hard to tie the score behind some great basketball by Robert
Horry, probably some of the best of his rookie year. He had two
dunks and two free throws in our comeback.

Inside two minutes, Derrick McKey gave the Sonics a two-point
lead with an 18-footer. Hakeem answered with a 12-foot turnaround. Our defense held on their next possession, and then we
worked the ball in to Hakeem again. They doubled quickly, and

Hakeem found Horry with a perfect hook pass on the weak side. Robert released a 16-footer as the shot clock went off. *Good.* Rockets by two with 32 seconds left.

Seattle posted up Ricky Pierce, who made a tough turnaround to tie it with 23 seconds remaining. We called timeout. We wanted to use as much of the clock as we could before shooting. Our strategy was to shoot with four seconds or less remaining. We were going for the win or, at the very least, we'd have a tie and overtime.

Seattle pressed as we inbounded the ball. We kept our poise and ran a post-up for Hakeem. Again, the Sonics doubled and Hakeem found Max, who quickly passed to Kenny in the corner. As the buzzer sounded, his shot hit the rim and bounced away. We were so close to advancing to the next round.

In the overtime, the lead seesawed until Sam Perkins made a big turnaround to put them up by three with 24 seconds to go. Hakeem's jump-hook in the lane put us down by one. There were 17 seconds left. We had to foul or they would run out the clock. The Sonics inbounded to McKey and we grabbed him, putting him on the line. He missed both free throws.

On the next possession, we again went to Hakeem. He passed out to Maxwell, who dribbled left and let the shot go. His jumper hit the rim and bounced away. We fouled in desperation on the rebound, and two Seattle free throws made it 103–100. We had a chance for a final shot, but Hakeem's desperation three-pointer didn't come close. We had ended the season the way it had begun—with a loss to the Seattle SuperSonics.

In our closing meeting of the season, I talked about the home-court advantage and emphasized the importance of all 82 regular-season games. "Never mind those last two games," I said. "What about other times during the year when we lost to low-ranked teams because we weren't mentally ready? That's what homecourt advantage is all about. We can't lose those games if we want to be champions. We have to get every possible advantage."

I just knew when I left the room that the message had sunk in. It was a simple talk, designed to show that a victory over Minnesota is just as important as a victory over Chicago.

As we broke up for the summer, I had a good feeling. I knew we had fared well against the four teams still playing. And I knew how close we had come to being in the Western Conference Finals.

The 1993–94 season could be very special, I thought.

The stage was set for us to put on a show the city of Houston would never forget.

15

IN THE SUMMER of 1993, we learned that the Rockets would be getting a new owner. Charlie Thomas sold the team to Florida businessman Leslie Alexander, ending Charlie's eleven-year reign as the head of the franchise. We had always been like a family with Charlie; we were comfortable in his presence. The news that the team had been sold came when I was in Utah for the Rockets' summer camp; general manager Steve Patterson and I returned home to meet Les for the press conference.

Right away, I could see Les was extremely upbeat about the team. He said he had a lot of respect for me, which, to be honest, was quite a relief to hear. So often new owners come in and have preconceived ideas about whom they want to have for their coach.

If a new owner questioned or doubted you, it would add a new complication to our team's development. But Les was supportive from day one, and I liked the things he was talking about. He said he was going to do everything he could possibly do as an owner to help us bring a championship team to Houston. I was also pleased when he told us the Rockets should be close to the community and give back to the community.

It was a good first impression.

Shortly after the announcement that Les was taking over, we acquired a key player in Mario Elie. It was a deal we had been working on all summer with Portland. I had watched Mario the previous year when he took over for the injured Clyde Drexler; Mario took the floor with such energy. He was one of the guys in this league that I really respected because of his warrior approach, and I felt he could be a great addition to our club with his versatility, attitude, and toughness.

The deal was similar to the one that brought us Scott Brooks. The Blazers needed room in their salary cap to sign free agent Chris Dudley, so we were able to get Mario for only a second-round draft choice.

The other key addition to our '93–94 club would be rookie point guard Sam Cassell. Sam had played on a very talented Florida State team; his teammate, Doug Edwards, was drafted by Atlanta, and his running mate at guard, Charlie Ward, was later drafted by the New York Knicks. Another young Florida State guard, Bob Sura, would eventually be drafted in the first round by Cleveland.

Sam was an exciting player who brought a lot of flair to the game. We hoped he would add penetration off the dribble to our attack. We were always trying to add different dimensions to our team; Elie and Cassell would add a lot of depth to the ballclub.

I asked Les Alexander if I could hire another assistant coach, and Les agreed. I was looking for a young coach to complement our veterans, Carroll Dawson and Bill Berry. Larry Smith came to mind; I loved his blue-collar approach to the game when he played. I didn't know if he was planning on playing any more or if he was even interested in getting into coaching. He was surprised when I called him out of the blue.

Larry told me he had been thinking about coaching for a couple of years. He had been saving scouting reports and studying them while watching a lot of videotape. He said he would be honored to work for the Rockets.

Before we got to training camp, there was a bombshell announcement that Steve Patterson was being relieved of his duties. I had a great relationship with Steve, and we worked well together. I had expressed this to Les early on, and he was willing to give it a try for a while, but after a month or so he made the decision to release Steve.

It was a loss. I have to admit that. But when I talked to my Ann Arbor attorney, Phil Fichera, he explained to me that it's very common in any business that when new management comes in, things like this are going to happen.

I had to respect our new owner's wishes to come in and do it his way. So, while it was a loss not to have Steve, we just had to move on.

By the time we gathered in Galveston, I felt strongly that every member of the preceding team had left the '92–93 season with a lesson deeply embedded in his mind: We had to go out and try to beat *every* team. The effort had to be there not only against the plus-.500 teams, but also the lottery teams. We had a lot of hope and confidence that we were close. Sure, you're going to lose some in the course of a long season, but if we came to play every night and kept our eye on the goal of homecourt advantage, I felt we had a chance to do some wonderful, exciting things.

In our opening dinner after Media Day, I got up before the team and said that I thought we were a championship-caliber team. This was shortly after Michael Jordan's stunning retirement, which most people felt had opened the door to the title for a lot of teams. I said that I wasn't going to talk about championship possibilities a lot in public, but that I felt this team had what it took.

"Deep down inside, I think it's a realistic goal," I told our players. "Let's get to work. Let's become a better team. Let's go after it."

Why bring the word *championship* into our vocabulary right there? Because the teams in the finals of '93—Chicago and Phoenix—were clubs we had enjoyed success against. We knew we were in that category.

Training camp went well again. The players were receptive and worked hard. We opened with a solid home win over New Jersey and then went out west and won road games at Portland and Golden State. It's the old cliché, one game at a time; you just look at the problems presented by a specific opponent and go from there with tunnel vision. I knew this: We were going into each game with a lot of confidence, and our defense was the key. On offense, we had a meat-and-potatoes approach, especially when the game was tight in the fourth quarter. When you exploit

Hakeem's strength, the defense has a difficult choice: Do they cover him with one man or double-team and leave a spot-up shooter open? If we were close in the fourth quarter, we felt we had a great chance to win. And this confidence began to snowball.

After the win over Golden State, there was a press conference the next day to announce the club was extending my contract. Les was acting on the things he had said to me, and I felt we were establishing a strong, close working relationship. In that merry month of November, everything was positive. We didn't always play great, but we kept finding ways to win with different heroes stepping up.

One night, against a struggling Philadelphia team, we were 12 down in the fourth quarter, but reserve forward Matt Bullard came through with 11 points down the stretch and we pulled out the game by four. That was typical of what was going on; it seemed like we had a different star each game, and I felt great about that. It was a sign that we were becoming a true team.

Yes, we were going to Hakeem the majority of the time. But once the defense committed, the ball would start moving and the open man would get the shot. Bullard was a guy who we felt, with work, could be a solid player. His biggest attraction was that he was 6-10 and had excellent three-point shooting range. Once he was in his shooting motion, a guy rotating out wasn't going to block his shot because of the high release. Matt's strengths perfectly fit our system.

We were 10-0 when most people figured our streak would end. We were at Utah on a back-to-back assignment, and it happened to be my forty-fifth birthday. Well, our guys gave me a wonderful present with a gutsy overtime win. We were two points down with 2.1 seconds lift in regulation and needed a clutch play. There wasn't enough time to get the ball to Hakeem, so during a timeout we decided to let Mario take it and create. He made a strong drive, drew the foul, and canned the pressure free throws.

On and on it went. Different games, different heroes. It was exhilarating to see our basketball team play with such purpose and unity.

Wins against Sacramento, the Clippers, and Milwaukee made

us 14-0, and then came a much-anticipated trip to New York City. The Knicks were 11-2 and doing some talking in the papers about our streak. NOT IN OUR HOUSE, the tabloid headlines declared.

We were out to tie the 15-0 mark established by the 1948–49 Washington Capitols, who had been coached by Red Auerbach. For a regular season game on December 2 to have that much meaning was good for our team: As a coach, you always try to simulate the pressure you'll face later in the playoffs, and here was a situation where we all wanted that game and New York definitely didn't want to give it to us. We were going to see some playoff-type intensity, which was something I wanted our players to experience.

It turned out to be a game that we pretty much dominated. Hakeem got 37 points, and we doubled Patrick Ewing and forced them to take outside shots that weren't going down. We got a tremendous 14-rebound game off the bench from Carl Herrera, and Elie, who had a chipped bone in his right hand but was determined to play in his hometown, gave us 19 inspired minutes and scored his only basket with his left hand. Chipped bone or no chipped bone, there was no way we could hold Mario back.

The only problem that night was what happened *after* the game. The trip from New York to Atlanta turned into a nightmare.

We took a bus from Madison Square Garden out to the airport. But the guy in the truck who came to escort us to the plane didn't have the right papers. We waited for an hour to clear up the problem. When we finally got on the plane and made it to Atlanta, we discovered our bus was three terminals away and that the trains weren't working.

That took another hour. By the time we got to the hotel and flopped into our beds, it was 4 A.M.

With that kind of short sleep and with the emotion of winning a big game in New York, we just didn't have it the next night against the Hawks. They trampled us 133–111, so we had to be content with sharing that opening-act with the '48–49 Capitols.

We knew the streak had to end sometime, and if somebody was going to beat us, it didn't hurt as much coming from a Lenny Wilkens team. He's a coach I really respect. I've always admired the way Lenny's teams take on his personality: They play smart and with poise.

The really impressive thing was that we went on to win seven more in a row after the Atlanta setback. A couple of nights after losing to the Hawks, we were in Cleveland and down seven with 2:43 to go. "Hang in there," I said. "I believe we're going to win this game."

We scratched and clawed and found a way to pull it out. Maxwell hit a right-wing trey with 31 seconds to go, and we stole a game that Cleveland had led for the opening 47:28. These were the little clues that were telling us it was a different kind of season, a special season.

When we came home 16-1, a group of about two hundred fans met us at the airport to express their appreciation for our spectacular start. Everybody was contributing, and everybody was getting their share of the glory.

Otis Thorpe got on a roll a couple of nights later against Charlotte. I decided to leave Otis in at the end so he could reach that rare 40-point milestone. Otis was such an everyday worker, a guy who would grind out those double-doubles—double-figure points, double-figure rebounds. Always battling in the trenches. When a guy like that is having a big night, you want to give him every opportunity to enjoy the spotlight.

It seemed our winning streak was taking on a life of its own. When you're on that kind of roll, you need some luck to go with the skill. We were down by three to Miami on our home court on December 9 with 3.6 seconds to go. Miami's Harold Miner elected not to foul in that situation with Max about 35 feet away. *Boom.* Maxwell spun around and made one of his patented miracle three-pointers to send the game into overtime. Another dodged bullet, another magic moment.

But as well as we were playing, Seattle was doing just as well. The Sonics only had one loss when they came into the Summit on December 11. In an extremely physical game that reminded me of an old Detroit–Green Bay football game on Thanksgiving Day, we got down in the trenches and won, 82–75, holding the Sonics to .316 shooting.

The finishing touch to our 22-1 start came in San Antonio, when Maxwell's jumper beat the buzzer to give us a hard-fought win against an improving Spurs team. On the Riverwalk after the game, I ran into Rockets beat writers Robert Falkoff and Eddie Sefko at a favorite watering hole. We spent a couple of hours enjoying the evening. They commended the team on our great start, and I responded by saying, "Guys, there's something special happening here. There's a spirit on this team, a positive force that you can feel. They believe they can win every time they step on the floor."

After that seven-game losing streak the previous year, we had gone 63-12 in the regular season—a tremendous span of solid basketball. We had found our identity. We had learned how to win, and our confidence was soaring.

However, what goes up must inevitably come down.

We began to lose a few. Denver beat us at home and we got mauled at Phoenix on Christmas Day. The way we failed to run back on defense, we were just playing Santa Claus for the Suns.

We came to the start of the New Year 24-4, but from January 13 to January 20 we lost as many games as we had lost the entire season. We fell 120–102 at Washington and 82–76 to a Chicago team without Jordan. We came home and promptly lost 95–83 to the Celtics, then went back on the road and dropped our fourth in a row, a tough 111–106 loss to Denver in double overtime.

There was some talk within the team about shot distribution, as there always is when things are going poorly. But the biggest gripe was the way I was substituting, especially in the fourth quarter. I was doing things a little differently from other teams. Usually, starters finish the game. But we would finish some games with Hakeem and sometimes with as many as four nonstarters. I hadn't set out to change the way I used our personnel, it just seemed to happen.

We usually rested Hakeem late in the third quarter and started the final quarter with him and the reserves. We always seemed to be in close games; most of our fourth quarters were nip-and-tuck. With five or six minutes remaining, the customary time to get the starters back in the game, I'd have to start making decisions. Did the combination of players on the floor have control of the game? If this lineup had lost a lead or was struggling, the decision was easy: starters back in. But most of the time it wasn't that clear-cut. In a tense fourth quarter when every possession is crucial, I had to judge if the players in the game were attuned to the competitiveness of the situation. I had to appraise the lineup individually and as a whole. Sometimes a player didn't appear to be accomplishing much statistically, scoring baskets and getting rebounds, but he was doing the little things that help us win: setting picks, making good passes, playing solid defense. Just because a player isn't scoring shouldn't be a reason to take him out of the game.

A big factor is how the starter played earlier in the game. If he was having an exceptional night, he deserves to get back in the game. But sometimes, the replacement is also having a good game. This really makes it tough. I try to find a way to have them both in if there's a way to match up favorably with the other team, but if that isn't possible, I give the nod to the starter.

It isn't always fair to the reserve, but it's something a player coming off the bench must learn to accept. If the starter was having an average or below-average night and the reserve was getting the job done, I felt comfortable leaving the reserve in to finish the game. This sometimes meant a starter might not play at all in the fourth quarter.

I liked our starting lineup of Smith, Maxwell, Horry, Thorpe, and Olajuwon. But I also had some valuable role players coming off the bench. Scott Brooks could get the team under control and make sure we'd run a solid play. Mario Elie was such a fierce competitor; he loved the challenge of taking their toughest player at big guard or small forward and making him work for everything he got.

Matt Bullard was a streak shooter who could keep the defense honest when we passed inside, and Carl Herrera, an emotional player, had the ability to grab big rebounds and play aggressive defense. All of these guys, at one time or another, finished games. I knew every player wanted to play, especially when the game was on the line in the fourth quarter. I was sensitive to their feelings, but I had to keep my mind focused on my primary job, which was finding ways to win.

This approach was getting great results. We rarely lost leads and we pulled out a lot of games that could have gone either way. Our players dealt with it remarkably well when we were winning. I realized it wasn't easy for them and I appreciated their sacrifice. When we did start to lose games, it became more of an issue.

I talked to just about every player one-on-one about playing time and what his role was supposed to be. Kenny Smith was affected the most because I was generally going with Scott Brooks in the fourth quarter. It wasn't what Kenny was or wasn't doing; it was the calming effect Scotty had on the team late in the game. I felt secure when Scott was directing the team and I believed the players felt the same way, too.

I explained to Kenny that I felt he was a valuable part of our team and that he was helping us win games. But Scotty was helping us, too. I had to find ways to use all the players.

Kenny expressed his feelings in a professional way, and I understood his disappointment. Otis Thorpe's situation wasn't as drastic; there were only a few occasions when he sat out the last quarter. He had been a starter most of his career and was used to finishing games. He wanted to discuss my strategy.

Robert Horry didn't air any negative feelings when we talked, but he did express his frustrations to the media after a game in which he didn't play in the fourth quarter. "I'm a phantom starter," Horry said.

Vernon Maxwell came right to the point with me. "Rudy, I don't like it worth a damn," Maxwell said. "I'm a competitor. I want to be out there. I'll accept it when we win, but I still don't like it."

Actually, Max was very good about sharing his minutes if the game was in hand. He'd often tell me, when I was getting ready to put him back in the game, to let the backup stay in, especially when the reserve was having a good game.

Carl Herrera wanted a bigger role on the team. We were using him as our third big man, playing behind Otis Thorpe and when we rested Hakeem. But Carl also wanted to play some small forward. In a private meeting with Carl, I wrote on the blackboard the names of the players in their positions. I showed him he was the player behind our two big men. He was a very important part of the rotation. The only other player in Carl's position was Richard Petruska, who was a rookie and not ready to play regularly.

I pointed at the small-forward position: Horry, Elie, Bullard. Three players splitting 48 minutes. Elie did get some two-guard minutes, but there weren't enough minutes to keep three players happy, much less a fourth.

And who would fill Carl's role if he were playing small forward? Carl did have some small-forward skills, but I felt he had some big pluses at the big-forward spot. He had good speed and quickness and could outrun most big guys in the fast break. He was active and could outquick them in the halfcourt game.

At the other forward position, this advantage would be negated because small forwards are generally more athletic. I appreciated that he wanted to do more for the team, but I couldn't promise him any minutes at small forward.

The toughest thing a coach has to do is make his players understand the benefits of sacrificing for the team. They have to believe that what's being given up is fair exchange for winning. I want every player on the team to feel appreciated and be happy with his role. I began to realize I was being naive and too idealistic—and also forgetful. How could I not remember how much I had wanted to play and how it bothered me when I felt I got shortchanged?

It was almost impossible to have everyone on the team happy. You can only play five players at a time and you have twelve very competitive players on the team. It's natural to have some players dissatisfied with their roles. In fact, it's probably healthy. I wouldn't want players who could easily accept not playing and not strive to earn more time. But I also wouldn't want players who don't take the needs of their teammates into consideration. Everybody wants to contribute. There has to be a balance. Somewhere between those two extremes is the answer.

IN LATE JANUARY, we got a call from Detroit personnel director Billy McKinney. The subject of an Horry–Sean Elliott trade came up. We hadn't been looking to change the team at the time, but you have to listen to all possibilities. We hadn't found a replacement for Steve Patterson yet, which made it difficult to scan the league for these opportunities. Before we acquire any asset, we always do tape work, so we broke out tapes on Elliott. The image you have of a player is not always an accurate one until you put him under the microscope.

Elliott was a good offensive player. He really ran the floor well. He'd get layups or quick shots from the wing. He was a good outside shooter with three-point range and had an exceptionally quick first step on drives. When he was with the Spurs, they would clear a side of the floor and isolate him for one-on-one situations. He often exploded by his defender for a dunk or an easy shot.

Elliott was also an unselfish player. He'd give the ball up to the open man. We had heard he was a quality person and got along well with people. On the negative side, we felt Robert was a better defender and rebounder. Horry did a little bit of everything on the floor. He was versatile. He was a better than average defender. With a 6-10 frame, jumping ability, and great wingspan, he could be a factor protecting the basket with blocked shots. He was a better than average rebounder, but we felt he could improve there because he was taller than most small forwards. He passed the ball well, especially to the post.

I felt Robert was a good standstill spot shooter, but he wouldn't always shoot the open shot. When Robert first attended our summer workouts, I'd have players in three-on-three situations. Robert would constantly pass up open shots. I began urging him always to look at the basket.

"You're a good shooter; you can make those shots," I told Robert.

It was something the staff constantly had to drill into Robert's mind. He was unselfish, which was admirable, but you can't overdo it. Our offensive system was based on causing a double-team, then moving the ball until we found the open man. If the open man doesn't shoot and passes to a man more closely guarded, the effectiveness of the offense decreases.

Robert was such a good kid. He had so much respect for the veterans that he would often pass up his shots to put the ball in their hands. The defender on Horry would feel he could double our big man and not worry about being penalized because Robert wouldn't pull the trigger.

Horry didn't always play this way. There were games when he was aggressive on offense. But we didn't know what to expect from game to game. We wondered what it would be like to keep the defense honest with Elliott's more aggressive offense. But we also wondered: Could Elliott defend well enough to be a positive?

It came down to this: We felt it was vital to take some of the offensive load off Hakeem. We had to wonder if we could win a title by running our offense through Hakeem eighty percent of the time. Were we putting him in physical jeopardy by working him so hard? We knew Elliott couldn't defend or rebound as well as Horry, but he could give us different ways to put points on the board without going through Hakeem.

It was an agonizing time. I really liked Robert as a person. He was the first player I had drafted as a head coach. He was a good player with a lot of potential for growth. It wasn't a popular move with my family: Sophie had gotten to know Robert and helped him find furniture when he first came to Houston.

Matt Bullard also had to be part of the deal because of salary-cap considerations. I also had very strong feelings for Matt. The trade was announced on Friday, and by Saturday morning Elliott was at Stouffer's Hotel across the street from the Summit, waiting for a 5-P.M. practice.

Sean had taken his physical early in the day and some of the results were coming in. A problem with his kidney showed up on one of the tests. I spent sixteen hours that Saturday talking with kidney specialists from all over the country. There was no definite conclusion. His particular problem could cause him trouble in the future, but it was something you could not absolutely predict. He may go through life and not be affected by it at all. Some specialists said it was something he could play with; others said it was something we should not ignore.

I talked to Les Alexander and the whole staff, weighing the pros and cons. We decided the investment and the risk were too great to take. We would negate the trade. Not having a general manager to do the intensive research it takes to make a solid trade was costly. We were now in a terrible situation. Robert and Matt had to get on a plane in Detroit and fly back to Houston.

How would they deal with the fact that we wanted another player more than we wanted them? There was nowhere I could go to get advice on how to handle this situation because it hadn't happened before.

I had talked to both players immediately after the trade was made and said nothing but positive things to them. I also told them how much I liked them and what a tough decision it was. When they came back, I met with them individually and told them I could understand bad feelings toward me and management. I was willing to accept that.

Robert was the one I thought would be affected more, but he came back with a pretty solid attitude. It was almost one of relief. He told strength coach Robert Barr, "Man, it was cold up there."

I knew Robert was sensitive and that it hurt him to think we would let him go. Looking back on it now, I think the aborted trade triggered something in Robert. It changed his approach to the game. Later, when he got open shots, he'd say, "Screw it, I'm putting it up there. What else can they do? They've already traded me."

I always talk about turning a negative into a positive. That's what Robert did. Yes, there was definitely a scar there that had to heal. But Robert was giving the healing process a chance. It took great strength and character to come through this the way he did. Something like this could have completely torn the team apart.

Matt Bullard had a different reaction. He was openly bitter when we met. He was in the last year of his contract and felt he would have had an opportunity to play more in Detroit and increase his market value. He also felt betrayed. Matt had been a big supporter of our system; he had worked hard with our strength coach to develop the body he needed to be an NBA player. He appreciated that the organization had the patience to wait for his development. And now those feelings were gone.

I tried to be as positive as I could with Matt. I hoped his attitude wouldn't hurt his play.

The controversy had died down a bit as we headed into the

later part of the season. Our backcourt rotation changed; Sam Cassell was really coming on in practices and when he got into games. I put him into a game against Orlando on March 1 and he was fearless taking the ball to the basket. Sam led us to victory over Shaquille O'Neal and company, and I began to see how the rookie could add a penetrating dimension that we didn't have.

Sam's flamboyant style gained him many supporters. On my weekly call-in radio show, fans were singing his praises and asked about the possibility of Sam starting in place of Kenny Smith. I said that I had given the possibility some thought, but I hadn't made a decision. In hindsight, it was a mistake on my part. I shouldn't have publicly voiced that opinion. It got picked up by the papers and became an item. I had caused a distraction with a statement about a thought.

Kenny told the media he felt betrayed. In my attempt to answer a caller's question, it came out differently than I expected and was misunderstood. It was a valuable lesson. I had always been careful to handle things professionally with the media, but I had to remember I was always vulnerable.

Fortunately, this incident seemed to spur Kenny on. I decided that while Cassell wouldn't start, he would become part of the rotation. Smith responded well the rest of the regular season, and Brooks became the odd man out. You just can't find time in a 48-minute game for three point guards, and Scotty was very professional about it. He became the leader of our bench. Rather than sulking or pouting, he pumped everybody up and was still a big factor for us just by the way he handled his role as a supporter.

It's hard to believe that after a 22-1 start we were actually passed in our division race. Jerry Tarkanian had started the year as the San Antonio coach, but our old friend John Lucas took over early. Luke's enthusiasm rubbed off on a talented Spurs team, and they went on to an unbelievable tear through the middle of the season.

We were like a 400-meter man who sprints to the lead and gets passed late in the race. But at that moment of the race when the real pain sets in, we showed the courage and determination to get that second wind and charge back to win the Midwest Division race.

It just shows how competitive the league is. You'd think that a 22-1 start would enable you to cruise on through. It was a great sign of character for our team to come back and really meet force with force.

In late March, we went on a crucial five-game road trip. We lost the first game in Phoenix, and Hakeem received a one-game suspension for putting his hand on official Bill Spooner. Hakeem had hit the floor in a scramble for a loose ball. He felt he was fouled. On his knees, he gestured toward the official, trying to get his attention. Spooner was looking downcourt where a fast break was in progress. He began running toward the play and Hakeem's hand made contact. It shocked Spooner.

I knew Hakeem didn't intend to hurt the official in any way. He didn't even mean to touch him. But I believe the league acted properly in handing out a one-game suspension. The officials in this league must be protected.

So now we had to play Sacramento without our big guy. The problem escalated when Maxwell and Herrera were ejected in the first half. I wasn't a happy guy as I went to the locker room. We were down by five at the half and without three key weapons.

All we did in the second half with a shorthanded roster was score 74 points and win the game going away.

Rookie Eric Riley started at center and did a good job. Sam Cassell was phenomenal, using his size to post up their smaller point guards, Spud Webb and Bobby Hurley. Other guys pitched in, and it seemed like that game gave us renewed belief in our system. It showed that we had good players who could step up in a crucial situation. If we played defense and moved the ball around, we had plenty of guys who could put the ball in the basket.

As we headed down the stretch, the Most Valuable Player race boiled down to Hakeem and David Robinson, and I felt it shouldn't even be a contest. Hakeem's assists were at an all-time high and his turnovers were down. He had done it all against the great players with amazing consistency.

There was a big NBC game on April 9 pitting us against San Antonio, and the network played it up as a battle for the division and for the MVP trophy. When we won that one, it seemed to be the capper to Hakeem's MVP year. But it was really the next night at Denver when we broke San Antonio's back by storming from behind to beat the Nuggets on a last-second shot from Hakeem. On the game's deciding play, Cassell made a great penetration move, drew Dikembe Mutombo to him, and found Hakeem on the right baseline for the game-winner.

The division was ours and we still had a chance at getting the No. 1 overall seed until Seattle nipped us, 100–97, on April 16. Nevertheless, I felt good about our upcoming playoff situation.

We worked hard to get 58 wins, which meant we would have home court against anybody other than the Sonics. In the final week, our priorities were to get some key people a little rest and come up with what we felt would be our best twelve-man playoff roster.

We had been looking for a veteran center to spell Hakeem in the playoffs. Riley had done some good things for us, but he was still raw and inexperienced. We wanted someone who understood what the playoffs were all about. That someone turned out to be Earl Cureton.

Earl had been part of Philadelphia's 1983 championship team, and he knew how to play the game inside. Plus, we felt he would add a stabilizing presence in our locker room, much like Tree Rollins had done the past couple of seasons.

The thought of adding Earl Cureton was something I had never even considered earlier in the season. Earl had been away from the NBA scene, playing with Magic Johnson's touring all-stars. But as we looked at what we would have to face, having a guy out there who wouldn't make a lot of mistakes and understood his role was very important. We felt Earl could talk to young players, too, in a way that wasn't condescending.

Chris Jent had been with us at the end of our regular season and made the playoff roster. For a young player, he showed poise and was a willing defender. We felt there might be situations where a guy like Jent could go in for a few possessions in a playoff atmosphere and help you. Also, we added Elie to the playoff roster; Mario had missed the previous six weeks after suffering a hand injury at Sacramento.

It had been a purposeful regular season. We went in with the goal of trying to be as efficient as we could and not underachieve in situations that had been troublesome for us in the past. Then, to be the pacer, have someone catch you, and then regroup—that was satisfying, too.

Overall, I was very pleased with our approach to the '93–94 season. We didn't get the best record in the league, but we knew the West was tough. Winning our division and having the second-best record meant we were definitely in the championship hunt.

I had set some pretty high goals in early October, and we had almost reached them all. We had put ourselves in position. But now we had to go out and execute. The playoffs were upon us, and we had to find a way to get it done.

16

I FELT THAT the Portland Trail Blazers, our first '94 playoff opponent, were what I call "a man's team." They might not have been the greatest shooting team, but each of their players would physically challenge you. It was going to be a series where their offensive rebounding would be key, because a big part of their attack was the missed shot and the putback.

We also knew Portland was an athletic team and would take the ball hard to the basket with guys like Rod Strickland, Clyde Drexler, and Cliff Robinson. Robinson had made some brash comments, saying he would "kill" Robert Horry if he were matched against Horry as small forward. Horry wasn't the least bit intimidated, but he knew Robinson was a dangerous offensive weapon who could go inside and also hit the three-pointer. Robert would have his work cut out for him defensively.

At the power positions, the Blazers would come with Buck Williams, one of the best rebounders of all time, and X-factor Chris Dudley. After missing most of the season because of a knee injury, Dudley would give them an additional six fouls at center, and he could rebound and block shots. Another factor to consider.

On our side, we had Elie coming back from his broken hand. It's difficult to predict how a guy will respond after missing six weeks, but Mario is such a hardworking ballplayer that I felt if anybody could get himself physically ready to do it, Mario was the man.

In Game One, the Blazers came out committed to double-teaming Hakeem, which put the burden of proof on our outside shooters. Fortunately, the shots were going down for us. We shot .533, including 9 of 16 three-pointers. Vernon hit some big ones down the stretch, which simply meant we had executed our system in a 10-point victory. If people want to take away a high-percentage play inside, the payoff is the three-pointer. When we hit those, we're a very efficient offensive team.

"We have to change our strategy," Drexler said after the game. "We drop way down to cover Hakeem, and Maxwell shoots so quick. It's a matter of staying closer to home and not paying so much attention to Hakeem."

We weren't sure if the Blazer guards would actually do that on a consistent basis, but that's the way it worked out in Game Two. Portland gave our outside troops supreme respect by electing to single-cover Hakeem for the most part. Early on, Hakeem didn't shoot well over the long reach of Dudley, but as the game wore on, Hakeem warmed up. He got to the foul line 18 times, hit seven of his last nine shots, and finished with 46 points.

While Hakeem's offense drew most of the rave reviews, it was a tremendous defensive play late in the game that sealed the win for us. It was one of the most amazing plays I've ever seen by a big man. We were only up by six when Strickland stole an Olajuwon pass for what seemed like a cinch breakaway layup. Understand that Hakeem was standing flat-footed when Strickland cut off the passing lane with a full head of steam. Hakeem started back late against one of the quickest guards in the league. He caught him right at the basket and timed his leap perfectly to block Strickland's shot out of bounds. It took superhuman effort to make a play like that. A lot of players, when they throw a bad pass, drop their heads in disappointment and assume that's one that got away, especially when the stealer has a breakaway. But Hakeem never gave up. The enthusiasm generated by that play spurred us on to an 11-point win and a 2–0 lead in the best-of-five series.

So far, so good.

But we couldn't keep it going when the series shifted to Portland for Game Three. The Blazers were a team with a lot of pride; many of their players had been in title series in 1990 and 1992. When you're feeling pretty good about what you've done and the other team feels like a wounded tiger protecting its home territory, that psychology becomes all-important.

Our defense just completely broke down. Strickland had 25 points and 15 assists, and Buck Williams—never known for his shooting—was 9 of 10 from the floor. One of our main defensive rules involves how we're going to funnel someone. We try to keep the offense from coming down the middle, because when an opposing player penetrates the lane, nine times out of ten it'll make something good happen for his team; the dribbler either gets a high-percentage shot or he draws the defense, which opens passing lanes to his teammates. It also really exposes the offensive board for their aggressive rebounders. We were letting them go wherever they wanted, and we paid for it in a 118–115 loss.

The loss I could take, but the fundamental defensive breakdowns really disappointed me. I went over the tape and showed the breakdowns. If we didn't take away those strengths of theirs in Game Four, we were going to lose that one, too. And then it's a one-game deal where anything can happen.

We had two full days off in Portland to let the message sink in. We spent a lot of time on fundamentals, and we were back to our old selves in the first quarter of the fourth game.

With our defense swarming and helping, the Blazers could hit only 4 of 26 shots in the opening quarter and scored just 13 points. That set the tone for us to go on to a 92–89 clinching victory. As a general rule, the things we had worked on in practice had really paid off in limiting Portland's attack.

One rule about coaching that I had learned: You have to focus on a main theme in practice. If you think you can get five or six things done in a practice, you probably won't get anything done. Our main theme was controlling the penetration of their great athletes. By doing that, we were headed for the Western Conference Semifinals for the second year in a row.

When Strickland's desperation three-pointer missed the mark

at the buzzer, I embraced Blazers coach Rick Adelman, who wished me good luck in the next series. It turned out to be his last game with the Portland franchise. I've always had a lot of admiration for Rick because when the Blazers were winning conference championships, he was a hardworking coach who never drew a lot of attention to himself. He quietly and effectively did his job.

The system that the Blazers ran fit their personnel, but you're going to have cycles in this league. When you're on a down cycle because of injuries or age, it's always precarious, even for the better coaches.

Because we went four games with the Blazers and Phoenix swept Golden State, we had a quick turnaround for Round II. We had to take a long flight home in the wee hours of a Saturday morning because the Western Semifinals would start the next day.

By Saturday afternoon, our coaching staff had gathered at the office. Prior to our practice, we wanted to watch the end of the Denver–Seattle series. What a surprise! A most pleasant surprise.

The Sonics had run into a team in Denver that really gave us trouble, too. The Nuggets were young and talented and they were playing inspired basketball under Dan Issel. Somehow, the Nuggets pulled off a shocker in Game Five at Seattle; the sight of Dikembe Mutombo on the floor clutching the ball at the end of that remarkable upset will be remembered for a long, long time.

For us, the Denver victory was a gigantic break because now we were suddenly the team with homecourt advantage throughout the playoffs.

"That sounds good, but we still have to win the games," I cautiously said to the media.

Getting it done would mean beating some explosive Western teams. In the East, we wouldn't have to worry about the haunting presence of Michael Jordan, but clubs like New York and Indiana were playing well enough to earn championship rings.

Our next opponent was the Phoenix Suns. They were led by Charles Barkley. He was a flamboyant, big-personality guy. I remember scouting him on videotape when he was at Auburn; he was a unique player, only 6-5 and weighing about 270. He had more of a football player's body. Charles was extremely skilled. He could shoot from outside, but his primary strength was dominating the inside. He gave up height to his opponents, but he really knew how to use his body to get position and finish the play with a variety of shots.

The most amazing thing about Charles was his explosiveness when he jumped. It didn't seem possible that a man with his physique could fly above more streamlined athletes, but he did it all the time. The game I was scouting was close, and Charles got to the free-throw line late in the game for two important free throws. The camera zoomed in for a close-up. Right before Charles took the pressure shot, he looked at the camera and winked. Then he made the shot. I couldn't believe what I had just seen. I pushed the rewind button on the remote just to make sure. Yep—he winked!

Charles enjoys the game. He plays it with passion, but he always has fun. He was our major concern going into this series. He's tough to cover one-on-one, but when you double-team him, he's one of the best in the league at finding the open man.

The Suns were similar to us. They had dangerous three-point shooters in Dan Majerle and Danny Ainge. Kevin Johnson, their high-scoring point guard, was another big concern; he had blinding speed and was always dangerous when he had the ball. He was always looking for opportunities to penetrate. Coach Paul Westphal ran a lot of pick-and-rolls for him, but Kevin was just as dangerous bringing the ball down and spotting an opening to knife through on the dribble.

A.C. Green was a solid veteran at forward. He had won championships with the Lakers, and he brought a workmanlike attitude to their team. He was willing to do the dirty work—rebound, run the floor, play solid defense. They had good depth up front with offense-minded Cedric Ceballos and seven-footer Joe Kleine, who was an excellent outside shooter for a big man.

Our high spirits after the Denver upset were quickly dampened. The only positive thing I can say about Game One was that it came on Mother's Day, and I hope all the mothers had a great day because we sure didn't. There were about three-thousand empty seats at tipoff. We forged an 18-point lead, but the Suns fought back, and some clutch play by Kevin Johnson helped them gain a 91–87 victory. In just one game we had lost the homecourt advantage in the series.

The crowd story overshadowed the game story, and I understood how our players felt. Every playoff game you watch on television the arena is packed and the fans are going crazy but we didn't have that, so it hurt the players. Yes, it was a 2-P.M. game on Mother's Day and we knew a lot of people were doing other things, but the players felt that for such an important playoff game we deserved a full house.

Our team rallied behind that hurt feeling. When you have a cause like that, it gives you more energy and focus. As a coach, sometimes you don't care what's going to fire them up as long as *something* does. Anything to have a purpose.

Some of our players were publicly critical of the Game One support, and the emotion really came forth in Game Two. The Summit was sold out, and we scored 40 points in the third quarter. It seemed like a perfect scenario to heal all the hurt feelings. With 10 minutes to go, we led by 20. With 6:49 to go, we led by 17. With 2:37 to go, we were up by 10.

And when the game was over, Phoenix had won, 124–117, in overtime.

We had played with such intensity and fire, really taking control of the game. But mysteriously, in the fourth quarter we became tentative. We began to pass up good shots, and it became contagious. We would bypass an open opportunity, instead passing the ball to a covered teammate or driving into traffic. When we did take open shots, we were aiming the ball, trying to will it into the basket instead of shooting with the relaxed confidence we had in the first three quarters.

Momentum changed with the force of a tidal wave. They capitalized on every mistake we made on defense. If one of our guys was out of position, they not only scored, they scored a three-pointer. It was like a giant boulder crashing down a mountainside. We tried with all our might to hold it back, but it finally rolled over us. It was one of the most depressing moments of my entire career.

After the game, in the stunned locker room, we talked it over.

Some of the players admitted that even though we were playing well and had the lead, there was an underlying feeling of uncertainty, a lack of confidence. It baffled me. We had never lacked confidence in the past, especially in the fourth quarter. We prided ourselves on being a solid execution team late in the game. We had compiled amazing stats for holding leads or coming from behind to pull out a win.

Why now? Was the great confidence the veteran Suns displayed affecting our psyche, making us think we couldn't beat them no matter how big a lead we had? Those kinds of things had never bothered us before. I thought back to the New York game, when we were going for the 15-0 start; we had responded in a big way. I couldn't believe the theory that we were psyched out.

To make matters worse, after the game Matt Bullard criticized our offensive strategy down the stretch to the media. He said we ran the same play over and over, intimating that we just went to Hakeem and there was no diversity. It was out of character for Matt, but obviously the scar from the aborted Detroit trade hadn't healed. It was also wrong. We chart all the plays we run, and in the fourth quarter we ran 13 different plays. Most of them were designed to get the ball in Hakeem's hands, but this strategy had been the backbone of our success the whole season. Our system ran through Hakeem.

On some occasions, we went directly in to him, which was his favorite play. On other occasions, we started the play on the right side of the floor and swung it to him on the left. We also ran seven pick-and-rolls to try to get other players involved. The same shots we had in the 40-point third quarter were there in the fourth quarter, but we either passed them up or we missed them.

Losing causes so many ills. It's like a poison that can spread throughout the team. It eats away at the foundation and finally kills it. It causes all kinds of critical analysis from people away from the team—media, fans. The antidote for this poison is mental toughness—hanging together, relying on each other, and believing that no matter how bad things get, until that final buzzer sounds there is always a chance to turn it around.

We left right after the game for Arizona, and the flight out there seemed to take an eternity. That night in Phoenix, the coaches and I reviewed the tape of our disaster before going to bed. I was lying there around 4 A.M. when the phone rang. It was Sophie. She never calls at that hour on the road, so I first asked if everything was okay. She said, "Yeah, I just want to know if everything is okay with you."

She wanted me to know that even if we lost four straight, she would always know I gave it my best. She wanted to say that's all a person can do. When I got up the next day, that phone call gave me the extra strength I needed to deal with this tough situation.

We quickly heard about the same headline appearing in both Houston newspapers: CHOKE CITY.

That was about as low as you can ever get. As a coach, you think about labels that have a way of sticking to you and to your team. They can sometimes become a part of your identity well into the future. Losing big leads is a disease that coaches dread. That's how you lose your job. That's not to say people don't make big runs in this league, but somehow you've got to find a way to stop the bleeding. I know I wound up being the head coach of the Rockets because of that type of game, when we blew a 24-point lead.

I faced my greatest test. Could I get this team that I so strongly believed in refocused and believing in themselves again? It really is the essence of what coaching is all about: righting the ship, getting it headed back on course.

I contemplated what approach to take. I could see the players were in low spirits. They were wounded by being called "chokers." They needed to be encouraged, uplifted, and reinforced. I couldn't use falsehoods to convince them. It had to be based on logic and reasoning. I knew that if we could get big leads on the Suns, there was no reason we couldn't beat them. But words alone could not achieve the result we needed; I had to show the team the evidence. They needed to see for themselves the contrast in their aggressiveness from the first three quarters to the fourth quarter.

We had watched and edited the tape through the night, and there were many obvious examples. I wanted the meeting with the team to have more of a positive feel than a critical one, so we decided to show the edited video of the fourth quarter first, pointing out the situations where we didn't pull the trigger on open shots. I kept stopping the tape and saying to the players involved, "I believe you can make a high percentage of this shot and you know you can, too. You've made it a thousand times."

Then we put on the positive tape. It was more like a highlight tape. There were plays showing us executing with intense aggressiveness. We put in examples of our players taking shots with defenders hanging all over them and still drilling them. I started to see the brightness return to their faces. They began vocally responding to the plays on the screen.

"Way to take it to the hole, Max."

"Dreamshake."

"Nothing but net, Kenny."

We had three times as many highlights on the tape as tentative examples. The tape ended, and I began to speak.

"Amazing, isn't it? You all saw the difference. I know there is nobody here who can explain why something like this happened. Let's never let it happen again. We can never lose our confidence."

I saw heads nodding.

"You know we can beat these guys," I said. "If we can get up on them, we can beat them. You've all heard what they're calling us. People are jumping off the ship. All we have left is us. I want to tell you I believe in you guys and I believe we can win this series. I would say that even if we were down 0–3. You've proven it to me time and time again. Let's get back to being our old selves and turn this thing around."

For the first quarter of Game Three, it appeared the words had fallen on deaf ears. We shot a horrendous 4 of 17 in the opening period and trailed 29–15. The Phoenix fans were chanting about a sweep and some people in the stands were holding up chickens by the neck as illustrations that we were chokers.

I kept urging our guys to relax because I felt the problem was that everybody was trying *too* hard. It was now a matter of survival. We turned it up defensively. Seldom-used Chris Jent went in during the second quarter and made a couple of hustle plays. If the defense hadn't been there, we were going to go down 3–0, but the defense kept us afloat. To have the Suns' lead under double-digits at 48–40 was a positive going into halftime.

In the second half, our offense exploded behind Maxwell's 31 points. He kept driving the ball at their defense, and the Suns couldn't stop him. We kept running and scoring, building a lead that silenced the America West Arena. We wound up stunning them, 118–102, and it was about as emotional as I've ever felt after a game.

Enduring this crisis pulled our team closer. We had felt abandoned and isolated, and we could only look to each other for support. It was us against the world.

Believe me, it was one hell of a Friday the 13th for the Houston Rockets franchise. We were back in this series.

Still, we had to come back and do it again on Sunday. Winning once in Phoenix . . . maybe they weren't fully focused. To do it again would really require something extraordinary.

And extraordinary it was. With a show of great character and determination, we beat them again, 107–96, to even the series 2–2.

"It's not Choke City, it's Clutch City," owner Leslie Alexander shouted as we romped to the locker room.

Clutch City? It was a label we would happily have with us for a long time to come.

Late in Game Four, Hakeem made a block on a Charles Barkley shot that has to rank as one of the all-time best rejections. Barkley took the ball strong to the basket, and Hakeem met him high above the rim. The block was so pure and powerful that the ball slammed to the court with overwhelming authority.

It was symbolic: Hakeem had turned Barkley's attempted stuff around and the Rockets had turned the series around.

"The Rockets aren't chokers, they are men with a hell of a lot of character," I said in my media session. That comment came straight from the heart.

Otis Thorpe did a great job guarding Barkley straight up. We didn't want to double constantly because Barkley was too good at finding the open man. Even if we had double-teamed, we had made a coaching decision never to leave Dan Majerle alone. He was too dangerous behind the three-point line.

Vernon Maxwell carried out his assignment and didn't give Majerle many open looks. Majerle's confidence seemed to wane as the series wore on.

It was now being billed as the series with a homecourt *dis*advantage. Four games, four road wins. But we changed all that with a dominating effort and a blowout win in Game Five at the Summit. We won it, 109–96, and our big guys, Otis and Hakeem, led the way with 20 points apiece.

The fans were clearly back on our side, having met us at the airport when we returned from Phoenix. The pilot called me into the cockpit as we taxied into Hobby Airport and pointed out about five thousand people who were screaming and holding up signs. After all the negativity the previous week, this greeting really gave our guys that added spark to put on a great performance in Game Five.

Phoenix came back with its own gutsy effort in Game Six as veteran A.C. Green led the way. After three consecutive losses, we knew that the Suns would come out with high intensity in Game Six. Trying to beat a great team like that three times on its own court is asking a little much.

So it was do-or-die for both teams in Game Seven at our place. We had played all year talking about the importance of homecourt advantage, and this was a classic example of why you battle through those January and February games to stay a step ahead of the better clubs in the league. Being at home didn't assure us a win, but it certainly beat the alternative of having to play before a hostile crowd in Phoenix.

Hakeem was great with 37 points, but it was Sam Cassell's big game that really put us over the top. He came off the bench for 22 points and seven assists. We were up by five with 4:50 remaining when Sam hit a trey just before the 24-second buzzer. That was the shot that really put us in control of the game.

I've said it thousands of times that one of my favorite things in life is taking a negative and turning it into a positive. When Choke City turned into Clutch City, that was about as good as it gets.

I didn't know how much farther we were going to go, but I couldn't have been prouder of a team. I think we learned so much about ourselves in that Phoenix series. To go through those trials as a group and come out of it—it's something so great I wish everybody could feel that way just once in their lives. What a wonderful sense of accomplishment you have when a group pulls in the same direction and gets a seemingly impossible task done. That's what I think about when I recall that '94 Phoenix series. The sense of togetherness, of relying on the guy next to you is so special; basketball may be just a sport, but sports can say a lot about how the world works—or how it should.

We had to come out of the clouds pretty quickly, because facing the Utah Jazz in the Western Finals represented another strong challenge.

I have always been a big fan of Karl Malone. I was a scout when he broke into the league as a rather unheralded rookie from Louisiana Tech, and I watched him develop into one of the greatest power forwards of all time. I also scouted John Stockton at the college all-star tournament in Portsmouth when a lot of people didn't know who he was or where Gonzaga University was. I also happened to be scouting the Jazz in New Orleans during the preseason before Frank Layden stepped down and Jerry Sloan became their head coach. I spent an hour or two with those guys that night and really got a feel for how solid a guy Jerry is.

The Rockets and the Jazz share the same offensive philosophy, an inside-outside approach. We go in to Hakeem and they go to Karl; if the defense overcompensates, good ball movement gets you the open outside shot, and we each had the people who could knock it down.

I felt the big factor for Utah was when they got Jeff Hornacek from Philadelphia for Jeff Malone just before the '94 trading deadline. I remember when I first heard about that deal—it was like a nerve being hit. I thought it was a great deal for Utah because Hornacek would give them that pure outside shooter to go with a great assist man in Stockton and a great post threat like Malone.

This time, it was the Jazz who had to make the quick trip for Game One, and we took them down, 100–88. They didn't have fresh legs, and we knew it would be a much tougher challenge in Game Two.

May 25, 1994, was a day that Hakeem and the Rockets organization can reflect on with great pride. The day started with the news that Hakeem had won the MVP award. Commissioner David Stern made the trophy presentation prior to the game, and

Hakeem insisted that the whole team join him. I got goose bumps; it was another moment when I felt so proud of the gestures that our players were making for each other.

There's a picture of Hakeem passing the trophy up into the arms of his teammates. It was truly an inspiring moment for me just to be around people so giving. Hakeem then went out and used a 41-point, 13-rebound performance to give us a 2–0 series lead.

The Jazz came back strong with a 95–86 win in Game Three, so once again, Game Four would be pivotal for us. Either we would break their spirit a little by going up 3–1 or it would be a brand-new series.

Kenny Smith came up big with 25 points, and we were up by two with 13.5 seconds left. Utah inbounded the ball, and that's when all the craziness set in: As the Jazz were running their play, we noticed that the clock wasn't moving.

Horror. Shock. It's hard to describe the exact feeling when you look at the clock in that situation and it's not moving. Fortunately, we scrambled and got the stop when Tom Chambers missed a forced shot in the lane. We managed to run out what seemed like a never-ending clock, and the timekeeper, a guy named Wayne Hicken, was off the hook.

I never felt there was any foul play in the Hicken situation; it was just an unfortunate human error. Had Utah scored, it really would have been chaotic, but we survived and were now in position to wrap up the series in five.

Back in friendly surroundings at the Summit, the team and our fans were primed for a conference title. We made a statement right off the bat, jumping to an 8–0 lead. We led by 24 at the start of the fourth quarter and won, 94–83, to gain our first Western Conference championship since 1986. For us to beat a good Utah team, 4–1—a team with two guys headed for the Hall of Fame, a no-nonsense system, and a professional organization—it gave me the feeling that we were ready for the final, definitive step that could forever change the psyche of long-suffering Houston sports fans.

By finishing the series quickly, we had the opportunity to go back to Galveston while waiting for New York and Indiana to finish the Eastern Conference Finals. The Knicks made a gallant comeback to take it in seven. I thought back to the dreams I had as a kid growing up in my era: If you were out in the driveway and had the last shot of an imaginary game, it was against the Knicks at Madison Square Garden. Dave DeBusschere. Bill Bradley. Walt Frazier. That was what we dreamed about.

We had beaten the league's best offensive team—Phoenix—and now we had to take on its most physical defensive team—New York. The Knicks were coached by Pat Riley. We had had two play-off series against his L.A. Lakers, in 1986 and 1990. The Lakers were a freewheeling, fast-breaking team that could run you off the court. They also had the ability to execute the halfcourt game, directed by Magic Johnson and featuring center Kareem Abdul-Jabbar.

But Riley had totally different personnel with the Knicks, and they played a different brand of basketball. They would run when they had the opportunity, but basically, they were a grind-it-out, disciplined, halfcourt offensive team. The biggest contrast between Riley's Lakers and his Knicks was the type of defense they played: The Lakers played great team defense using quickness and finesse, while the Knicks used a much more physical approach.

If Portland was a man's team, New York was a he-man's team. Every Knick was a hard-nosed warrior. They were mean and proud of it. They should have been; it had gotten them to the NBA Finals. Some teams called them dirty players, but I wouldn't go that far, though I will say they pushed it to the limit. I'm not saying that as a negative statement. I respected them for their aggressiveness. Every team has to find its way to win. The Knicks were a big-body team; if they tried to play defense using only finesse, they would have wasted their biggest assets—physical strength and tenacity.

The true measure of a coach is if he can win with different personnel and with different styles. Pat Riley has my utmost respect. I was honored to be going against him and his tough team.

Patrick Ewing, their center, was always discussed in the same manner as Hakeem. They were similar in many ways; they are both versatile big men who don't have to rely on the inside game only. Patrick could move outside and knock down the jump shot.

He could also put the ball on the floor and make a move to the basket.

Charles Oakley is a great role player. He's always in the trenches doing the dirty work, constantly banging and trying to wear his man down. He and Otis would be a great matchup, power versus power. At small forward, they were not that small. Charles Smith, at 6-10, started, but he was more of a big forward. In fact, he had played a lot of center earlier in his career with the Clippers. His strength was posting up.

Anthony Mason backed up both forward spots and was a player on the rise. He had knocked around in the European League and the CBA for several years. Now he was establishing himself in the NBA. Mason had surprising ballhandling skills for a player his size, and he was a versatile defender. He could match up against either forward and even defend centers.

The Knicks had two aggressive guards in John Starks, a streaky shooter like Max, and Derek Harper, whom we knew well from all his years at Dallas. The Knicks had acquired him right before the trade deadline, feeling he could be the final piece to a championship puzzle. We definitely had our work cut out for us.

The day before the finals opened, we noticed that the number of media members was staggering. People with microphones and notepads had gathered from all over the world. I tried to stay with my basic routine to keep a sense of normalcy. The assistant coaches and I ate our pregame meal at the same place we always did, and we even said the same words that were part of our superstitious regimen on game days.

"Good luck, big guy," Carroll would say. I knew exactly what he was doing. He had to say it and I had to answer—because that's what we always did—"Good luck to you, big guy." We didn't want anything to change our normal operation, even if it was the championship series.

Game One was just what we expected—down and dirty. Thorpe came through with 14 points and 16 rebounds, and our defense limited New York to 34-percent shooting. We won it, 85–78, in a classic defensive struggle. But the national media didn't see it as classic, bemoaning the lack of points as bad offense.

We took a lot of "uglyball" criticism, which seemed unfair to me because this was New York's preferred style, and we had to meet that challenge. It's just like in a war: Whether the war is in the jungle, the mountains, or the desert, you have to do whatever it takes to win in that environment.

Harper stepped up big in Game Two, hitting four three-pointers to fuel the Knicks' 91–83 win, which gave them the homecourt advantage.

In Game Two, after all the things we had been through, I saw something that disturbed me. Because of the constant physical pressure they put on us, I felt our unity wasn't what it should be. There were some little exchanges in the huddle, with guys saying things like, "Why don't you hold up your end?" We were slipping into a bit of a negative team mentality.

I sat on an ice chest in the locker room after the game, not speaking for a couple of minutes. Finally, I said, "If a team is going to behave the way we behaved to each other out there, I don't think we should be champions. If that's the way you get there, I don't think I want to be part of it. The way we have to do it is by always staying together. Let's not let this opponent turn us against each other."

By the time we arrived at Madison Square Garden for Game Three, we were determined to take back that homecourt advantage. We jumped out on them, 42–26. But the Knicks responded behind their thunderous crowd and took an 88–86 lead on Harper's jumper with 52 seconds left.

On our next possession, we worked the ball to Hakeem, who made his move and noticed at the last instant that Cassell's man had drifted too far away. Cassell never hesitated after accepting Hakeem's pass; he reared up and stroked that three-pointer as though it were a summer day in the park. Nothing but net.

What a gutsy, gutsy shot—a shot that, in retrospect, may have been the key to the whole series. We were up 89–88, and a courageous call by Jake O'Donnell—who whistled Ewing for a moving pick—kept the Knicks from getting off what might have been a winning shot. Cassell iced it with four free throws, and our 93–89 victory meant we were at least certain of getting back to Houston for Game Six.

What a great sports week it was in New York. On the nights we were off, the Rangers were playing Vancouver for the Stanley Cup title. My family was there with me, and we were taking a lot of walks and enjoying the exciting atmosphere of the big city.

I'll never forget what my youngest daughter Melissa said as we were walking through Greenwich Village and commenting on the people you would usually find in the Village—people with mohawks in leather, drag queens, you name it. I was thinking maybe I should be protective, but Melissa's eyes lit up and she said, "God, I love it here."

The only things that spoiled our exciting week in New York were the losses in Games Four and Five. We were in position to win both times, but the Knicks made some big plays when they had to have them. In Game Four, we had a real scare when Robert Horry soared high and was bumped in flight by Anthony Mason. Horry landed hard on his tailbone, and we didn't immediately know his status for the remainder of the series.

Horry was able to come back in Game Five, and we were up 80–78 with 3:12 remaining. But Starks drilled a key three-pointer, and the Knicks took the game and a 3–2 series lead. It was an eerie night for most people trying to watch the game, because NBC cut away from it for the O.J. Simpson Bronco chase. We knew something strange was going on outside the lines, but we had to maintain focus. We were right there at the end, but we allowed them to sneak away for a couple of late breakaways, and that was it.

One of the subplots in this series was Mario Elie's playing time. In the previous series, I was playing him a lot at both the big-guard and small-forward positions. But because the Knicks had so many big "threes" (the number by which we label the small-forward spot), chiefly Smith at 6-10 and Mason at a very broad 6-8, I felt I could only use Mario at big guard, and it cut a lot of his minutes.

It was a tough situation, because Mario is a New Yorker and I knew how much he wanted to play. We also had a delicate situation with Kenny Smith, who had been having trouble with the physical Harper. I just kept supporting Kenny, feeling he was going to break out of it. To criticize Kenny or get into a "Smith or

Cassell" debate at this point would not have served any purpose for us.

Going back to Houston down 3–2, we heard a lot of questions on another topic of strategy. We have always run a lot of pick-and-rolls, and the Knicks double-teamed the ballhandler on every pick-and-roll and rotated out of it to pick up the open men. As we reviewed the tape after each game, we heard some of the commentators on television criticize us, saying the Rockets just aren't going to get what they want against New York's pick-and-roll defense. But they didn't know what we were trying to accomplish.

In this series, whenever we went to the strong side and just threw it in to Hakeem, he had to burn up a lot of energy just getting position—fighting Ewing and especially the physical Anthony Mason. If we continued this strategy, Hakeem would be worn out by the end of the game when we needed him most. We had to relieve that constant pressure on him, so we started running pick-and-rolls with Otis setting the pick and Hakeem positioned on the opposite side close to the basket. When we ran the pick-and-roll on the left side of the floor, Otis would roll wide to the left corner. When the guard dribbling to the middle was double-teamed, he would flip the ball to Otis, and the man guarding Hakeem would have to run all the way across the court to pick up Otis. Meanwhile, the man who double-teamed the dribbler quickly had to rotate to Hakeem, who was posting up near the basket. While this rotating was taking place, Hakeem didn't have to absorb the physical pounding; he was saving energy.

Otis would pass the ball crosscourt, all the way over to the right side of the floor. Then we'd pass in to Hakeem down low. We were getting better position by using this indirect method of getting him the ball, rather than dribbling down into the teeth of the defense, and meantime were saving wear and tear on our MVP.

It seemed that everyone was critical of this strategy. "Why are you running so many pick-and-rolls?" I heard over and over. "You're getting nothing out of them."

Everyone on the outside judged the play on whether it got quick results—either the dribbler or the roller scores. But we were privately pleased with the results we were getting. It just took a

little patience on our part and two extra passes. I didn't explain
this strategy to the media. Why tip our hand? I just said we were
satisfied with our pick-and-rolls.

The media looked at me like I was crazy or just plain dumb. An
ex-NBA coach came up to me in a restaurant. "Rudy, I can't believe
you keep running that play with Otis setting the pick," he said. He
then gave me advice on how he'd do it.

I courteously thanked him. One of the most appealing things
about sports is that they're not only entertaining to watch, but
spectators get to play coach. Everyone has an opinion on how to
win the game. It's times like these when a coach has to stand
firmly on the principles he believes in.

We got another great airport reception when we came home,
and I felt good even though we were down 3–2. If someone had
told me in October we could win a championship by winning our
last two games on the home court, I would have taken that.

Game Six was nip and tuck, as Starks put on a great shooting
performance for the Knicks with his buddy Spike Lee cheering
him on from the stands. We were up, 86–84, when the Knicks set
up for their final play. Ewing set the pick for Starks, who veered
left on the perimeter. He was going for the win and the title with a
three-pointer.

But here came Hakeem to keep the series alive. With an effort
almost beyond belief, he lunged at Starks and his fingertips just
grazed the ball, causing it to fall short. Hakeem had actually lost
his balance and regrouped. It happened right in front of me, and I
could see the flight of the ball. If that one went in, the guys in New
York would be wearing those '94 rings. But the ball fluttered short
of the rim and I ran off the court with my right arm held high. It
wasn't a feeling of victory; it was a feeling of survival. We had given
ourselves a chance to play another day and possibly become the
champions of the world.

Game Six was on a Sunday afternoon, and we wouldn't play
Game Seven until Wednesday night. Would there be overwhelming
anxiety? Would the long wait be stressful?

Surprisingly, a calm came over me for the entire series. Yeah, I
was emotional about the games and I knew I was up against a

great coach in Pat Riley. But while I'm usually something of an insomniac, I was sleeping very well.

The Knicks were a basic team. They weren't going to surprise you. I felt we were prepared, even if they changed their pick-and-roll defense. If there was any pressure on me at all, it was basically going to be in my substitution patterns.

I was leaving nothing to chance. I had a black suit and a black-and-red tie that I hadn't lost in all season. On my radio show, more than a handful of people said, "If you're a good coach at all, you've got to know to wear that black suit and black-and-red tie." We got everything back from the cleaners just in time.

Game Seven was again tight and tense, and we held a narrow lead most of the way. As hot as Starks had been in Game Six, he was that cold in Game Seven, finishing 2 of 18 overall and 0 for 11 from three-point range.

We were up, 78–75, when Hakeem dropped in a jump hook at the 2:51 mark. The Knicks couldn't answer, and then Hakeem got the ball to Maxwell, who squared his shoulders and dropped in a three-pointer that put us up by eight at the 1:49 mark. Maxwell happily plopped to the floor, Kenny Smith swung his arms in glee, and our whole team ran out to pound Maxwell as timeout was called.

The pictures at the end were, as they say, worth a thousand words. As the clock was ticking off, one of our ball boys, Ricky Rosa, had me in a bear hug. Sophie ran onto the court, and I could see the expression on her face. She's such a strong person, and when she shows emotion, I just can't hold it back.

I grabbed my son, Trey, and it was truly a golden moment. Nine long months of sweat and tears, and now this great mission had been accomplished by a special group of people who just kept believing.

This was the first time an NBA championship presentation was being made on the court, with the fans right there. I had to compose myself and find a way to express my feelings in front of everybody.

"Houston . . . you wanted it so long," I said. "You've finally got it. I'm proud to be part of the team that got it for us. And when I say team, I mean it in the truest sense of the word."

These were spontaneous words, straight from the heart. I knew there had been a lot of frustration in Houston because none of its major sports teams had ever won a championship beforehand. This was for our franchise, our fans, and our city.

The 1993–94 Rockets didn't have a guy whose hands you could just put the ball in and have something happen one-on-one. We had to be a team—distribute the ball and play defense. When most people think of teamwork, they think about guys passing the ball around, but in order to have a good defense, teamwork is essential. All five guys have to help each other.

When the champagne celebration at the Summit died down, we all made our way over to Cafe Pappadeaux for a victory party. There was a numbness in my body as I visited with all our friends and supporters. That numbness didn't pass for days and days. We had a championship rally before 50,000 people in the Astrodome, and then a championship parade through downtown Houston. It was all a happy blur. I was getting very little sleep because my nerve endings were so excited. I thought about it and I wanted to be able to put into words what it all meant.

When you grow up in an era of dynasties and you see the Boston Celtics, you think, These are the guys who win championships. The Yankees win. The Packers win. For those who don't win, I think you start to believe it's always somebody else who gets the ring.

We learned that the impossible dream can come true. It's not only for someone else. It takes hours and hours of hard work; it takes sharing and sacrifice. There will be many tests along the way, and it takes the strength of character to face adversity and overcome it. It takes believing in yourself and the men who stand with you.

But it can happen. It *did* happen.

The 1993–94 Houston Rockets shared this impossible dream. This championship wasn't for the Knicks or the Suns or the Bulls or some other team.

This was Houston's time. Why not us?

17

IN THE AFTERMATH of those euphoric championship experiences, it didn't take me long to get a true picture of what life in the celebrity fishbowl is like.

I had been on a golf outing one summer day, and after our round a couple of buddies and I wound up going out and having a couple of beers at a couple of places in Houston. It turned into a late night. After we left, I drove one of my coaches back to his car. We had a good conversation about his contract, which took about thirty minutes. He brought up some interesting points and, as we separated, I wanted to think about what he had said.

When there are things in my head that I need to mull over, I like to do it late at night. So instead of just getting on the freeway, I thought I would drive through town; it would take me maybe ten minutes longer to get home, but by the time I got there I would have the issues we had talked about clear in my mind.

As I passed the entrance to the freeway and went underneath it, I could see flashing lights a hundred yards away. There were two or three cars being pulled over, and the street was lit up like a Christmas tree or the Las Vegas strip.

"What the heck is going on?" I wondered aloud.

After having seen those other cars pulled over, I noticed a light flashing at me. I had no idea why I was being pulled over. I put on

227

my blinker, pulled over to the curb, and waited to get out of the car. I always keep my wallet in my front pocket, and it had fallen out behind the seat. I was back there reaching for it and finally retrieved it after, I'd say, about five seconds. Then I handed my license to the officer.

"Why did you pull me over, officer?" I asked.

"For speeding," he replied.

Speeding, I couldn't believe it. I had seen all the flashing lights ahead and, like most people, I slowed down as I approached them, thinking there was probably an accident. I couldn't have been speeding. This was either ridiculous or a mistake.

"What's the speed limit here?" I asked.

"It's thirty miles per hour, and you were going over that."

I now knew what had happened: I was caught in a speed trap. The officer asked me where I had been. I told him I had been out with friends. He asked if I had been drinking. I was honest and told him I had had some beer.

The officer then asked me to take a Breathalyzer test. I could see taking a Breathalyzer test if I had been driving recklessly or going way over the speed limit. But I was driving in the 35-miles-per-hour range, and I didn't feel that a test was warranted.

"Do I have to take it?" I asked.

"No, you don't have to take it. But if you don't, you'll have to go to jail."

The officer was performing his duties to the letter. I was going over thirty, I had admitted to drinking beer—but something about the whole situation bothered me. I felt I was driving carefully, and their pulling over several cars en masse didn't sit right, either. I hadn't seen any cars moving at a fast pace. I felt it was unfair. And now there was the Breathalyzer question.

I didn't think I was intoxicated. I didn't feel I acted as if I was under the influence. Would he have asked me to test if I had lied and told him I wasn't drinking? I let my emotions get the best of me and I said, "I don't think I should have to take the test. I was just on my way home. I wasn't driving recklessly."

He took me down to a small police station where they asked some questions. I called Sophie and explained the situation. Of course, she was concerned about what was going on; I just explained to her I wasn't going to take the test because I didn't feel it was proper. I then called Robert Barr, and he said he would come down as soon as possible.

Then I retired for the rest of the night at the West University jail. As I lay in my cell, I tried to calm myself down. I couldn't shake the feeling of frustration. My intention that night was to take a leisurely drive through town and think, and I wound up in jail.

I knew if I had taken the test I probably would have avoided all this. But at the moment of my decision, I felt it was extremely unfair. That belief would not let me give in. Was it the right thing to do? Absolutely not. But you couldn't tell me that at the time. I was committed.

Robert showed up and called an attorney, Rusty Hardin. When Rusty came to see me, I explained what had happened. He told me, "They have a videotape of the arrest and the questioning at the station." When Rusty told me this, I felt reassured.

"If there was something on the videotape that suggests I was reckless or my behavior and speech were not proper, I will plead guilty," I said.

As we left the jail in the morning, I was completely shocked by the media mob outside. There were twenty to thirty reporters gathered around the station. They hadn't been warned that I was coming out. As I stepped outside the door, they started running, tripping over each other, and fighting for position. We've all seen a thousand movies where there are scenes of a frenzied media throng with people yelling out questions. That's exactly what was happening to me. The questions were the most ridiculous I had ever heard, and it became like a B-movie.

"Rudy, was the pressure of the championship so much for you to deal with that you had to be driving drunk through this town?"

I wasn't going to answer any of this stuff. I just said I would make a statement.

"I respect the law and the justice system," I said. "There is a difference of opinion between the arresting officer and myself. I will let it go to court and accept the decision which comes from that."

One media member yelled out that it was "reported" I went over the yellow line three times and was swerving and slurring my words. Now, this wasn't even close to the way I remembered it. "The videotape shows this," one of the reporters insisted.

I got in my car and went home. It was very distressing, because you learn that when something like this happens, many people presume that you're guilty.

We had a lot of wonderfully supportive telephone calls at our house, but it was tough on Sophie and the kids. All I could do was be honest with them; I said I had had some beers that night, but I felt I was fine and that I handled myself in a very respectful manner with the officer. I wasn't ashamed of anything I did. When I talked to my son, Trey, I did get emotional.

"When we were on top, everyone was praising me," I said. "Now, you might hear some nasty things from some people. I'm still your same Dad. I'm sorry if any of this causes you pain."

The television footage of my coming out of jail broke in on soap operas and all the afternoon programming, like this was the assassination of a president or something. As I watched some of the news programs, there were statements like, "What about these sports figures? O.J. Simpson and now Rudy Tomjanovich."

I couldn't believe what I was hearing.

On one of the radio talk shows, they even dedicated an hour to the topic of "What's wrong with these high-profile people? Are they above the law?"

Crazy stuff.

Nobody really came out and jumped on me—but on the other hand, nobody defended me, either. Nobody said, "Wait, let's see what the video shows."

It was a revelation to me. When you're on top, a lot of people love you. But a lot of people also love to see you trip and fall.

Some callers to the talk shows felt the charges should be dropped simply because the Rockets had won the championship. That's the stupidest thing I ever heard. I've always wanted to be just a citizen. I don't want favors. That would be wrong. All I wanted was to be judged fairly.

The district attorney and Rusty Hardin went down to see the

videotape. I never did see it, but this is how my lawyer later described the video to me: There was footage of my jeep going down the street in the middle of a lane. If it did move, it was only about six inches, which is normal. You could see the light shine into the car, and I put on the blinker and pulled over to the right.

The tape showed the officer coming over, and there was a slight delay while I got my wallet. I was making the same gesture I make on the sidelines: hand through my hair. There was no staggering. I went to get the license out of my wallet, and it took a little time to find it. I get so many calling cards each day that sometimes my license gets caught in there with all these cards.

The tape shows that it took six seconds—maybe less—to get the license out. Later the officer said the time it took to get the license out was reason to suspect something was up.

Then there was a conversation you couldn't hear on the tape. All of a sudden, I'm asked to turn around for handcuffs and put in the police car.

The tape continued after I was in the police station. The officer asked me if I would take the tests. He went through about six or seven test requests, and my answer was always, "Officer, I prefer not to take this test."

This was the videotape. No slurring. No behavior to indicate intoxication.

The district attorney told Rusty he didn't see any evidence to convict me of driving under the influence. The charges were dropped, and I made a statement that the proper legal channels had decided the issue and I was grateful for that.

I also felt I had to say something about the people who presumed guilt. I vented some of that frustration; I understood that it's not a fairy-tale life, but it's amazing how bad news can instantly be perceived as such big news, while good news can, at times, be perceived as no news.

All around the country, there had been mug shots of me in different publications. The farther away from Houston it was, the more bizarre the stories were. One story had me running off the road.

Once it was over, an all-news radio station in Houston reported for the first few hours that the charges against me had been dropped, but after these first three or four hours I noticed that it wasn't mentioned the rest of the day. People who missed the initial broadcast didn't know the next day that the case had been dropped. Quite a contrast to the media coverage when I spent a night in jail.

It's sort of a disappointment to me that people love controversy, violence, anything on the negative side. I learned that during the Kermit Washington incident, and this situation reminded me of that one.

There are probably some people who still think I got off because of my celebrity status. There's no way in the world that district attorney would do something like that. In fact, I felt he was in a position where—if there was anything to the charges, he had to deal with the public scrutiny and pursue the case. It would have been the right thing to do, and I understood that.

Fortunately, the arrest incident didn't linger for me through the summer of '94. Occasionally, I'd hear a wisecrack that would trigger bad feelings, but as fall approached, my full concentration was on finding a way to get us in the right frame of mind to defend our title like the Lakers, Pistons, and Bulls had done before us.

"Winning the championship was tremendous, but the great teams go out there and do it again," I told our players as we reconvened in Galveston.

I knew that if I was getting so much attention during the summer, our players had to be getting even more. It does something to you; when you're patted on the back all the time, it can take some of the steam out of you.

I thought we had a good training camp, but when we went out for our preseason games, our defense just wasn't there. We addressed it over and over, and by the time the regular season started, it was like someone had turned the switch: The defense was back, the guys were tough, and we got off to a 9-0 start.

I'll never forget opening night against New Jersey, when we unfurled the championship banner and received our championship rings. It was one of the greatest feelings ever. I was standing next to Hakeem and, as the banner floated by us on its way to the rafters, Hakeem and I made eye contact; no words were spoken, but we each knew what the other was thinking: After all the years of striving, that banner represented the ultimate moment of accomplishment.

I knew I would notice that banner each day I came to work, and it was so special to see it hanging up there. The rings were special, too, but I'm not a jewelry person. I looked at my ring and put it in my sock drawer.

"Why don't you wear the ring?" people ask me.

"I don't need to wear it. The ring is just a symbol. I've got the feeling right here," I tell them, pointing at my chest.

After our 9-0 start, the team began to go flat. I think what happened is that we had won a championship, we had enjoyed a great November, and then the complacency set in. All of a sudden, cruise control became a habit. It was as though we assumed we would win just by stepping on the floor.

If you look at our record from the middle of '92–93 through the 9-0 start in '94–95, we were an astounding 107-35. But we began to lose some of that edge, and there wasn't an obvious cause. At times, the players would even talk about it themselves. It just wasn't happening for us in December and January.

On January 16, we were horrible in a 94–75 loss at Minnesota. A couple of nights later, in a championship rematch against the Knicks, we were solidly whipped, 93–77. Then we hit rock bottom in an NBC game at Chicago on January 22. This was a good Chicago team, but remember that the Bulls still didn't have Michael Jordan back. Yet they embarrassed us, 100–81, and that one really struck a nerve. The Bulls were matching up with a smaller team against us, with Toni Kukoc at power forward. We talked about using size to our advantage, but we went out and completely humiliated ourselves in the first half. We got outhustled. They beat us to every loose ball.

I try to be very observant, especially when we're having troubles, and the reaction I was seeing from some players riled me. They weren't looking inward at themselves, facing the fact that they weren't playing well; they were making remarks about other players or the strategy we were using.

That was it. I had had some days when I got on them, but this one hit me hard and I exploded. I moved into our United Center locker room very aggressively, yanked my coat off, and sort of twirled it over my head before throwing it in the corner.

I told our guys how I felt about their whole approach to the game. I questioned whether we were worthy of carrying the "champions" label. It was the most volatile display I had ever had at halftime, and then we went back out in the second half and did nothing to show the pride of champions. I decided to call a meeting the next day before practice.

"There is no intensity on defense," I told the team. "We're not playing together on offense. I don't see any unity out there. Everyone's bitching. We're playing losing basketball, and we've got to get that fixed. Now's the time to bitch. Let's clear the air."

I wanted everyone to get his complaints out in the open so we could deal with them.

One statement directed at me was, "You don't want us to run." This is a common complaint, one I had heard even back in the days when I was playing; whenever a player is struggling offensively, he wants to get some easy scores.

"Where did you get that idea?" I responded. "When have you heard me say 'Don't run'?"

"You're always calling plays," the player said.

"I'm always calling plays because the other team is constantly scoring and we have to take the ball out of bounds. We need to play some defense and stop somebody to get some fast breaks."

My philosophy has always been to look to run first and get an easy opportunity; if it's not there, then we set up. Even if I've called a play, if the defense doesn't get back quickly, we should take advantage of that breakdown. This was emphasized from the first week of training camp. Before every game, when I put our game plan on the blackboard, the first option under offense is always "look to run and run hard."

I explained this philosophy, but everyone knew running wasn't the core of our problems. We had lost our togetherness.

"Why is there constant bickering?" I asked. "We've been through so many tough times together. Why are we pulling apart?"

A couple of players responded, making positive statements, emphasizing togetherness. Then Hakeem spoke: "Everyone is saying the right things, but do we honestly feel those things? We say we like each other, but we don't play like it. We have to make the decision to really be a team or to admit we have problems."

The meeting ended on that note. I didn't know what to expect. I knew all the players' feelings were not expressed in the meeting, but I felt it was a step in the right direction.

We played Milwaukee the next day, and it was amazing: The Bucks had a talented, young team under Mike Dunleavy, but we took the floor with a purpose. The intensity was back and our defense was as good as it has ever been.

I actually felt sorry for Mike, my ex-teammate, because our team was in such a zone that day. If we had played like that against the Bulls on national television, people would have been raving about the defending champs.

The 115–99 win over Milwaukee sparked a resurgence. We won three of the next four games, and my intention at that time was still to keep the nucleus intact. Coming into the year, owner Leslie Alexander, vice president of basketball operations Bob Weinhauer, and the entire staff had talked about how to go about defending the title; it was my feeling that, yes, we should look at all the opportunities that come to the organization, but I thought these guys—because they had shown such great teamwork in winning a championship—deserved a chance at defending the title. That didn't mean we weren't going to try to add to the squad, but I wanted the main people to be the same.

As the year went on, however, some things seemed to be missing. Subtle things. The spark that was always there the previous year would come and go. On a telling four-game western road trip before the All-Star Game, our inconsistency was magnified. We started the trip by playing great in Phoenix and blowing the Suns out by 24 points. The next night, we went to Portland and were crushed 120–82. Then we regrouped for a solid win at Sacramento. But twenty-four hours later, we were lethargic in a 122–107 loss to the L.A. Clippers at the Sports Arena.

By the middle of the year, we hadn't taken any steps toward pursuing a trade. High-profile guys like Scottie Pippen and Clyde Drexler had publicly requested trades, and our names got linked with theirs strictly through rumors. There was no truth to any of it.

Prior to February 6—three weeks before the trading deadline—I was intent on finishing the year with the same nucleus as last season. But Drexler's name was now starting to be mentioned in our staff meetings. Clyde's salary for 1994–95 would fit somebody's cap, but he had a big balloon payment coming in '95–96. I didn't think there was any way in the world it would happen for us.

The Blazers, though, were somewhat under the gun. If they failed to trade Clyde before the trading deadline, the balloon payment would have been on their cap, and the chances of trading him would have decreased considerably.

When we talked to Portland, the player they were interested in was Otis Thorpe. His '94–95 salary could match up with Drexler and one other Blazer player. We wanted them to throw Mark Bryant into the deal, but the Blazers refused to do that. Still, we kept talking. The more I thought about it, the more I felt that Clyde was the only star in the league who could make a quick adjustment to playing on our team. One big factor was Clyde's relationship with Hakeem. With any other star in the league, there might have been a negative effect because we go to Hakeem so much. Chemistry was an issue, but it was less of one with Clyde.

Nobody had ever repeated as champions by making a major trade in the middle of the season. But in looking at it, Clyde—for his relationship with Hakeem and his hometown connections with the city of Houston—made a lot of sense. The final reason for making the deal was that he was a guy who had come close before and now even more passionately wanted to win a championship.

Thorpe had been a solid, reliable worker with an iron-man approach; night in and night out, he was there for you. Out of all the guys on the club, Otis was the one I had been around most away from the court. I'm not saying we were buddies, but we had played golf three or four times in the summer and had a good relationship.

On the night of February 6, something happened in Portland that pushed us closer to pulling the trigger on the Drexler deal if the Blazers were truly serious about it. The Blazers were slaughtering us, and the fans at Memorial Coliseum were giving it to us pretty good because we were the champs and it meant something to beat the Rockets.

Following a timeout, as I came out of the huddle, I saw two of our staff members—Robert Barr and Larry Smith—coming out of the stands along with Horry and Maxwell. At that point I had no idea what had happened.

One of the officials came over to me and said, "Those four guys have to be ejected for going into the stands." It was then that I found out Max had gone up there allegedly to confront a fan who'd been razzing him. The other guys were there merely as protectors, but we didn't contest the ejections.

When Maxwell drew a ten-game suspension from the NBA, that got us thinking about the stability of our starting big guard. What could we expect from Max? He was a fiery guy who had had his share of incidents on and off the court. In a year when we were struggling, putting your team in that kind of jeopardy really got me thinking about making a deal.

Clyde had enjoyed a great All-Star career, and handled himself with an air of class. If we got Drexler, he would eventually have to take over as the starting two-guard. I was going to let nature take its course in terms of Maxwell; my thought was that Maxwell, in that situation, would say, "I'm going to do whatever it takes to be out there." I thought he was such a tough competitor that he would work to become the guy who could play point guard beside Drexler. In fact, I had brought up the idea of Max playing some point guard to him the previous summer. I felt he had the quickness to defend at that point, but he needed to improve his ball-handling. Drexler and Max at the guard positions would be an interesting combination. Few teams in the league could match their physical strength in the backcourt.

Bottom line? Maxwell had done a great job for us. But he had become someone I couldn't rely on as a foundation block for the future.

It was a tough decision that was made easier by that last Maxwell incident in Portland. Who knew what the next incident might be? We needed the stability that Clyde could bring. If Max would accept the new program and fit in with Clyde, so much the better.

We ended that western road trip with the depressing loss to the Clippers that brought us to the All-Star break. We were ready to hammer out a deal by the time we got to Phoenix for the weekend's festivities. Executives from the Blazers and Rockets had some intense negotiations, and my input in Phoenix was, "Let's go for it."

Two days after the All-Star Game, the deal went through. In order to make the salary-cap numbers fit, Tracy Murray was added to the Thorpe–Drexler deal. I liked Murray's shooting ability; there was a chance that he, too, could help our team.

I wanted to get the news about the trade to Otis before he came to the arena for our game that night against the Clippers. Because the deal wasn't finalized until the players had showered and left our shootaround, I had to try to contact Otis by telephone.

It's not the easiest thing in the world to do, to tell a guy who has been part of your championship nucleus that he's moving on. Otis was classy about it.

"Who's it for?" he asked.

"Clyde Drexler."

Otis was surprised. He felt that if he was going to be traded, it would be for another power player. That's what everybody was asking: "How are you going to become a decent rebounding team when you lose a solid power forward?"

As crazy as it may seem, we felt that with Clyde at the two-spot (he was probably the best rebounding big guard around with Jordan gone), we would improve our overall board game. I knew we had some hardworking role players ready to help us at the four-spot.

We put a lot of faith in Carl Herrera. He wasn't an Otis Thorpe, but per minute played, their rebounding numbers were pretty close. We also had Pete Chilcutt and newcomer Chucky Brown to throw into the power-forward mix.

And that was just the rebounding issue.

After looking at the tapes, we saw that Clyde wasn't just a good passer; he was a *great* passer. He would get guys layups off a halfcourt set. Our fast-break efficiency would also improve with Clyde running the wing or pushing the ball; before Clyde, we had all this speed, but we didn't consistently make plays on the break.

Clyde was also a guy who had to be double-teamed when he would post up. That created open shots for our perimeter people.

Our first game with Drexler was a beauty. He couldn't enter the game until the second half because we were still waiting on word from Portland that Thorpe had passed his physical. Our guys kept it close until halftime, and Clyde gave us a burst of enthusiasm as we pulled away from the Hornets in the second half.

We beat Washington in our next game and then had the special treat on a Saturday morning of meeting President Clinton at the White House in honor of our '94 championship. It was too bad that only five of the players who had made up that '94 title team were on the trip. The short list included Hakeem Olajuwon, Sam Cassell, Scott Brooks, Kenny Smith, and Mario Elie. Otis Thorpe had been traded, Vernon Maxwell was suspended, Robert Horry and Carl Herrera were injured, and the others had been released. That just illustrates the changing nature of life in the NBA.

Those players who were able to attend really enjoyed it. We came in a side door of the White House and were taken to the Oval Office. I remember feeling that it was so much smaller than you think when you see it on television.

President Clinton read an address to the nation on his radio broadcast, and then met with some young children with physical disabilities who were there at the same time as our team. When he met us, the president struck me as a very affable, relaxed, sincere man. He made us feel he was a regular guy, and we quickly found out he loves to talk basketball, especially Arkansas Razorbacks basketball.

We went out to a press conference and made some presentations. As President Clinton was fooling around with the basketball and the jersey we gave him, Carroll Dawson broke the formality in the room by saying in his folksy voice, "Now all you need are the trunks."

Everybody laughed, including the president.

"A shot," President Clinton said with a chuckle. "I need a shot."

As the press conference ended and President Clinton was leaving, the White House press corps yelled out a couple of political questions. The president was on his way out the door, but he turned and answered those queries. It really gave me an insight into what his job is all about: Even on a Saturday morning, attending a ceremony for a basketball team, there were serious matters for this man to address. I thought about my own daily meetings with the media and how small-scale it is when compared to this type of constant scrutiny on such heavy topics that affect the nation and the world.

We went from Washington to New York and lost for the first time with Clyde. For the rest of the year, we were an injury-marred, sub-.500 team.

Here was the situation I was faced with: I felt this Drexler trade would make us a better team, but the players at Clyde's position—because he could play both small forward and big guard—weren't really happy about the deal. This great player coming in was going to take some of their playing time, and time is everything to a player.

There was some public criticism of the trade from the team, mainly from Robert Horry and Mario Elie. Other players felt that when Maxwell joined in the mix after his suspension, that would take minutes from other backcourt people, too.

Though I was convinced the deal made us a much more versatile team, we never got a chance to prove it in the regular season. We had too many injuries, with guys coming in and out of the lineup; Horry, Herrera, Hakeem, and Maxwell were all hurting. Clyde had some outstanding games, but our offensive plan was changing with all the shifting of personnel.

I think we only had one game in the last month when Horry—plagued by a bad back—was in there with the entire cast. There were flashes of brilliance, but none of these guys were in great shape or completely healthy.

We couldn't find a comfort zone as we came down the stretch. In fact, there was tension surrounding the whole team. Fortunately, it was eased somewhat by the things Clyde was doing on the floor; he won the respect of our guys, especially through his unselfish passing. I give Clyde a lot of credit for ultimately making this deal work through his professionalism and his approach. In reality, there was a hell of a lot of pressure on Drexler and on the organization.

The incumbent players now had a built-in excuse: *They made a trade, screwed up our chemistry, and we aren't better than before. We traded a power forward for a big guard. How are we supposed to win when they do stupid things like that?*

That had to be what was going through guys' heads. That's the way it is in this league.

But Clyde's positive approach changed the negativity to the point where we felt that, Hey, maybe it can happen for us if we can get everybody healthy.

In early April, we lost both Hakeem and Maxwell for a couple of weeks because of anemia. Hakeem had looked sluggish for a couple of weeks; he was trying, but something was missing. We thought maybe he was just tired from back-to-back long seasons.

It turned out that Hakeem's anemia was a reaction to anti-inflammatory drugs. His red-blood-cell count went way down, and the doctors felt we would see a different, lively Hakeem if we gave him some rest and got him off the anti-inflammatories.

In the standings, things didn't look good at all. We finished 47-35, which was 15 games off the pace set by Midwest Division champion San Antonio. Many people were passing negative judgments on the Drexler trade, but we held firm to the belief that the deal had made us a better team.

But would we have enough practice time to meld everybody together and prove our point?

We got everyone healthy by the end of the regular season, and now we would have a few crucial days in Galveston to get Clyde familiar with the entire system.

There was a long, tough road ahead for a No. 6 seed. But as I made that drive to Galveston, I truly believed we had the personnel to give those higher-seeded teams one heck of a run for their money.

When you talk about having room for improvement—well, nobody had more room than the Rockets.

18

THOSE UNEASY FEELINGS I had about the Jeff Hornacek trade the previous year were reinforced in '94–95 when Utah fully blended the pure-shooting Hornacek into their system and won 60 games. Even without center Felton Spencer, who missed most of the year because of a knee injury, Utah was really tough. And we were still a team searching for an identity.

Because we never had our full team together because of injuries after the Drexler trade, we, the coaches, were going into the playoffs not with doubts but with questions about whether our guys truly *believed* in the revised team.

Did we *believe* we were legitimate title contenders?

Yes, we had struggled and not gotten the results during the last month of the regular season. Still, I felt a lot of positive things had been happening, and I wanted the players to buy into the notion that, yes, a 47-win team could take a 60-win team if we came together with the precision I had envisioned the day we traded for Clyde.

We had finally gotten healthy, which gave us a fighting chance. After an intense week of workouts in Galveston, we went out to Utah and hung right in there during Game One at the Delta Center. It was a typical Houston–Utah affair, with good execution on both sides. Who would make the key shot at the end?

With the score tied at 100, Utah went to its pick-and-roll with John Stockton directing traffic. Stockton managed to get all the way to the basket, and his layup bounced tantalizingly on the rim before falling through to give Utah a two-point victory and a 1–0 lead in the best-of-five series. After Stockton's layup with a couple of seconds remaining, we had one last chance: Following a time-out, we inbounded from midcourt, and Vernon Maxwell—the guy who had made so many miracle shots for us—wound up taking a three-pointer for the win.

This time, no miracle. Max's off-balance shot hit the rim and bounced away. At the time, there was no way I could have imagined that last shot by Maxwell would be the final shot of his Rockets career.

But that's the unfortunate way it turned out.

I had heard after the game that Max had been cussing me out on the bench while the game was going on. The main issue was playing time, and it was brought to my attention. We had basketball matters to go over in preparing for Game Two, but our staff felt strongly that Maxwell had stepped over the line, and it couldn't be ignored.

Let me say that I understand players are going to be upset when they aren't getting as much time as they believe they deserve. I dealt with that myself as a player. But I felt the Maxwell situation had to be addressed. We had a day off between games, and I took some time and talked extensively with members of our staff. The problem had to be handled the right way.

I couldn't go on other people's word about what had happened on the bench in Game One; I just had to think about it in a general way. Before we had our shootaround for Game Two, I took Vernon aside and we talked about the situation.

"I understand how competitive you are," I said. "I know you want to play."

Still, I couldn't tolerate what I heard had happened.

"I didn't see it," I told Max. "But if it happens again, I'll have to deal with it."

It was in the best interest of the team to let players know that kind of behavior wouldn't be tolerated. We didn't have a loud, verbal fight, but the point was made. Maxwell admitted to me he was angry. He said he had lashed out because he was so competitive.

I didn't feel Vernon had played very well in Game One, and we didn't flourish when he was on the floor, although it wasn't all his fault. I was going to give him another shot the next game. I never predict how many minutes a guy will get, but there certainly was a chance that Max would play even less in Game Two. If that situation came about and Max lashed out again, I wanted him to understand I would have to respond in a disciplinary way.

The main theme of our conversation was that I understood Vernon's frustration. "I believe in you," I said. "I believe you can work your way back and be a big part of this team."

When we made the Drexler trade, we knew that Clyde would be the eventual starter at big guard and Robert Horry would be the small forward. But the situation never came to a head in the regular season because of all the injuries. Now it looked like Max was finally seeing the writing on the wall.

I urged Vernon to work his way through it and play such good basketball that he would still get ample playing time. Even in Game One, I had tried playing him at the point a little bit.

"If you play well, the minutes will be there for you," I said.

I repeated that theme several times during the conversation. At the end of our talk, Vernon said, "Rudy, it's so damn hard to play like this. I'm used to being a starter. I feel I have to do certain things out there and I need consistent minutes to get my rhythm and play my game."

Maxwell had always been an aggressive player, always willing to take a chance and take the big shot. He felt it was making his game worse to be in a role where he was coming off the bench.

"Don't live for the moment," I urged. "Work your way into this thing. I'm pulling for you. You've done so many great things for this team. I'm on your side. You've been down and come back so many times."

I said all those things to try to get him to hang in there and not overreact. If he reacted the same way as in Game One, I didn't know what would happen, but I stressed that it wasn't going to be like the first game, where I was wrapped up in the action and hadn't actually seen what Max was doing.

At that point I went into the locker room and addressed the team. We talked about the basketball adjustments we would have to make against the Jazz. As we went out onto the floor for our walk-through, Maxwell went up to Bob Weinhauer and told Bob he had a pulled hamstring and couldn't play that night.

Max didn't join the shootaround, and I went ahead with the business of preparing the team for Game Two. After the shoot-around, the situation was explained to me, and Weinhauer, Robert Barr, and I decided that Max would go home.

I felt this was Maxwell's reaction to our talk. What I had to say to him didn't register at all. There was no need for me to talk to Vernon again, because I had done as good a job as I could do. I was honest. I believed he had the ability to work his way through it.

But Vernon didn't buy it.

As I took my pregame walk that day, it was the only time in my life I ever prayed for our team to have success. Usually, I just ask the Lord for our guys to do the best they can. But on this occasion, my soft prayer was, "Just let the right thing happen."

Here was a guy who had been a big part of our success and a guy I believed in—a guy I felt was part of the family—and he was leaving the team under very unpleasant circumstances. Vernon had never been a Boy Scout, but I had learned to accept the idio-syncrasies of all our players. I genuinely liked Max.

I didn't know how our team would react to the Maxwell exodus. "Just let the right thing happen." I didn't pray for a championship. It's just that I had given this situation a lot of thought, and I felt I handled it with professionalism, sensitivity, and respect. If Vernon left and our team cratered because of it, I just didn't feel that would be justice.

From a personal standpoint, I was very disappointed in the choice that Vernon made. But I was also relieved, in a way, that this festering problem had come to a head. I think Vernon made an honest decision on how he felt. He didn't want to be part of it. He couldn't take it.

Trying to win a championship in such a competitive environment is tough enough. If a guy doesn't have that total commitment to the cause, it just adds to everyone else's burden. Yes, we were losing a talented player, but with the tension and the negative feelings that were swirling around us, this could easily turn out to be addition by subtraction. It was possible this was going to take away a negative that could hold us back.

Before we took the court for Game Two, I made a brief statement to the team that Vernon wouldn't be here. Then we went about our business of preparing for the game.

From the opening tip-off, it was beautiful. I couldn't have asked for a more positive reaction. We wound up hitting 19 of 28 three-pointers, a record at the time. Kenny Smith had a career-high 32 points and hit 7 of 8 from beyond the arc. Each time the Jazz went to double-team Olajuwon, we moved the ball expertly and got great outside looks. On their court, in a pressure situation, the offensive display was simply phenomenal in our 140–126 victory.

We were a happy bunch as we boarded our flight for the trip home. This was the team I had visualized after the Drexler trade, except that Maxwell wasn't in the mix. We had Kenny and Clyde at the starting guards, with Hakeem in the middle and Robert Horry and Pete Chilcutt at forwards. We had Mario Elie, Chucky Brown, and Sam Cassell ready for important reserve roles, and cagey veteran Charles Jones around to provide some defensive help against certain pivotmen.

I still didn't know how the public would receive us when we came home 1–1. There had been all this fan feedback about how the Thorpe trade would kill our rebounding. Deep down, I still wasn't convinced that the public—or the team—truly believed we could repeat.

The Jazz had a few days off to adjust to their homecourt loss. Karl Malone was sensational with 32 points and 19 rebounds in Game Three, and Utah pulled away for a 95–82 victory to take a 2–1 series lead.

Karl Malone is an opposing coach's nightmare. Here's a guy with a strong inside game—a power move to the middle and a great turnaround shot. He can go outside and score even beyond the three-point line. He's great on the pick-and-roll with one of the best point guards of all time in Stockton. Besides all that, Malone's a sensational passer; if you consistently double-team, he'll pick you apart.

Utah uses a splitting action when they pass the ball to Malone. When guarding a splitter, if you turn your head and don't see the ball, it's going to be an easy layup. Malone can deliver that pass.

So we had to pick our spots to double-team Karl. A lot of our strategy meetings were about how we were going to do it and when we were going to do it. Sometimes you can play almost perfect defense and Malone will still destroy you. He did it to us in Game Three, and if he did it one more time we were going to be on early vacation.

The media flipped back through the records and found that no reigning champion had gone out in the first round since Philadelphia in 1984. We were down to the moment of truth, and it was only then that I began to learn how much our guys wanted to cling to their territory at the top of the NBA mountain.

The veterans—Clyde and Hakeem—were spectacular in Game Four—as we blew out the Jazz, 123–106. Clyde finished with 41 points and Hakeem had 40. We were simply not going to allow ourselves to give up that crown on our homecourt.

"When Hakeem and Clyde both have it going, there's not much you can do," Jazz forward Antoine Carr lamented.

So it had come down to one game. Forty-eight minutes of pure intensity to see which team would earn the right to move on to the Western Conference Semifinals.

The Delta Center was rocking for the decisive game, but we came out strong and got a lead. Then a series of breakdowns by our guys just before the half enabled the Jazz to come back, and Hornacek hit a three-pointer at the halftime buzzer to give them a two-point lead. Their emotions were running high, and that momentum carried over to the second half. It didn't look good when the Jazz built a 12-point cushion, and with four minutes remaining, they were still up by seven.

The crowd was going bonkers, and I had to call some timeouts to stop their runs. As I went into the huddle and looked at the faces of our players, I could see that we were focused, but there wasn't energy there or anything that suggested we were going to get this thing done.

We talked about hanging together, getting some stops, and executing at the offensive end. The music and the celebration had already begun at the Delta Center. Sometimes, when you get in that situation, the players can get in a festive mood a little too early. Maybe that happened to the Jazz. I think we came out ready for serious business, while everybody else in that arena was thinking about whom the Jazz would play in the next round.

There weren't a lot of flashy steals or turnovers that changed the game around. We were just grinding it out. David Benoit took several jump shots for them down the stretch, simply because he wound up with the opportunities after our defense took away Utah's primary options. We double-teamed Malone and rotated out in time to check the better perimeter shooters. When they swung the ball, it was Benoit who had the good shots, but he couldn't hit them.

It was a flashback to the grit and determination we had shown in our '94 championship run. We were dead in the water; we were on a great team's floor, and the Jazz certainly knew how to execute under pressure, but somehow we hung in there. With Hakeem scoring 33 and Clyde getting 31, we roared back for a 95–91 victory that finally convinced me that our players felt in their hearts this team could win it again.

I wish I could say it was something I said or something that a player said. But there wasn't much you *could* say, because the crowd was screaming so loud we could barely hear each other in the huddle. When it was quiet enough to say a few words, it was basic stuff: "Hang in there, it's not over, don't stop believing in yourselves." Our guys met this test of courage in magnificent fashion. It took tremendous mental toughness not to fall apart in this situation. Instead of playing desperate and forcing things, we kept our blue-collar mindset. It was a game I'll never forget; when I think of the epitome of our determination, it was Game Five at Utah.

Our charter plane was headed one of two places on that Saturday: Either we were going home for the summer or to Phoenix for the second round. What a special ride it was to take the short trip from Utah to Arizona. We were a rejuvenated ball-club. Utah was so tenacious, so good—and we had survived it and bought some time for the new chemistry with Drexler to become even better.

As we made our descent from the sky and touched down at Sky Harbor Airport, Phoenix had never looked more beautiful. We were in a seven-game series now, with margin for error.

FRANKLY, I felt there was very little chance we were going to win the first game at America West Arena. Coming off the emotional and physical strain of the Utah series, our batteries were low.

Phoenix had energy and fresh legs. The Suns trounced us, 130–108, in Game One. It didn't help that we only had Drexler for a little more than one quarter. Clyde was shockingly ejected by Jake O'Donnell early in the second period, and it was all downhill from there. Clyde had made what looked like a clean steal in the open court and was on a breakaway when a delayed whistle was blown. Jake called a foul. Drexler looked at him in disbelief. A technical was called. Then, as Clyde rushed at O'Donnell, a second technical was called, which meant Clyde was gone.

Clyde handles himself with professionalism on and off the court. He rarely gets overly demonstrative when he's playing. He didn't make any overt gesture when whistled for the foul. The first technical was called from over thirty feet away; Jake wouldn't have been able to hear what Clyde said even if Clyde did say something. It was a bizarre incident. It all happened so fast. It was ironic, because Jake O'Donnell was an official I respected a great deal. He was one of the best officials in the league for many years. When he worked a game, I would feel comfortable that we would get a good effort and, most of all, consistency. That game turned out to be the last game Jake worked in the NBA.

Clyde was back for Game Two, but we had a similarly dismal result. The Suns went to 5–0 in the playoffs with a 118–94 victory, and Charles Barkley, the self-proclaimed CEO of "Butt Kickee, Inc." surmised that business was good. Who were we to argue after those first two kicks in the seats of our pants?

But at least we were coming home.

"These guys have only held serve," I told the team. "We've been in situations worse than this, but we've got to get into the series. We've got to get the next one and put some pressure on them."

We felt Phoenix was a good front-running team. The Suns had super confidence and a high-powered offense. We had to put some doubt in their minds.

One adjustment we made when we got home was to put 6-10 Robert Horry on the 6-5 Barkley. Charles started Game Three by missing his first 10 shots, and we went on to rout them, 118–85. With Barkley, we were dealing with basically the same situation as with Karl Malone: Charles is a very clever passer who can really read defenses. What we wanted to do, because they had such good three-point shooters in Dan Majerle, Danny Ainge, and Wesley Person, was to try to get a player on Barkley who wouldn't give him a high-percentage shot. But Charles is so powerful and explosive that he's capable of scoring sixty or seventy percent of the time if he's single-covered.

We couldn't get too excited about that Game Three win, because Game Four was the next day and we knew the Suns would come back strong. Barkley hit his first eight shots before cooling down in the second half. Kevin Johnson, however, stayed hot the whole game, and his 43 points on 18 of 24 shooting carried the Suns to a 114–110 victory.

Here was the strategic decision we had to consider: Phoenix runs a lot of pick-and-rolls, and because the Suns had the three-point shooters and Barkley, we decided not to double-team the point guard and open up those other avenues. Our game plan was to stay man-to-man on their perimeter shooters and try to have Kevin shoot the outside shot over the pick-and-roll. He not only did well on that, but he was so good in the open court. Our philosophy and game plan was, "Let's not overextend on this guy," and it hurt us in that particular game.

Do you change philosophies after a performance like that? We decided not to.

I felt we had to stick to our guns and not worry about what the critics would say. By doing it this way, at least we weren't creating a bunch of other problems to deal with. Yeah, we were giving Kevin a bushel of points, but we wanted to cut off the other people and limit their options over the entire series.

The Suns had to be feeling good with a 3–1 lead. But Kevin Johnson cautiously said something after the game that stuck with me.

"The Rockets have the heart of a champion," he said, talking about how tough it would be to deliver the knockout punch.

Heart of a champion? That statement by K.J. would eventually prompt me to say, "Never underestimate the heart of a champion." The phrase would wind up on T-shirts, but it wasn't planned or marketed; it was just a spontaneous response that stayed with me after hearing what Kevin Johnson said about our team after Game Four.

It looked bad, being down 3–1 and having to go back out to Phoenix. But I believed in our team because we had been in a similar predicament the previous year. I talked about our being in the same locker room as last season's great escape.

Our problem was that we didn't have the whole team in that locker room when we arrived for Game Five. Drexler was so sick with the flu during the day that he could barely get out of bed. Our bus left for the game without Clyde, and we prepared to play without him. But about thirty-five minutes before tip-off, Clyde showed up despite his throbbing head and aching muscles.

His coming into the locker room was an inspirational moment for our team. What a classy professional! I got goose bumps myself.

"I've got to be here," Clyde said. "I'm going out there to give whatever I've got."

We hung in there, but it looked like the Suns had us in the final minute. Barkley was at the line for two shots with his team up by one. He missed one of two, meaning we could try for a two-pointer instead of taking a three-pointer to force overtime.

When it's a two-point game, it means the issue is still in Hakeem Olajuwon's hands. On the make-or-break possession, Hakeem showed the stuff legends are made of: a quick fake, a jump hook, all net. There were 8.2 seconds left when Hakeem's pressure-packed shot tied the game. When Wesley Person's long jumper rattled out at the buzzer, we had reached overtime with momentum on our side.

It was like Barkley had said about us: "The Rockets are like a big ol' Texas roach. You put your foot on it, you hear the crunch, you think it's gone. Then you pick up your foot and see that thing scurry away."

In overtime, Robert Horry drained a big three-pointer that really got us over the hump. We won it, 103–97, and I couldn't have been more admiring of a group of men. What a gutsy effort—especially considering that Clyde could barely stand.

When you win in a game like that, you don't just walk off the floor. You run off the floor with heads held high. Making that trot down the corridor at America West was one of the best feelings you could imagine.

They couldn't drive the stake through our heart. We were still alive.

Back in Houston for Game Six, the Suns played us on even terms for three quarters, but then we exploded with a barrage of three-pointers in the fourth quarter to win going away.

History was still on the Suns' side, because no road team had won a Game Seven since Philadelphia defeated the Celtics at Boston Garden in 1982. During that span, the home team had gone 20-0 in Game Sevens.

But we were confident because we had been in the pressure cooker so many times. Over the last two years, we'd been in seven games in which we'd faced elimination, and had won every one of them. We were mentally hardened at that point. Now the Suns would have to prove they could thrive in an elimination situation for the first time.

Phoenix came out with a vengeance in Game Seven, rolling up a 44–29 lead in the second quarter. Our offense was really out of sync, but we battled away and chipped to within 10 at the half. It was a case of not letting the dam break. If you keep fighting and keep the game within reach, the psychology changes; closing out a series is so damn hard to do.

I didn't feel uncomfortable at all being down 10 at the half. This was going to be a battle all the way to the wire. Again, Kevin Johnson was the focus of their offense with his penetration. Things were not looking good when Hakeem picked up his fourth foul with five minutes left in the third quarter and the Suns leading by nine, but Clyde and Sam picked up the offensive load. Clyde became our post-up threat and hurt them inside with 14 big third-quarter points. Sam came off the bench and gave us a great spark, scoring on penetration from the outside. He knocked in 12 points that period. We actually took the lead with Hakeem sitting out, and we entered the fourth quarter leading 81–79.

Hakeem was well-rested and inspired by the heart his teammates displayed. We started pounding the ball inside to him in the final period. He responded with 14 clutch points. Our biggest lead was five points, but the Suns kept fighting back. Kevin Johnson was a one-man wrecking crew; he was relentless attacking our basket. With 20 seconds left, K.J. was fouled, and on his 20th consecutive successful free throw, he tied the game with his 45th point. But he missed his 21st free throw, giving us a chance to shoot for the win.

We were going to run the clock down and take the final shot to win it or go into overtime.

Paul Westphal, the Phoenix coach, decided to employ a trap defense on the critical possession. We were poised enough to find the open man, and it was Mario Elie deep in the left corner. With 7.1 seconds on the clock, Mario threw in the shot of his career—a beautiful three-point rainbow that seemed to hang in the air for an eternity before plopping through the net.

I wasn't surprised at Paul's strategy. He was saying, Why let these guys do exactly what they want? Make them be creative. By trapping, Paul knew everything we had focused on in the huddle would be thrown out the window; with the trap, we just had to react and make the right play. Also, the trap would speed up the process. Even if we scored on a quick shot, they would have a chance for another offensive possession.

But the fact that we made a three instead of a two changed everything. Now we were in position to foul. After they made two free throws to cut our lead to 115-114, Danny Ainge intercepted a pass in our frontcourt. As Ainge let it fly from three-quarter court, I had a premonition of disaster. Ainge was a guy I had been having nightmares about.

"Oh, no, not this way," I muttered.

The ball sailed high and wide. We had done it! We were only the fifth team in NBA history to win a playoff series after being down 3–1.

The Phoenix Suns must have been thinking, How could lightning have struck for the second year in a row? They had us—and then they didn't.

We had such great respect for that Phoenix team. When they said we were special, it made us *feel* special. We celebrated and got on an airplane bound for Texas—but instead of going home to clean out the lockers, we were off to San Antonio for the Western Conference Finals.

THE SPURS HAD WON 62 games, best in the NBA. They won 55 of their last 66 under Bob Hill and had beaten us five of six times in the regular season. As happy as we were about the Phoenix series, we had to come back to earth quickly and get ourselves prepared for the task ahead.

In one of those games during the regular season when they were taking care of us, I remember Sean Elliott, who had been traded by Detroit to San Antonio during the off-season, standing by our bench and saying, "Coach, you had your year. This is *our* year."

Sean didn't say it in a cocky way. He's a class guy. He was just emphasizing how much the Spurs wanted to occupy that mountaintop that we had climbed the year before.

The Spurs had been romping through the league with Dennis Rodman around to help David Robinson inside. Avery Johnson had become such a positive for their team at point guard, and the Spurs had a nice complementary cast.

San Antonio had us, 93–92, with 26 seconds to go in Game One, and Elliott—an .807 foul shooter—was at the line. But Lady Luck was smiling on us as Elliott missed both attempts. With the door of opportunity wide open, we went with our post-up play to Hakeem. Everybody went to their spots, and Robert was open as they closed down on Hakeem. The great thing was that Robert had the confidence to step up and take the shot, even though he hadn't made a basket all night. Horry's 16-footer with 6.5 seconds to go gave us a 94–93 win and a 1–0 lead in the series.

We felt we had stolen Game One. Coming off an emotional series and having to travel, you don't really expect to win one like that.

As we huddled in our locker room, a lot of positive things were being said. "We've got to stay hungry," someone shouted.

"We've got to stay humble, too," another player yelled.

Hungry and humble: This became another rallying cry that was born in our locker room. These slogans weren't developed in advertising meetings; the words that stick are the ones that are said with true emotion in the heat of battle. These words that followed our championship successes were genuine, and I hope people understand it wasn't something that was manufactured to sell T-shirts.

You've got to stay hungry. You've got to stay humble. These are things that all coaches want to say to their teams, and it's a great feeling when the players say it for themselves. They're hitting it right on the button.

Prior to Game Two, Commissioner David Stern was on hand to present David Robinson with the MVP trophy. I don't think anyone could quarrel with Robinson getting the award, based on his performance in the regular season. He's a spectacular, athletic player; end to end, he might be the fastest big man in the game today. Some people are critical of his lack of inside power, but I feel David Robinson uses his quickness and speed as well as anyone. He can pull off the block, face up and drive by bigger defenders, not only for scores but for foul-shooting opportunities. He was at the top of the league in free throws attempted. He's a very tough man to defend.

Robinson had led his team to the best record, and his numbers were superlative. But as we were standing there watching the ceremony, I had a feeling that Hakeem would be especially pumped up. There was no way in the world I'd have to give a pep talk for that game.

The 1994 MVP went against the 1995 MVP and showed the moves of a ballerina and the strength of a weight lifter. Hakeem finished with 41 points, and we jumped on them early and held on for a 2–0 series lead.

Through the first two series, Hakeem had been so consistent and so reliable, but in the San Antonio series he hit a peak. I've never seen anything like it. Olajuwon was in another world. When we would watch the tapes after the game and see the things he was doing against a great defensive player—it was just amazing. When I'm on the porch with the grandkids talking about the greatest performances of all time, the series that Hakeem had against San Antonio will be at the top of the list, you can be assured of that.

In Game Two, Drexler was able to utilize his speed and height against Vinny Del Negro, and Horry had a big game with 21 points and five three-pointers.

Coming home with a 2–0 lead, we were determined to keep the eye of the tiger. But I have to give San Antonio credit: The Spurs showed they were a heavyweight team by beating us twice on our court to even the series.

"In the first two games, we stank," Spurs guard Doc Rivers said. "Winning is a great deodorant."

We were up by 11 in the third quarter of Game Three, but the Spurs began to get great play from their perimeter people—Elliott, Del Negro, and Avery Johnson. "A.J." is one of the fastest advancers of the ball in the league. He keeps you back on your heels. If you don't get back quickly enough on defense, it's a layup drill for him and their athletes. This time, they had the answers down the stretch.

Game Four was a blowout because we didn't attack the boards. The Spurs had a 64–39 rebounding edge, including 24 offensive rebounds. Rodman's 12 offensive rebounds were two more than our whole team. Rodman is an amazing player; he can be a significant factor for his team. He does all the hard stuff, like banging the boards on every shot, playing tough defense, and setting picks.

He has an uncanny knack for knowing where the ball will bounce, and he has quick feet to get him there sooner than his opponent. A lot of times, he doesn't even jump to try to get an offensive rebound, but the man assigned to box him out doesn't jump either—he's too busy trying to find Dennis to put a body on him.

Rodman is a lot like the Phantom of the Opera. He's there . . . then he's not. He might not score a lot of points, but the extra possessions he gets for his team are a big bonus. It's an element that every team would love to have.

Suddenly, the roles had been reversed: The Spurs were doing what the Rockets were supposed to be doing. It was like a slap in the face for us, letting us know that the team with the best regular-season record wasn't going to roll over. Four games, four road wins. We just wanted to keep that trend going for one more game.

Sure enough, we went back down Interstate 10 and won our third in a row at the Alamodome. Hakeem got 42, and Sam Cassell had a monster game off the bench with 30 points and 12 assists. San Antonio was so confounded by the road dominance that coach Bob Hill had his team spend the night in a San Antonio hotel. But nothing was working for the home team.

Now we had to figure out a way to break that road cycle. There's really no way to explain the home team losing the first five games of a playoff series, but with San Antonio and Houston only two hundred miles apart, both clubs had their fair share of supporters for the road games.

From our standpoint, at least, I think that helped. We were experiencing a relationship with Rockets fans at the San Antonio Marriott River Center that we never would have experienced at home. When you're home, guys drive to the arena and park underneath the Summit. You don't have that much contact with the fans.

When we came down those San Antonio elevators for each road game of this series, it was very emotional and inspiring. The lobby was jammed with well-wishers as we made our way to the bus.

At one point, a security man called me and asked, "Do you want to go down a back corridor and avoid all these people?"

"As long as you supervise them, we're going right through the lobby," I said. "I think this is helping us."

In Game Six back at the Summit, Hakeem finished what he had

started. His 39 points and 17 rebounds lifted us to a 100–95 victory and a 4–2 series triumph. For the six-game set, Olajuwon averaged 35.3 points. All you can say is that his series against San Antonio will be legendary.

I was sort of dazed as I walked off the floor. Here we were again, with a shot at the big prize. Any doubts about our being a championship team were completely gone. The dream I had about this team—the vision I had when we made the Drexler trade—was being realized.

Over in the Eastern Conference, the Indiana–Orlando series was going down to the wire, so we went back to our Galveston training camp and awaited the result. As our scouts edited the tapes of both teams, we saw that both teams presented problems. The high draft picks of Orlando—led by Shaquille O'Neal and Anfernee Hardaway—had been tough on us. Shaquille was such an awesome physical presence, and Hardaway had the height to give us matchup problems at the point. But then you looked at how well Reggie Miller was shooting and how well Larry Brown had the Pacers playing, and it figured to be a rough deal either way.

The Magic won the seventh game in Orlando. They were the new kids on the block. What a collection of young talent! They had the two major positions—point guard and center—filled with young superstars. Hardaway was constantly being compared to Magic Johnson; at 6-7, he was a versatile player with outstanding ballhandling and passing ability, and he was an improving outside shooter. He could play point guard, shooting guard, and small forward. At point guard in particular Hardaway presented big-time matchup problems. Kenny and Sam would have a big challenge dealing with Hardaway's post-ups.

Shaq was the kind of player, when you looked at his future, you knew the sky was the limit. He was so big and athletic. I didn't like to think about Hakeem riding off into the sunset and Shaq coming in to take over. Shaq is so powerful you can feel the force of his strength by just standing on the sidelines. But he was still learning how to add more finesse to his game to complement his raw power. He has a chance to become one of the most dominating players of all time.

Orlando had other talented players such as Nick Anderson, who started at big guard, and small forward Dennis Scott. Nick was strong as a bull; he could overpower most guys at his position inside and could also shoot from behind the three-point line. Scott was their best pure three-point shooter. He was a bomber, very streaky and very dangerous. Horace Grant, the former championship contributor with the Chicago Bulls, added leadership and a workmanlike attitude to this very young team.

The Magic were still flying high from their clutch victory over Indiana when our series began in Orlando.

Our starting lineup in the finals evolved from something that had happened earlier in the playoffs, when Horry guarded four-position players like Barkley and Dennis Rodman; with the rangy Horry at the four-position, we could start Mario Elie at small forward beginning in the San Antonio series.

As I said earlier, I had no plans to make Horry a four-man when we made the Drexler trade, but with the teams that we drew in the playoffs, we felt this lineup matched up better. Dennis Scott was a small forward who liked to stay on the perimeter and take three-pointers; it was a good matchup for the 6-5 Elie. We also felt Horry could handle himself defensively against Horace Grant. Horace is an intense, aggressive guy, but I wouldn't really call him an inside force. He's more of a face-up power forward. Also, Robert would be in position to help on Shaquille and still rotate out to their three-point shooters when playing the four-spot.

We were showing some rust from our six-day layoff as Orlando danced to a 20-point lead in Game One, but with Drexler pushing the ball relentlessly, we squared our jaws and came back on them, eventually going up by nine in the second half. Back came the Magic in a seesaw game, and it looked like we were goners with 10.5 seconds remaining.

With Orlando up by three, Nick Anderson missed two free throws. He hustled in to grab his second miss and was fouled again at the 7.9 mark. But Anderson's third shot of the sequence was off and so was the fourth. According to a mathematician contacted by NBC-TV, there was better than a 99-percent chance that Anderson would make at least one of those four free throws.

We wanted to win the game, but you had to feel for Nick Anderson when that one-percent came through for us. We were still breathing. Even so, we needed a three-pointer to force overtime. The odds of making a three-pointer when the defense knows it's coming aren't too good, either.

But Kenny Smith, who had already converted six treys, made a great individual move. We had called a play designed for him to come off a pick-and-roll. Instead, he made a nice crossover dribble, went away from the pick, gathered himself with Hardaway on him, and nailed the three-pointer with 1.6 seconds to go.

In overtime, we had the final possession and made it count. Drexler made a hard drive, and Hakeem was right there to tip in the miss with 1.3 showing on the clock. Just as in the San Antonio opener, we had stolen one. The way the bizarre finish unfolded simply had to be devastating for a young team like Orlando.

The NBA had us out for a party at Universal Studios after Game One, and everybody had a great time. It was almost *too* comfortable: great weather, great entertainment, a comeback victory on the road.

When we gathered for our Game Two shootaround, our guys looked like they were out for a day at the beach. They were feeling good about themselves, but the truth was that Orlando controlled that first game and we were fortunate to win. Still, we were acting like we had control of the series.

I waited and waited for a change of that cavalier attitude, but it didn't come. When we came together after the shootaround, I told the players how I felt. "I can't believe the way we're acting," I said. "Did we forget what happened in Game One? We were very fortunate to get that one. Now here we are in a situation where we can really put the pressure on, and we're not focused. They're probably going to kick our ass big-time."

Well, we came out roaring. I don't know if what I said made a difference, but I felt it was the right thing to say, and Game Two turned out to be the only one-sided game in the whole series. Whereas Smith had gone off for seven treys in the opener, Game Two belonged to our other point guard. Sam Cassell reared up for 31 points, and we were up by 22 at the half. The Magic made up some ground in the second half, but our 117–106 victory made for a great plane ride home.

We got a big lift from the old pro Charles Jones in Game Two; he went into the pivot for 15 minutes and helped hold the fort against O'Neal. He disrupted Shaquille a little bit while Hakeem was getting some valuable rest. Charles was a true professional, as were his many Jones brothers who played pro basketball. Earlier in the playoffs, Charles had played solid minutes against Karl Malone and David Robinson. Also, unsung Chucky Brown played 12 minutes in Game Two and hit 4 of 5 shots. It was a total team effort. Each guy who went out there made a valuable contribution.

I wasn't writing off Orlando by any means as we headed home. Game One had shattered their confidence, and then we really came out focused for Game Two. We knew the emotions they were going through were a big factor. I felt if they ever got a win, it would change everything. There was tremendous potential on that Magic team.

The Magic played very well in Game Three, but they made only 8 of 31 from three-point range. That glitch was just enough for us to squeak through and win it, 106–103. The big shot belonged to Horry: With a 101–100 lead and less than a minute to go, Horry set his feet for a three-pointer that clinched the game.

At this stage, we were on a Magic carpet ride, no pun intended. We were making the big play, doing all the little things it takes to win a championship. What a transformation it had been: When the playoffs started, we didn't know who we were, but the pieces had come together and our belief grew stronger as the playoffs went on. With each playoff series, our chemistry got better and better.

We won Game Three on a Sunday and had to wait until Wednesday for Game Four. There was a lot of "sweep" talk going around Houston, and I wasn't happy about that. Again, I want to emphasize how scary I thought Orlando could be if they broke through with that first victory. It could have triggered a volcano of confidence.

In Game Four, we were only up by one heading into the fourth quarter. But Mario Elie had an outstanding game, hitting 9 of 11 shots. We took over down the stretch, and the championship hoopla began building to a great crescendo. As the game was winding down, I made my way toward Orlando coach Brian Hill.

"Everybody is going to talk about a sweep, but this series was a lot closer than that," I said to Hill.

This championship was special for so many reasons. It was especially great to see Clyde and Hakeem celebrate the ultimate moment of victory together. Twelve years earlier, they had fallen short in that memorable Houston–North Carolina State national championship game. Now they were like two kids in a candy store.

For Clyde, it was his first championship, and that dream I had the day of the Drexler trade was realized. He wanted a championship so badly, and he paid the price to get it. When Hakeem and Clyde embraced, it was an emotional, storybook ending. Yes, fairy tales can sometimes come true.

One of the best moments I've had in sports was when Hakeem found me on the court in the aftermath of Game Four. He grabbed me with a show of emotion that you don't often see from him. It wasn't a situation where we were thrown together in a small area; he sought me out in the mayhem, and that embrace on our court was one of the greatest feelings of my life.

Once we got healthy and survived that first tough series against Utah, our belief in ourselves was back, and we never stopped believing after that. This championship was another example of the wonderful things that can happen when people work together.

There were so many different heroes because we shared the ball. Different players had big nights. That was really gratifying. Everyone had their time in the spotlight.

Most of all, it was about heart, and I expressed that feeling when I got the chance to address our crowd in the postgame ceremony.

"Nobody has ever done what this team has done . . . come from the sixth seed . . . down in the series. We had nonbelievers all along the way," I said. "I have one thing to say to those nonbelievers: Don't *ever* underestimate the heart of a champion!"

The '95 Rockets are going to have a legacy. They will be symbols for every underdog. For every high school or college team that struggles through the regular season and starts with a clean slate in the tournament, they can look at us to see that the underdog can put it together at the eleventh hour and become a champion.

The "Twoston" Rockets. It had a wonderful ring to it as the city of Houston celebrated another title.

For anybody who faces adversity and overwhelming odds, remember this '94–95 team. Remember the hurdles it overcame and the courage it displayed time after time. Miracles can happen. The '95 World Champion Rockets were proof of that.

19

IT'S GAME NIGHT for the Houston Rockets. The building goes dark, the spotlight focuses on the five starters who trot out for the pregame introductions, the houselights come back, and the officials toss the ball into the air. For the next two hours or so, the fans see what I believe to be the greatest sport in the world.

The focus is usually on the players and the head coach, who often patrols the sidelines. But there are so many people behind the scenes who play instrumental roles in the high-speed drama.

When I started playing in the NBA under Alex Hannum, the head coach did all the coaching. But the league has changed a great deal since those days of the solo coach or the coach and one assistant.

Most teams today have at least two assistants and other helpers. The fact is, you can't do it by yourself because there's so much that goes into running an NBA team. I've been blessed to have had a lot of quality people working by my side.

When the game begins, I have three assistants sitting beside me. Prior to the 1996–97 season, those men were Carroll Dawson, Bill Berry, and Larry Smith. In the fall of '96, Carroll moved into a front-office position and Jim Boylen moved from video coordinator to an assistant coaching job.

C.D. and I have been together for seventeen years. Del Harris hired him as an assistant in 1979, and Carroll coached me for two years before we both spent ten years as assistants under Harris, Bill Fitch, and Don Chaney.

Carroll and I have become as close as brothers. He has affected my life as much as anyone. He's truly a special person, a man of great integrity. He'll always try to do the right thing. To do anything less wouldn't even enter his mind.

Carroll and I have a common philosophy of life: The only way to get the things you want is to work for them. Just wishing and hoping won't get it done. There is no trick, no shortcut, no substitute for hard work.

Those close to the Rockets know Carroll is one of the funniest guys around. He has a quick wit and loves to turn words around and give them a double meaning. Some people have a jagged edge to their humor; they may hurt someone's feelings just to get a laugh. C.D. is just the opposite. He'll use humor to make people feel good about themselves or to make them feel welcome.

It's amazing that Carroll and I have become so close, since we come from completely different backgrounds. I was a city kid, and Carroll was from the country. He grew up in a small town in east Texas called Alba. I've never met a person prouder to be a Texan.

Fittingly, Carroll loves country music. On our rides out to the airport when Carroll was coaching, the person doing the driving had control of the radio dial. I would just stare in amazement when Carroll rattled off a list of facts about a song on the radio. He'd know where the singer was from, who was singing background, and so on. Once he even asked, "Rudy, I'll bet you can't guess who's playing that fiddle in the background?"

"Carroll, I don't *care* who's playing the fiddle. Could we please listen to some normal music?"

I shouldn't be pointing fingers about musical taste, because mine isn't exactly Top 40. I like rhythm and blues and even reggae, the music that originated in Jamaica.

One day, I happened to have a reggae tape in my deck when Carroll looked over at me and said, "Is this that spaghetti music that you like?"

"Spaghetti music?"

"Yeah, isn't this ragu?"

It took me about a year to understand Carroll's accent. At first I was completely confused. Early in our relationship, I asked him for directions to a gym.

"You go down this freeway until you see a tar," Carroll said.

"You mean, there will be tar on the road?"

"No, it's a tall structure."

"Oh, you mean *tower.*"

"You take that exit and go down the road a piece until you come to an open field filled with fliers."

"Carroll, what kind of fliers? People with kites? Or is it an airport?"

"No, beautiful fliers that grow in the ground."

"Oh, *flowers.*"

"Now, make a left and take that road all the way past the far house."

"Past the last house?"

"No, the *far* house. The *far* house where they have the *far* engines."

"Oh, *fire* engines."

I threw up my hands. "Carroll," I said, "just pick me up and we'll go together."

The two things Carroll really cares about—besides his family, of course—are basketball and golf. He's a tremendous golfer. For a man who's 6-6, 260 pounds, he not only has a power game, but also a soft, finesse game. When Carroll has a club in his hands, there's nothing he could do that would surprise me. I've witnessed so many of his miraculous shots. The highlight was a shot he made on a Salt Lake golf course one summer while we were attending our rookie camp there. He was over 220 yards away from the green after his drive on a par-five hole. Carroll nailed a two-iron and asked, "Where's it going?"

"It's going toward the flag," I said, watching the flight of the ball. "It's on the green. It's in the hole!"

The reason Carroll asked me where the ball was going was that he has lost sight in one eye, and if conditions aren't perfect, he has trouble seeing out of his working eye. One of our good friends said after seeing the double-eagle shot, "If I gouge out one of my eyes, will I be able to hit the ball like that?"

Basketball remains Carroll's first love. He played at Baylor and later coached there for fourteen years. Unlike me, Carroll always wanted to be a coach. It was his calling. He has the perfect personality to deal with people. Most of all, he loves to teach and is great at it. Nothing gives him more satisfaction than helping a player learn something new to add to his game.

Carroll understood he would rarely be recognized for his help. It didn't matter to him; he was just happy that the player got better.

I believe Carroll was the best big-man coach in the game. When he taught his men the fundamentals of the inside game, every detail was covered: how to get position, how to give a good target, how to catch the ball, locating the defense, making a quick decision on what shot to use.

He drilled the centers and power forwards each day: jump hooks, step hooks, drop-steps, turnarounds, face-ups. I've seen him do wonders with players who came to us without a basic shot.

Every player should have a basic. Some big guys never learn to play with their back to the basket in college, and when they get the ball in good position close to the basket, they don't have anything in mind—no plan. Usually this results in a weak shot. It's frustrating for the player; he catches the ball in a high-percentage area, but he feels awkward and doesn't have the maneuverability to get the ball in the basket.

After working with Carroll, players began to have confidence in their inside moves. They began to feel more and more comfortable using those shots in a game.

I believe Carroll played an instrumental role in the development of Hakeem Olajuwon. With all the constant drilling, he helped Hakeem become one of the most feared inside players in the history of basketball.

I realized what a great teacher Carroll is when I was still playing. He was born to be a coach. I can only imagine the disappointment he felt when his time came to move up to head coach, and it was blocked by his health situation. I would have loved being a helper with Carroll as the head coach; it would have been the natural progression in Carroll's career.

A lot of people would have been bitter about the situation. Not Carroll. He knew that Steve Patterson was right in expressing concern about Carroll's health if Carroll had been elevated to head coach in 1992. Carroll understands the tremendous amount of stress with which a head coach must contend. He could have felt sorry for himself and sat around moping; instead, he read the situation and, as always, tried to do the right thing. He encouraged me to take the job.

The first thing he did was to help me start thinking like a head coach. I had to establish a philosophy, a belief system; that's why we spent those many hours up at Lake Conroe talking about all the facets of coaching.

I realized early on how lonely it gets being a head coach. When things go wrong, either you're blamed or you're expected to fix the problem.

It's amazing how people react to coaches when the team is losing. Some people think everything that happens on the court is something the coach has control over. Every bad pass or missed shot is the coach's fault: He should have *made* them do it the right way. It's as if the players are robots and the coaches have the controls. People forget that there are finely conditioned athletes wearing the other uniforms who are doing everything in their power to stop us from doing what we want.

When you need support, it's important to have people you can confide in and lean on. Having Carroll is like having a family member on your staff.

WHEN most fans think of coaching, they think of the guy standing on the sidelines, giving hand signals to his players and ranting and raving for one reason or another. Bench coaching during the game is probably the most critical part of the job, but it loses all its importance if all the hard work and preparation hasn't been done beforehand in practice. What good is it to signal for a particular play if you don't know your team can do what you ask of it?

There are numerous decisions a coach must make during a

game, especially if he calls set plays, which I happen to do. I usually make an average of fifty calls a game; the rest of the time we're fastbreaking or in a transition game, looking for easy opportunities to score. In addition to the plays, the coach has to decide who to substitute and when, and when to call timeouts. There are also the decisions we have to make before a game, in our morning shootaround or pregame meeting; these usually involve our defensive game plan: How will we play the opponent's pick-and-roll plays? Which post-up players will we double-team, who will be the double-team man, and when will we bring the double—on the pass, on the dribble, or when he gets to the lane? As the game progresses, we watch and make adjustments if these plans don't work out as we'd hoped.

There are three basic areas that a coach can try to control during a game: tempo, matchups, and momentum.

Tempo describes the pace of play; you want the game played at the pace your team plays best. The Rockets have had very athletic players while I've been coach here, so we like to take advantage by running the fast break whenever we can. We do this either by causing a turnover or by running when the other team misses a shot and doesn't get back on defense quickly. But since we haven't been as effective making plays on the run when the other team does get back, I prefer to see us show some patience rather than firing up quick, low-percentage outside shots; that's when we want to work the ball inside, ideally before their defense is totally set.

When the other team scores, we generally run a set play that I've called from the bench. Again, the key word is patience; we don't want to take a quick shot unless the defense has broken down and we can get a layup or a wide-open shot.

On defense, we want the opponent to do the opposite of what we're trying to accomplish on offense: We try to take away their fast break by getting back and making them set up in the half-court, and then we apply pressure to force them to take a low-percentage shot or, better, commit a turnover.

The perfect tempo would be a fast break for us, forcing them to take the ball and letting us set up the defense, which sets up another stop and a fast break, etc. Most games won't turn out so neatly; you don't get a lot of blowouts in this league. Usually, the tempo shifts from team to team.

What can a coach do when the tempo is unfavorable for his team? Here's an example: Say we're playing the Lakers during the Magic Johnson era. Their best tempo was a lot quicker than ours. Say they've gotten into their Showtime fast-breaking game: they're getting layups and easy shots, and their fans are pumped up, encouraging them to pour it on.

The NBA isn't like college ball, where you can slow down the game just by taking a lot longer to shoot. But there are a number of things that I can do. Normally, we have two people back on defense when we shoot; we can add another man to try and slow down their fast break, sacrificing some manpower on the offensive boards. We can also challenge the man who rebounds the ball, getting our hands up so he cannot make a quick outlet pass.

Another way is to deny the ball to their key player on the break—in this example, Magic Johnson, their playmaker and push man. We want to make him come back for the ball instead of getting it on the run, which breaks up the rhythm of their fast break.

The best way to keep tempo under control is to execute well on offense and score. They now have to take the ball out of bounds, which gives us time to set up our defense. I'll usually call one of our most reliable plays at these times.

Matchups, which you can affect through substitutions, is another factor of the game a coach really has to stay on top of. We have control of who we match up with defensively; how they play us is out of our control. We're always looking for matchups we can win, where our player can get the best of theirs. At worst, we hope for a standoff.

This is the part of the game that's like a chess match. When a starter needs a rest, do I have a substitute who can win the matchup, too, or at least hold his own? I may be matching a reserve against a starter, but the reserve is fresher; the opponent's starter has to be tiring, too. But usually it's reserve against reserve.

There are times when a reserve might not play against certain teams, because of the matchups. I've always believed in using the bench a lot; I believe it's an important factor in having a successful team, especially for team morale. I know that being a reserve is not an easy role; the starter has the luxury of playing right from the jump ball, when everything is equal, while the reserve is coming into a game that's established its own energy level, its own flow. We might be ahead, and need the reserve to keep the energy level high. Or we may be trailing, and he needs to inject enough added energy to pick everybody up. And he won't have the luxury of slowly adjusting to the game; he has to do it immediately. A lot of players have a hard time performing this role, especially if they're used to being starters.

There are six basic reasons for a substitution. The first and most obvious is to rest a player who's in the game. The second is foul trouble; I want to make sure I have the best players available at the end of the game.

The third reason is matchups. I may feel I have a better-equipped player coming off the bench to handle a particular matchup. Fourth is game situations: At the end of quarters, say, we like to put in another three-point shooter in place of an inside player and run an isolation, hoping to draw a double-team and create an open three-point shot. I've used players like Pete Chilcutt and Matt Bullard in these situations. This also applies to the late-game situations when we need three-pointers.

The fifth reason is when we need a player's special ability. We may need a good rebounder in the game if we're getting hurt on the boards. Late in the game, when we're trying to protect a lead and the defense is fouling, we'll insert all our best free-throw shooters.

The last reason for substituting, which I hope rarely happens, is because of poor play. With the vigorous schedule that NBA players have to endure, even the great ones have occasional terrible nights, and you have to sit them down.

Momentum is what you hope you'll get from controlling the tempo and having the right matchups. You hear people talk about momentum all the time in sports, and it's something you can't see, but you sure can feel it. It's real; it's like a great tidal wave crashing into you, trying to wash you away or pulling you along with it.

When it's in your favor, you feel invincible; when it's against you, you have to find a way to get it stopped. It's a very big concern for coaches.

The number-one way to deal with momentum running against you is by calling a timeout—not only to break the opponent's rhythm and to let the adrenaline level die down, but more important, to reaffirm our game plan and objectives. I believe my behavior is very important during these timeouts; I have to show I have confidence in the team and not show frustration or panic—though if we're not hustling or applying ourselves, I'll become a little more aggressive and I might throw a couple of adjectives into my sentences to get us refocused.

Sometimes, timeouts alone won't do it. Usually, I have to make coaching changes to get things turned around, either by substituting or by making a decision to change our defensive or offensive approaches to the game. This is usually when you employ your pressing defense.

What do you do when momentum is on your side? You smile.

Players win games. But a coach can help by putting them in situations where the players can do the most good.

LOOK DOWN the Rockets bench on game night and you'll see assistant Bill Berry. Bill was working with the Rockets as a regional advance scout on the West Coast when I was an assistant. My role was to prepare our team for what the other team was doing, and I would work with the advance scout to prepare a report that the players could understand. Bill did a great job; we spent a lot of time on the telephone, going over strengths and weaknesses. I felt we communicated well.

When I got the head-coaching job, we needed another assistant to fill my old role as preparation coach. Bill was the logical choice. He's a meticulous guy who pays attention to detail. His written scouting reports are neat and thorough, and he does his assignments like clockwork.

Prior to the game we're playing, Bill takes the scouting report prepared by our advance scout and pares it down to five or six basic plays that our opponents run. He watches at least two of their most recent games to make sure they haven't added anything new since our scout last saw them.

Bill diagrams these plays on a scouting pad and presents them to the coaches on the morning of the game. We decide what defenses we'll employ and talk about what we think the opponent would have trouble defending. After this meeting we have a shootaround, preferably at 11 A.M. It really should be called a preparation practice. The first thing we do with the team is watch an edited videotape of the opponents' plays in our locker room. Then we go onto the floor, where Bill assembles the scout team.

We tell our players what the opponents' play is called and then literally walk them through the routes they'll run, letting our players know any special tendencies the opponents may have.

While Bill is doing this, the other coaches address the defense on how we should defend the play. For instance, if we were playing the Orlando Magic in previous years and we decided to double-team Shaquille O'Neal when he got the ball in the post area, we would have the defense walk through the rotations: Who will be the doubling man? How would we rotate out to cover their dangerous three-point shooters?

I feel we're a well-prepared club, and Bill Berry is an integral part of that. Bill had been an assistant coach at Michigan State during the Magic Johnson era. Bill was also the head coach at San Jose State, where he coached his very talented son, Ricky Berry, who was drafted by the Sacramento Kings in the first round. Bill also became an assistant coach with the Kings and has done advance and personnel scouting. He has a well-rounded knowledge of basketball. He helps me in many ways, from suggesting various drills to analyzing our play to counseling others. He has a keen eye for recognizing talent. In practice, Bill coaches the guards and small forwards. His shooting drills are always executed with a lot of enthusiasm and competition. Three-point shooting is a very important part of our offensive system, and Bill always has our guys sharp and confident. With the success that we've had, Bill has been considered by other teams looking for a talented, experienced coach. I always want my assistants to have an opportunity to advance in this profession. Fortunately for us, Bill has not accepted an offer. It would be a great loss to me and to the team if Bill went elsewhere.

My other assistant, Larry Smith, is one of the youngest coaches in the league. I enjoyed coaching Larry when he played for the Rockets because he had a no-nonsense approach to his job as a rebounder. I knew he would carry that approach over to his job as a coach.

It's not easy making the transition from player to coach. I've gone through it, and I understand it takes time. Larry is constantly growing as a coach. He loves the game and he loves working with people. He's developed strong relationships with some of our players, and they feel they have a supporter in him: someone who's willing to listen to them, someone who's willing to give them extra time after practice. I've gotten to know the man they call "Mr. Mean," and he *does* look mean, but I've found he's one of the most caring people I've ever met. Everything I believed about Larry's work ethic was true, and then some. He truly hates to lose. I couldn't find anyone more loyal to me and the Houston Rockets. With C.D. moving up, Larry has taken over the role of big-man coach. He's doing a great job, especially in the rebounding area. Larry has gained valuable bench coaching experience by coaching our rookies and free agents in our summer league program.

The young players really respond well to him. He always manages to have a winning record, regardless of our talent level. He is well respected and has a very bright future as a coach in the NBA.

Besides the assistants on the bench, there are many other people who influence the result of the game.

The late John Killilea was the personnel scout in our drive to two world titles. John had been an assistant coach at Boston, Milwaukee, and New Jersey, and also coached in the CBA before joining our organization. John scouted colleges, international players, and other NBA teams, looking for possible assets to make the Houston Rockets stronger. I would have our whole staff help out during training camp, and that was when the coach in Killer came out. He loved to help teach defense.

A ROCKET AT HEART

I was a player when Killer coached in the league. I wasn't known for my defense, and I know Killer had serious doubts about my being able to get the Rockets to become a good defensive team. I really soaked up the things he talked about, especially how to teach defensive technique. His input helped me develop our defensive philosophy.

Killer liked to tell jokes. He had a habit of punching the guy to whom he was telling the joke, I guess to add emphasis.

I began to notice a pattern during John's joke-telling: If there was more than one person listening to the joke and I was in the group, the recipient of the punch was always me. It was like I was the only punching bag.

I brought this up to the other guys on my staff, and they would say they hadn't noticed the habit. Why should they notice? They weren't getting hit.

John's punches weren't hard; it was just that he was always telling jokes, and the ensuing jabs came so often. I tried to figure out a way to avoid the punches. Even better, to find a way for him to adopt a new punching bag.

Once I thought I had the perfect plan. We were on the road, and Killer was driving. There were three passengers: Steve Patterson, Carroll Dawson, and myself. Because I was the tallest, I usually sat next to the driver in the shotgun seat. This time, I told C.D. I'd rather sit in the back and stretch out.

I then asked Killer to tell us a joke. Now, I figured, Carroll would be the logical recipient of the punches.

I couldn't wait. This was going to be great.

Killer begins: "Three guys walk into a bar . . ."

He gets to the punch line, and the son of a gun actually reached into the backseat and punched me. I couldn't believe it.

I finally asked Killer if he was doing it on purpose. He was genuinely surprised. He didn't realize what he was doing.

"I won't do it anymore," Killer promised. Of course, the next time he told me a joke he hit me again.

Basketball was in Killer's blood. He was always on the road. If not in some college town in our country, Killer would be in Europe looking at international prospects.

275

We grew increasingly concerned about Killer's health the last couple of years. He had diabetes, so he had to be careful with his diet and not get too fatigued. We wanted him to cut down on the travel. It was proposed that he only do games in the Midwest, close to his suburban Milwaukee home, or do one game a week and scout the other games at home off videotape.

Killer came into my office one day and shut the door behind him.

"Rudy, I appreciate your concern," Killer said. "But I feel fine. I know how to take care of my health problems. Basketball is my life. It's what I do. I want to work. I'd go crazy just sitting at home. You don't have to worry about me. If something did happen, that would be okay."

Killer then leaned forward and whispered something to me that I'll never forget. He had a premonition.

"Rudy, I know I'm going to die on the road. That's the way it should be. Just like my friend Jack McMahon."

I hated for Killer to talk this way. But I deeply admired his love for his job and the game of basketball. We did cut Killer's work load. But two years later, just as he predicted, he died while on the road.

Another guy who has an influence on whether we're successful on game night is Joe Ash, our advance scout. I met Joe at the Portsmouth (Virginia) postseason all-star tournament, and we would sit in the balcony and exchange opinions about players we were scouting. I quickly gained respect for Joe's feel for a player's chances of making it in the NBA. One of the players Joe was high on when we first started conversing was an unheralded kid from Iowa State named Jeff Hornacek. Everything that Joe saw in Hornacek was later borne out, as Hornacek went from being a low second-round pick to one of the top shooting guards in the league.

I would sometimes see Joe on the road when we were both advance-scouting; we'd go out to dinner after games and talk basketball. We had good chemistry. Joe had been a small-college coach, but spent a lot of years primarily as an educator. He also did part-time scouting for several NBA teams.

When I got the Rockets' head-coaching job and we needed a scout, Joe's name came to mind. He has done a terrific job as our advance scout. He gives detailed reports on our opponents and also does some college scouting. He has been invaluable in keeping us informed, and we've benefited greatly from Joe's efforts.

Jim Boylen became our video coordinator in 1992. He, like Bill Berry, was an assistant under Jud Heathcote at Michigan State. When we hired Jim, he had already been working with computerized video machines. Jim helped update our video department. His duties included editing our opponents' strongest plays from previous games so the coaches could prepare the game plan and the players could see them before our shootarounds.

I've always felt that players get a better feel for their opponents when they can see the man on video. We sometimes draw plays on the blackboard to show the problems an individual opponent presents, but when our players can see the people they'll be matched up against, it really gets their attention.

Until his move to a bench-assistant role, Jim worked in conjunction with Joe Ash and Bill Berry to keep us well prepared. At home games and during the entire playoffs, he would break down games while they were being played into offensive and defensive edits.

This really allows us to focus on what's going on. Sometimes Jim had a tape ready for the team to view at halftime so we could make quick adjustments. After the games, the coaches didn't have to wait around to pick up edited versions: Jim already had done it.

Jim is a friendly, open guy. He's excited to be in the NBA. He knows how difficult it is to break into the league, and he's very appreciative of the opportunity we've given him.

As a video coordinator during our championship seasons, Jim worked hard at his job. It's not an easy one; I know, because I used to be a video guy. It's so time-consuming. Even with state-of-the-art editing machines, it still takes about two hours to break down a tape. Then the video coordinator still has to put the data into a computer. He describes every play and punches it in. With the new machinery, we have a lot more options on what we want to take out.

If we're being hurt by the other team's pick-and-roll, all the video coordinator has to do is punch in a request to take out all the pick-and-rolls, and the computer quickly does it.

As game time approaches, players need to have their equipment taken care of so they can fully concentrate on the job at hand. David Nordstrom is our equipment manager, the only one the Houston Rockets have ever had. David was just a kid when we hired him in the late 1970s. He's been through great seasons with the Rockets and he's been through the tough times, too. He's part of the Rockets family. He has made it his goal to take care of the players' needs. With D.H., they don't look at him as an equipment manager; they look at him as a friend.

So many people are a part of the mental and physical preparation for a game. They aren't often in the limelight, but they have a passion and a drive to help make the Rockets the best they can be.

Ed Bernholz and his wife, Marge, were season-ticket holders for many years. They were hard-core fans, very loyal. They would get to games early, as soon as the doors to the Summit opened. A lot of the players get to the arena early to work on their shooting, and the Bernholz family enjoyed watching players tune up. When I was an assistant, Ed made it a habit to come down to the floor and tell me a new joke. It became a ritual. I used to look forward to seeing him so I could get a good laugh and break the tension.

Ed was in his sixties then, but he had the outlook of someone much younger. He enjoyed life and enjoyed working with people in the business world. Unfortunately, his great outlook on life was tested when his wife suddenly became ill. After a courageous struggle, Marge passed away.

Losing a soul mate is one of the toughest things we have to deal with in life. Ed did a remarkable job coping with it. He threw himself into basketball even more intensely. If there was a good pickup game anywhere in Houston, Ed would be there to see it.

Our coaching staff was always interested in seeing how our players were doing in the off-season pickup games, so I often ran into Ed. He had a zest for the game that I really appreciated.

We became close friends. Ed had time on his hands after retiring from his business career, and he asked me if there was anything he could do to help the Rockets. It didn't matter what it was. He just wanted to be close to the team he loved.

Money wasn't an issue. Ed said he would do it on a volunteer basis.

Well, I was just an assistant coach; I couldn't make that kind of decision, so I talked to Bill Fitch about Ed.

Bill has a big heart and really liked Eddie when he met him. Bill was known as Captain Video around the league, so Ed suggested that he could help us obtain tapes by recording them at his home, where he had a satellite dish. He also organized a system so that we would pick up every game we needed by going to a local television station or using the service the NBA provides.

Ed loved his role with the Rockets and helped us stay on top of what our opponents were doing. Our video department eventually grew as we added satellite dishes and hired people to record and edit them, but when video was in its infancy for the Houston Rockets, Ed was the guy who made our jobs so much easier.

Over the years, he hasn't lost any of his enthusiasm for basketball. He still spends his spare time watching whatever basketball action is going on around the city. I have respect for Ed's opinion; when we had a shortage of players for our summer-league team a few years back, Ed suggested we look at Tim Breaux, a young player he had watched in some of the pickup games. Tim wound up having an outstanding summer league and eventually made our team.

I don't know how many teams have a guy like "Coach Ed," a man who volunteers himself to the team. But I'm grateful for his dedication. This man has had a hand in helping us win two championships, and he has made life easier for all of us. Ed Bernholz is a giver.

Another extremely important member of any athletic team is the trainer. The health and welfare of the players loom large in determining what success the team will have. The knowledge and skill of a trainer make a big difference.

Ray Melchiorre was our trainer for nine years, including the back-to-back championship seasons. Ray is a veteran who broke in with the Buffalo Braves the same year I joined the San Diego Rockets.

Ray grew up in Philadelphia and has held many jobs in the East: Buffalo, Pittsburgh, Boston. When he moved to Houston, something strange happened: He became an urban cowboy. He fell in love with horses, especially cutting horses. He owns one and keeps it on a ranch outside of Houston.

These horses are like athletes with great agility; they cut a calf away from the herd, then play defense on them. Ray has ridden in rodeos. He wears cowboy boots and big, shiny belt buckles. He now considers himself a Texan.

I'll always have a special place in my heart for Dick Vandervoort, the Rockets' trainer throughout my playing career. Dick stood only 5-3, but he was a giant in the players' eyes. He always made you feel well cared for and did a great job connecting with the players.

Here's just one example of how much Dick meant to the Rockets: During our 1985–86 Western Conference championship season, Hakeem Olajuwon suffered a scary knee injury one night against the Los Angeles Clippers. There was talk of a quick surgical procedure, but Dick, relying on his years of experience, didn't overreact to the situation. He chose to send Hakeem back home to our doctor, and it was later determined that surgery would not be required. After a month of rehabilitation work with Dick, Hakeem was back to full speed and wound up leading us to the NBA Finals against Boston. It was a tremendous loss to everyone who knew Dick when he was killed in a farming accident shortly after the 1986–87 season.

If you happen to catch a glimpse of a muscular guy seated directly behind me on game night, you're looking at another key member of the Rockets' organization.

The first time I saw Robert Barr he was a weight lifter with arms as big as most guys' thighs. He was Ralph Sampson's personal trainer. Bill Fitch was impressed with the work Robert was doing with Ralph, and he hired Robert as the Rockets' strength coach.

Robert is blessed with a warm personality. He's a people person. After a few minutes around him, you find yourself drawn closer to him. I guess you could say he has personal magnetism.

What really wins people over is the fact that Robert genuinely cares about them. They feel they have a friend they can trust and that he'll be there when they need him. The effect Robert has had on our players is amazing. His job was to push them harder than they've ever been pushed. Pain was a big part of his program. He pushed players to the point of exhaustion, and the players loved him for it. They came to depend on him.

During the summer, when a lot of players take it easy, Robert had our guys working out five days a week. He couldn't even think about taking a vacation.

"What would my guys do without me?" Robert would say.

Robert's weight-lifting program helped all our players. Two guys who benefited greatly were Jim Petersen and Matt Bullard. Both of them came into the league with great potential; they just didn't have what we call NBA bodies.

During my playing career, there wasn't a lot of weight training. Only a small percentage of players were serious lifters. I learned the benefits of weight training from Robert. It helps conditioning. It helps prevent injury. It makes you stronger, which in turn gives you confidence.

The confidence certainly became evident in Petersen. Only a small percentage of third-round draft picks make it in the league, and Pete was one of Robert's hardest workers.

Pete loved to use his newfound strength. One night, in a game at San Antonio, he got into a skirmish with Artis Gilmore. Artis went about 7-2, 280 pounds, and was considered one of the strongest players in the league.

After the Gilmore–Petersen altercation, players were separated and there were free throws to shoot. As the rebounders lined up, there was still a little talking going on between Artis and Pete.

"Are you crazy?" a San Antonio player said to Petersen. "Why are you messing with Artis? He's the strongest player in the league."

"He's not stronger than me," Pete shot back. "I'm not backing down."

We heard this conversation from our bench. Later, Bill Fitch pulled Barr aside and said, "Robert, you've created a monster.

You've made Petersen stronger. But can you now make him smarter before he gets himself killed?"

Robert's summer program brought the players closer. In the past, our guys didn't see each other much in the off-season. Now they were seeing each other five or six times a week. They encouraged each other to push it to the max, and it had a tremendous bonding effect on the team.

My wife, Sophie, worked out with Robert for a while.

"Robert is usually a sweet guy, but when he gets in the weight room, he's *mean*," Sophie told me.

After one of her workouts, Sophie stopped by a doughnut shop. Robert was waiting outside with a stern look on his face.

"Sophie, I hope those are for someone else," Robert said. "My people don't eat doughnuts."

Over the ensuing years, Sophie and Robert have developed a close friendship. But she won't work out with him anymore.

Robert and I didn't get off to a flying start. When I was on the road as an advance scout and the team was at home, Bill Fitch had Robert do my job of editing in the video room. When I came back off the road one time, I was surprised to find Robert positioned in front of the video monitor.

"Hey, Rob, what are you doing back here?"

"Bill wanted the job done right, so he asked me to do it. Coach said I do a much better job than you."

"Okay, Robert, quit messing around. I've got work to do."

"I'm not kidding," Robert said. "I know exactly what he wants. Relax and watch an expert at work."

I was losing my patience.

"Dammit, Robert, the game is starting. Move over."

"Don't talk to me in that tone," Robert responded.

Robert got up. We squared off and danced around the room with our hands in the boxer's position. We never threw a punch. Instead, we exchanged insults.

"You can't take it because I'm better at editing than you, chump."

"I don't come into your weight room and interfere. That's where you need to stay, musclehead."

"You can't come into my weight room because we don't allow wimps in there," Robert said.

"Just because you look like Mr. T, you don't scare me. I know you're just a teddy bear."

While Robert has the ability to bring people together, he also has the talent to be an agitator. He used this skill to push players to goals they never dreamed possible. He'd say, "How are you going to battle those big guys if you can only lift a hundred fifty pounds?"

With me, he agitates because he enjoys getting on my nerves and seeing me react. I guess it's part of our chemistry.

That first confrontation ended with both of us bursting out laughing and me resuming my job with periodic verbal jabs from him.

Not a day goes by that we don't have a playful confrontation, and the players have noticed. When things are quiet, a player might say, "Hey, T, Coach Barr is getting out of line."

"What's he going to do? He can't whip me," I'd say. And then Robert and I would be off and running.

Through the years, our relationship grew closer and closer. We started spending more time together off the court. As I do with Carroll, I consider Robert the brother I never had. Robert's wife, Valerie, is a wonderful person who loves to laugh, and she really hit it off with Sophie.

Once when the Barrs were at our house, their daughter Kristy somehow managed to lose her Floaties while swimming in our pool. Kristy was only four years old, and she began to sink to the bottom of the pool. I happened to be barbecuing at the time, and I was watching the youngsters. I threw down my fork and was on my way in when my son, Trey, suddenly came to the surface with Kristy in his arms. Kristy was gasping for air and Trey was all smiles, especially when we all praised him for his heroic deed.

To this day, Kristy looks up to Trey, flutters her eyes and says, "My hero."

Robert and I began to do a lot of fishing. We'd either go north to Conroe for freshwater fish or south to Galveston, when the trout were running. Neither of us will win trophies for our fishing ability, but that time together gave us a chance to talk about a lot of things. Or maybe we wouldn't talk; we'd just quietly spend several hours together, building a strong, silent bond.

One of the subjects we would debate for hours was religion. Robert was very devoted to reading and understanding the Bible. He got me interested, and I enthusiastically took it from there, reading not only the Bible, but also many diverse books about religion. It's something I'll continue to study for the rest of my life.

Robert also opened my eyes to improving my diet. I'm an eater. I really enjoy food. Steaks, baby-back ribs, Sophie's pork chops . . .

I like to experience different foods, but it takes a toll when you live our lifestyle. The travel, the lack of sleep, no workout time, and a rich diet can lead to poor health. So I became more particular: no red meat, occasionally some chicken, a lot of fish, and tons of vegetables.

Since the change in my diet, my weight has been consistent and, for the most part, I've felt great. In fact, I feel better than ever.

Robert Barr is a connector, a link between the coach and the players. And it works the other way, too; he lets me know how the players are feeling.

When Les Alexander bought the team, he had a two-hour meeting with Robert. They really hit it off. As Les got to know Robert better, they developed a special relationship with a lot of trust. Robert is now the link between the owner and the team. When anyone has a problem, Robert is the guy to see. He's a good listener, a caring person, and he tries to solve whatever problems come up. His people skills have been invaluable in making us a proud organization. Les understands these talents and how important they are. He has promoted Robert to the position of senior executive vice president of basketball. Whether the strength coach or the man next to the owner, Robert always gives all of himself to the team.

I also want to say something about the broadcasters who have been part of the Rockets over a long period of time. Gene Peterson, Jim Foley, and Danny Gonzalez are our radio voices, and Bill Worrell is our television man, along with Calvin Murphy, whom I've already discussed in great detail.

I truly appreciate the loyalty that these people have shown to the Rockets organization. I understand that they have a job, too; if we aren't getting our jobs done on the court, it's up to Gene, Jim, Danny, Bill, and Calvin to report it. While doing that, they have shown great understanding. They have a feel for how hard it is to get a team to do the right thing. I also want to salute the work of our team doctors through the years: Charles Baker, Walt Lowe, Bruce Moseley, Jim Muntz, and Tom O'Brien.

All of the people I've talked about in this chapter have been vital in making the Houston Rockets franchise what it is today. I can't emphasize that enough.

The head coach is just the front man. Without the diligence and commitment of the people around me, game night wouldn't be much fun.

20

THREEPEAT! THREEPEAT! THREEPEAT!

That sweet term rang in our ears as we approached the 1995–96 season, and I really felt we had a legitimate chance to win our third consecutive NBA title. All of our key performers were returning, and we had added free agent Mark Bryant to fortify the power-forward position.

Our players still seemed hungry and humble. Our fans were pumped, knowing that only the Minneapolis Lakers, Boston Celtics, and Chicago Bulls had ever won three championships in a row. This was truly an opportunity for us to establish ourselves as one of the great teams in NBA history.

But there's an element in sports that nobody can control: No matter how much the players and coaches want it, no matter how skilled you are or how hard you battle, injuries can take away your fondest dreams.

That's exactly what happened to the Rockets in '95–96. An avalanche of injuries to key players simply proved too much to overcome. We fought hard and defended our consecutive titles with honor, but it just wasn't in the cards for us this time around.

Things had looked good at the beginning. As reigning NBA champions, we took a preseason trip to London and won the

McDonald's Open against worldwide competition. Our second ring ceremony on opening night was just as impressive as the first, and I had those happy goose bumps as we watched the second banner being hoisted to the Summit's rafters prior to our victory over Golden State.

We started 10-1, and that made our Thanksgiving turkey dinner in Indianapolis taste especially good. All the stories were about how the Rockets had carved out a niche as November's darlings: We had been 14-0 in November of '94, 9-0 in November of '95, and now 10-1 to start this season.

Our confidence had carried over from the '95 Cinderella playoff run, and Clyde Drexler had had an opportunity to fully indoctrinate himself into our offensive and defensive systems during training camp.

Yeah, we were rolling.

But the first major clue that this wasn't going to be our year came on December 19 when we were playing the Phoenix Suns at home. Clyde collided with Charles Barkley and had to be carried off on a stretcher while holding his knee and writhing in pain. Fortunately, it turned out to be a severe bruise rather than a ligament tear. But the Drexler injury was a preview of coming attractions.

In mid-January, Mario Elie took a nasty fall in Denver, and an arm injury would sideline him for most of the second half. On and on it went. Sam Cassell, Hakeem, Clyde again. Key guys were dropping out of our rotation left and right, and all we could do was keep our hot line going to the CBA as we searched for replacements.

San Antonio and Utah sped away from us in the Midwest Division race, and when the Lakers got a dose of adrenaline from Magic Johnson's return, we found ourselves in the No. 6 playoff spot as the regular season was winding down.

Our hope was that lightning could strike twice. If we could get everybody healthy in time for playoff training camp and if we could survive a couple of rounds, maybe—just maybe —we could repeat our late heroics of '95.

But in the final analysis, that was stretching the law of percentages too far. Our 48-34 season meant we would again open the playoffs without even one homecourt advantage. Teams just don't stay on top of the mountain forever by taking that route.

I was really proud of the way our guys came together in the first round against the rejuvenated Lakers. We got a split at the Forum, and then really played well to win Games Three and Four on our court. Keep in mind that this was a Lakers team that had won 36 of its last 48 regular-season games. Robert Horry did a great job on Magic in the final two games of the series, helping to hold Johnson to a combined 4-of-17 shooting mark on our court.

I was surprised at how emotional I became in the waning seconds of that Laker series, just thinking about how much our guys had been through all season. It was a source of great pride to see us come together under such adverse circumstances and play so well against a worthy opponent.

While we were battling the Lakers, the Seattle SuperSonics had thrown the gorilla off their backs by getting past Sacramento in four games. After first-round losses to Denver and the Lakers the previous two years, the Sonics broke through a huge mental barrier. By breaking the ice and getting through the first series, they could now take a deep breath and just play basketball.

That's exactly what they did when we met them in the second round. Finally, the Houston Rockets had met their match.

We had little preparation time for the opening game, and they blew us out on a Saturday afternoon. Because Seattle had such an aggressive defensive approach with a lot of trapping and switching, they're a team for which you really need preparation time. The Sonics aren't going to give you what you want on the first option, and you have to be patient and move the ball to the weak side. We worked on that after the opening game and really played well enough to win Game Two—but we didn't, because Seattle happened to put on the greatest three-point shooting display I've ever seen. The Sonics made a record 20 of 28 treys, and that was the difference in a close game. It was as if they had trumped our best hand.

That second game was really the key to the series. Had we

gotten out of Key Arena with a split, maybe the Sonics would have tightened up a bit. But they came to Houston loose, and the fact is that we never really got them stopped, even on our home court.

Gary Payton and Shawn Kemp really emerged for the Sonics as Seattle went on to sweep us. Payton was spectacular the entire series, and Kemp did the job for them on the inside. After they won Game Three by three points, we started the fourth game trying too hard. The Sonics built a 20-point lead in the fourth quarter, and it looked like we were going to end our two-year championship reign without much of a struggle.

But the fourth quarter of Game Four was a statement of what our team was all about. Our guys got caught up in the game and fought back like true champions. We made an incredible run to send the game into overtime, but Seattle held us off in the extra session.

We had not gone quietly. We had raged against the dying of the light.

"Listen to the sounds in their locker room," I told our players when we gathered for the first time as ex-champions. "Remember how we felt in that position. Listen to the sounds and think about how much you want it again."

As we look to the future, I still think the Houston Rockets have a championship-caliber nucleus to build around. Hakeem Olajuwon and Clyde Drexler have a lot of basketball left in them, and we were fortunate enough in the 1996 off-season to make a trade with Phoenix for Charles Barkley, one of the great players of all time.

Our window of opportunity is only here for a couple of years. We knew there would be a steep price to pay, but I thought we owed it to the championship-caliber players on our team to go out and maybe take a chance. I'd say to both the fans and to ourselves that an opportunity like that couldn't be passed up.

A lot of people looked at it one way: Because we gave up Sam Cassell, Robert Horry, Chucky Brown, and Mark Bryant for Barkley, they just said, "Four for one." But a lot of that has to do with the salary cap. You have to make the numbers fit to consummate a trade in this era. But we also made some additional moves to fit our chemistry. Brent Price fits with a Charles Barkley because Brent is a spot shooter. Price also fits with Hakeem and Clyde. Because the price was so high for Barkley, we had to find some backup strength, and we were very fortunate to get Kevin Willis. So now it looks like we wanted to make wholesale changes, but that wasn't the plan; it turned out that way only because the cap dictated the price for Barkley, and then we had to cover up the holes.

People asked me, "At what point of the ['95–96] season did you feel you had to make these big changes?" But I never felt like that. To get the prize, we had to figure out what the cost was. And to analyze it, you have to look at what's going to happen to this team in the future.

We have a window of opportunity. If we had stuck with our '95–96 team and used up our cap room to keep our players, what happens when our older stars are gone? How do we change our team? There's no way to compensate when the two great players, Hakeem and Clyde, are gone if we've committed huge chunks of salary even to excellent players like Horry and Cassell. So what we have here today is a solid, strong opportunity to go for a championship. If it doesn't work, in two years we can go after primary big-time players because we'll have money on the cap, assuming Charles only plays two more years.

If we had kept the same team, when it faded away into the sunset there would have been no way to change the team except through the draft. And I don't think we'll be drafting lottery picks for a while.

When the '95–96 season ended and it became apparent Charles would not be returning to Phoenix, he said publicly how he would feel about coming to Houston. We got great input from Clyde, who had been a friend of Barkley's, and Hakeem, who got to know him during their five weeks at the Olympics. Hakeem raved about Charles's work ethic and leadership qualities in those practices with the Dream Team.

Everything that was said about Charles has been true. He's a special person. He radiates positive energy. Be it confidence, be it team togetherness, intelligence, getting guys to talk about the game.

We have great leaders on our team. Clyde is a phenomenal leader. So is Hakeem. The way they've done it as leaders by example is perfect, because that's who they are. They're good at it. Charles brings us something a little bit different with his outgoing personality. So now we've got all these different ways to get it done.

I've talked about how each coach has to coach to his personality. Everybody has to live to their personality, too. Charles is so outgoing and positive, it's amazing.

Certainly, it was not an enjoyable thing to tell four guys I really love and who have helped us win championships that we had decided to do something different. I have strong feelings for every one of those guys. When I had to break the news to them, it was one of the toughest days of my career.

Those four guys knew when they were with me I was behind them a hundred percent. That's part of the appeal of our team: I like the players and I want them to do well.

I wish it didn't cost that much to get a Charles Barkley. But that was the price, and we felt it was an opportunity we couldn't pass up.

It was painful. People don't understand the personal aspect in professional sports. I preach family, and all of a sudden you're saying, "We're having a divorce." It's tough to take. I didn't have to go through that in my playing career. Thinking about losing those guys, before and after the Barkley trade, was a trauma for me. It's almost like a death. We care about our players, but that's the sacrifice you make. You say, "I've got to put those personal feelings aside and do what I think is the right thing for the franchise."

As far as my coaching future goes, I plan on doing this for a while. As a member of the "forties" club, I still consider myself a young guy, and I made a long-term commitment to Les when I signed a contract extension last season. That extension calls for me to coach into the next century.

When I line up for the national anthem and find that I don't have the same competitive urges that have driven me all through the years, that's when I'm going to find something else to do with my life. But I don't expect that day to come for a long time.

BEFORE CLOSING, I'd be remiss if I didn't mention how much I owe to my wife, Sophie. Whatever I've done in my career would never have been possible without her.

When I've felt down, when I've felt those doubts late at night lying in bed, she has always been the one to say, "You know you can do it." It's not that she's saying *she* knows I can do it; she's saying *I* know I can do it. I remember her humor when I was in the hospital after the Kermit Washington punch, when she had to be more scared than I was. I remember the "pennies" story that helped me relax before my first pro game in Houston.

I know it hasn't been easy for Sophie. I've been the one out there getting the stories written about me and getting my picture in the paper. But it's always teamwork. If we put it in a basketball context, I might be the one getting the points, but the MVP of our family is Sophie.

She's the pillar. She's the foundation. The Tomjanoviches all draw our strength from her.

While I've been on the road, jetting from city to city, Sophie has been the guiding force in raising three wonderful children: Nichole, Melissa, and Trey.

I related a story in the opening chapter about Nichole's concern for me when I took the interim head-coaching job. She touched me with her concern for my well-being, and we've always had that type of relationship. My other daughter, Melissa, also recharges my battery whenever it's low. Recently, when I was feeling stressed out, I went out to Los Angeles and spent some time with Melissa; a couple of days of seeing her smile and I felt great again.

My son, Trey, was, as they say, "born cool." He loves basketball, but he never got caught up in all the hoopla when we were winning those championships. He takes everything in stride.

I've talked about how the pressure of "Choke City" was tough and how that label can stick to you. Nobody wants that. But let me tell you where the most pressure came for me: During those '94 playoffs, I was working very late. One night, long after my son had gone to bed, I walked into his room, which is like a basketball museum. He had pictures of stars and role players on his wall, and little hoops here and there. As I walked in there and checked on him, I looked at the wall, and he had the brackets for the playoffs posted. I could see he had moved certain teams up. Every team was done in two colors, like the Portland Trail Blazers in their red and black. My son never said a word to me, but seeing him with that bracket on his wall made me want so much to move the Rockets through those brackets for him. He wasn't putting pressure on me, but something deep inside of me really wanted him to be able to move us up in his bracket.

As a husband and father, I couldn't have been more blessed.

I chose to write this book not out of any kind of ego trip; I'm not into that. On the contrary, I wanted to write it precisely because I consider myself a regular guy.

I think there's a general feeling in the world that regular guys don't wind up with the big prize in life. It's as though the big trophy is always for somebody else.

I just want people to know that's not true. My story and the Rockets' story are examples of how something truly wonderful can happen to regular people if you're willing to work hard and give it your best. We won back-to-back championships, and we're doing everything we can to win a third; if our story can be an inspiration to one regular guy or girl out there—if it can reinforce the message that any person who truly gives it his or her all *can* come out on top—then I'll feel as though I've really accomplished something special.

Index

American Airlines®

BOARDING PASS

NAME OF PASSENGER

BENTLEY/TARA LEIGH

			MILES

FROM XIO HOUSTON HOBBY

TO XIO DALLAS FT WORTH

AMERICAN AIRLINES

CARRIER FLIGHT CLASS DATE TIME

AA 3538 OCT1430P

REVALIDATION

GATE	BOARDING TIME	SEAT	SMOKE
C22	400	10A	NO

ADDITIONAL SEAT INFORMATION

PCS	CK WT.	UNCK WT.	SEQ NO.	PCS	CK WT.	UNCK WT.

BAGGAGE ID NR.

COUPON	AIRLINE	FORM SERIAL NO.	CK

BHK /HOU TICKETLESS

PASSENGER TICKET AND BAGGAGE CHECK

PASSENGER COUPON

NOTICE

This portion of the ticket should be retained as evidence of your journey.

Mullin, Chris, 19, 21
Muntz, Jim, 285
Murphy, Calvin, 80, 81–83, 88,
    100, 117, 135, 155, 284, 285
    as college player, 81–82
    competitiveness of, 86
    as member of Basketball Hall of
        Fame, 87
    as Tomjanovich's roommate, 85–
        87
Murphy, Vernetta, 85–86
Murray, Tracy, 238
Mutombo, Dikembe, 204, 209

National Basketball Association
    (NBA), 13, 260
    free agency rules of, 108
    Tomjanovich's contract with,
        57–60
    and violence in basketball, 105,
        106
National Collegiate Athletic Asso-
    ciation (NCAA), 47, 53
National Invitational Tournament
    (NIT), 57
NBA Finals:
    1980–81 (Rockets vs. Celtics),
        117–20
    1985–86 (Rockets vs. Celtics),
        149–50
    1993–94 (Rockets vs. Knicks),
        220–25
    1994–95 (Rockets vs. Magic),
        259–63
Nelson, Don, 19, 20, 75, 150
Newell, Pete, 59
Newlin, Mike, 80, 88, 91–92, 93, 107
    aggressiveness of, 219
New York Knicks, 55, 74, 79, 192–
    193, 218–20
    Rockets vs., in NBA Finals
        (1993–94), 220–25

Niagara University, 81–82
Nissalke, Tom, 80, 88, 89, 95, 108,
    109, 112, 120
Nordstrom, David "D.H.," 14–15,
    278
Notre Dame University, 143–44
Novak, Mr. (neighbor), 31

Oakley, Charles, 220
O'Brien, Tom, 285
Odom, William "Hawk," 32–34
O'Donnell, Jake, 221, 249
offensive plays, 171, 176, 177,
    179–80, 183–84
Olajuwon, Hakeem, 20, 21, 22, 23,
    150, 154, 168–74, 177, 186,
    187, 200, 207, 212, 262, 289,
    290
    competitiveness of, 172–73
    drafted by Rockets, 141–42
    injuries of, 158, 159, 160, 280
    in NBA championship series
        (1993–94), 221, 223, 224, 225
    as rookie, 170
    strengths of, 169
    in Western Conference Finals
        (1985–86), 148
    in Western Conference Finals
        (1994–95), 256, 257–58
    in Western Conference First
        Round Playoffs (1984–85), 146
    in Western Conference Semi-
        finals (1993–94), 215, 216
    in Western Conference Semi-
        finals (1994–95), 246, 247,
        248, 251–52, 253
    as winner of MVP trophy, 203–4,
        217–18
O'Neal, Shaquille, 23, 126, 202,
    258, 261, 273
Orlando Magic, 202, 209, 258–59,
    273